The American Bibliography of Slavic
and East European Studies for 1967

The American Bibliography of Slavic and East European Studies for 1967

Editor: Kenneth E. Naylor

Assistant Editors: Craig N. Packard and Zorianna M. Paschyn

Assisted by: Olga C. Shopay

Ohio State University Press

TABLE OF CONTENTS

INTRODUCTION

The present volume of the American Bibliography of Slavic and East European Studies continues the series of bibliographies published since 1957 by the Indiana University Press under different titles, the most recent of which appeared under the title American Bibliography of Russian and East European Studies. This Bibliography is the first volume to be published by the Ohio State University and its Center for Slavic and East European Studies. The present editor assumed responsibility for the Bibliography when it was moved from Indiana University to the Ohio State University in 1969.

SCOPE

The 1967 Bibliography attempts to list all of the relevant material on Russian and East European Studies published in the United States and Canada and by Americans abroad during the course of the year, as well as listing works in English published anywhere in the world outside of the Soviet Union and Eastern Europe. No item with its sole place of publication in a newspaper has been included. The journals listed on pages 7 through 19 have been checked for relevant articles, although not all journals have contained material suitable for inclusion in the Bibliography. Additional works of scholarly interest published elsewhere have been included when brought to the attention of the editor. Books related to the field published in England have been included whenever possible, as well as books in English published outside the Soviet Union and Eastern Europe. We have also included reviews of books published in 1967 wherever we have found

references to the reviews. Also included are unpublished doctoral dissertations defended in the United
States during the years 1966 and 1967 as far as we
could locate references to them and citation of the
publication of abstract in Dissertation Abstracts has
been included whenever possible. Original works of
literature published either in the countries of the
area or in emigration are not included.

The Bibliography lists books and articles and
reviews of books included as main entries. We do not
list the reviews of foreign books, i.e., those which
are not included as main entries, unless the review is
itself substantial enough to be considered an article
in its own right. Republications, new editions of
works out of print, and editions with new introductions have been included. Unless otherwise indicated
all items listed in the Bibliography carry a publication date of 1967.

In the future volumes of the Bibliography it is
hoped that we will be able to include more in the way
of international scholarly production published in
English of interest to the Slavic and East European
scholar.

ORGANIZATION OF BIBLIOGRAPHY

The Table of Contents should be considered a
broad subject index including all subsections of the
Bibliography. Items have been grouped generally according to subject rather than according to discip-
line. Items belonging in more than one section have
been assigned first to the primary area of interest,
with a cross reference to the other relevant sections.
The amount of material in some sections has led us to
make more detailed divisions than in fields where less
has been published. Generally, the arrangement has
been according to subject in the Social Sciences, with

the divisions being made according to country. In the
sections dealing with Language, Linguistics and Literature, division has been made by language family rather than by country, going from the Balto-Slavic languages to other Indo-European languages to the non-
Indo-European groups.

An article in an analyzed collection has been
listed separately with the number in square brackets
[ ] used to indicate the number of the collection itself. Reviews have been cited under the work reviewed
with the same entry number and a small letter following the main entry. Only the author and place of publication of a review have been cited, even though it
may have carried a title in the original journal. Comments to articles have been treated as reviews.

For works printed in Cyrillic the title (and
author's name) has been transliterated according to
the scholarly transliteration system used in the Slavic and East European Journal, Indiana Slavic Studies,
and the International Journal of Slavic Linguistics
and Poetics. When the author's name has a more common
English spelling than that of the transliteration,
this has normally been given. Translations of titles
have normally been given only when the English is
given in the original. Titles of items in English or
French have been recorded as printed, although the
spelling of foreign words may differ from that of the
transliteration system used.

The Author Index lists the authors, editors, and
translators of all items included in the Bibliography.
The spelling used is that which is found in the body:
no effort has been made to give the common spelling of
names, such as Chekhov for Čexov.

FUTURE BIBLIOGRAPHIES

It is requested that colleagues send the editor

(American Bibliography of Slavic and East European
Studies, The Ohio State University, 1841 Millikin
Road, Columbus, Ohio, 43210) reprints, copies of publications, or complete bibliographic data concerning
their publications for 1968, 1969, and 1970 for inclusion where appropriate in the Bibliography for those
years. This is of special importance for works published outside of the United States and Canada and
articles in journals which are not regularly searched
for material relevant to the Bibliography (see the
list of Abbreviations, page 7). Suggestions of other
journals which might be searched will be welcome inso-
far as they can be expected to include articles dealing with Slavic and East European Studies of scholarly
interest during the course of a given year. Articles
and books published in 1967 inadvertently omitted from
this Bibliography should also be brought to the attention of the editor; wherever possible, they will be
included in future volumes.

       Comments concerning the changes made in this vol-
ume of the Bibliography will be most welcome. The
editor believes that the expansion of coverage to include more of the international scholarly production
in Slavic Studies can only increase the value of this
Bibliography as a research tool by bringing the work
of foreign scholars to the attention of their American
colleagues.

ACKNOWLEDGMENTS

   The 1967 Bibliography, like its predecessors, has
benefitted from the generous .cooperation and support
of numerous persons. The editor wishes to acknowledge
with thanks the support of the Department of Slavic
Languages and Literatures, the Center for Slavic and
East European Studies, and the College of Humanities
of the Ohio State University, which made possible the
compilation and publication of the Bibliography. He

wishes to express special appreciation to the following contributing editors, whose assistance in the collection of material in their special fields has been
invaluable:

> Nellie Apanasewicz and Seymour M. Rosen, U.S.
>   Office of Education (Education)
> Rolfs Ekmanis, Arizona State University
>   (Baltic Studies, especially Latvian)
> Roger E. Kanet, University of Kansas
>   (International Relations)
> Felix J. Oinas, Indiana University (Folklore)
> John B. Quigley, Jr., The Ohio State University
>   (Law and Political Science)
> James P. Scanlan, The Ohio State University
>   (Philosophy)

The editor is especially grateful to the assistant
editors, Craig N. Packard, and Zorianna M. Paschyn, of
the Ohio State University for their conscientious de-
votion of time and effort as chief bibliographic as-
sistants, and to Olga C. Shopay, University of Missouri at Columbia, for her assistance in the beginning
stages of this project. He also wishes to thank Mrs.
Jane Ott for the care which she took in the demanding
job of typing the final manuscript.

To all his colleagues and to others too numerous
to mention who assisted in the compilation of the 1967
Bibliography, the editor wishes to acknowledge his
special appreciation.

Kenneth E. Naylor
The Ohio State University

ABBREVIATIONS

AA	American Anthropologist
AAAPSS	Annals of the American Academy of Political and Social Sciences
AAAG	Annals of the Association of American Geographers
AB	Acta Baltica
Acta Balto-Slavica	
ACQ	Atlantic Community Quarterly
AD	American Documentation
AE	American Economist
AER	American Economic Review
AfA	African Affairs
AH	American Heritage
AHR	American Historical Review
AHY	Austrian History Yearbook
Aidai	
AJA	American Journal of Archeology
AJCL	American Journal of Comparative Law
AJES	American Journal of Economics and Sociology
AJIL	American Journal of International Law
AJP	American Journal of Philology
AJS	American Journal of Sociology
AJSc	American Journal of Science
AJY	American Jewish Yearbook
AkDz	Akadēmiska Dzīve
A&L	Art and Literature
AL	American Literature
AM	The Atlantic Monthly
America	
American Journal of Psychotherapy	
American Philosophical Society Yearbook for 1966, 1967	
AnL	Anthropological Linguistics
Anthropologica	

Antioch Review
Antiquity
AP   .American Psychologist
APSR   American Political Science Review
AQ   American Quarterly
Archīvs
ArchL   Archivum Linguisticum
ARP   Annual Review of Psychology
ASch   American Scholar
Asian Folklore Studies
Asian Outlook
AsP   Asian Perspectives
ASp   American Speech
ASQ   Administrative Science Quarterly
ASR   American Sociological Review
AsSu   Asian Survey
Atlas
AUA   Annals of the Ukrainian Academy of
                    Arts and Sciences in the U.S.

BA   Books Abroad
Balk   Balkania Quarterly
BAS   Bulletin of the Atomic Scientists
Behind the Headlines
BHe   Baltische Hefte
BISUSSR   Bulletin of the Institute for the
                    Study of the USSR
BMLA   Bulletin of the Medical Library As-
                    sociation
BNYPL   Bulletin of the New York Public
                    Library
BR   Baltic Review
B-S   Byzantino-Slavica

CA   Current Anthropology
CAJ   Central Asiatic Journal
CalSlSt   California Slavic Studies
CAR   Central Asian Review
CD   Comparative Drama
CEF   Central European Federalist

CEJ/SB	Central European Journal/Sudeten Bulletin
Celi	
CER	Comparative Education Review
CH	Current History
ChiR	Chicago Review
CHM	Cahiers d'Histoire Mondiale
ChQ	China Quarterly
CHR	Catholic Historical Review
CJEPS	Canadian Journal of Economics and Political Science
CJL	Canadian Journal of Linguistics
CJWB	Columbia Journal of World Business
CL	Comparative Literature
CLibJ	Cornell Library Journal
CLRev	Columbia Law Review
CMRS	Cahiers du Monde Russe et Soviétique
ColumJTransnatL	Columbia Journal of Transnational Law
Com	Commentary
Communist Affairs	
CompP	Comparative Politics
ConP	Contemporary Psychology
ConR	Contemporary Review
Cooperation and Conflict	
CPS	Comparative Political Studies
CS1P	Canadian Slavonic Papers
CS1St	Canadian Slavic Studies
CS1StB	Canadian Slavic Studies Bibliography
CYIL	Canadian Yearbook of International Law
DA	Dissertation Abstracts
Daedalus	
Dance	
DC	Drama Critique
Diogenes	
Dissent (U.S.)	
DLZ	Deutsche Literaturzeitung
DM	Dance Magazine

DOP   Dumbarton Oaks Papers
DR   Duquesne Review
DS   Drama Survey
DT   Dancing Times

Econometrica
EcHR   Economic History Review
Economic Bulletin for Europe
Economics and Business Bulletin
The Economist
EDCC   Economic Development and Cultural
                                Change
EdF   Educational Forum
Education (U.S.)
EE   East Europe
EEQ   East European Quarterly
EG   Economic Geography
EHR   English Historical Review
EJ   Economic Journal
ELG   East Lakes Geographer
Em   Ethnomusicology
Encounter (England)
EP   Economics of Planning
ESEE   Etudes Slaves et Est Européennes
ETJ   Educational Theatre Journal
Europa-Archiv
EW   Eastern World

FA   Foreign Affairs
Far Eastern Economic Review
Finance
FLg   Foundations of Language
FLi   Folia Linguistica
Focus
Fortune
FR   The French Review
FSUSP   Florida State University Slavic
                                Papers

Gazette

Geo   Geography (England)
GerQ   The German Quarterly
GerR   The Germanic Review
GJ   Geographical Journal
GL   General Linguistics
Glossa   Glossa: A Journal of Linguistics
GM   Geographical Magazine
Godišnjak Društva Istoričara Bosne i Hercegovine
GR   Geographical Review
Grani

HBR   Harvard Business Review
HEQ   History of Education Quarterly
HER   Harvard Educational Review
Historian   The Historian: A Journal of History
HJ   Historical Journal
HLB   Harvard Library Bulletin
HLR   Harvard Law Review
HMg   Harper's Magazine
HO   Human Organization
HoLJ   Howard Law Journal
HR   Hispanic Review
HT   History Today
H&T   History and Thought
HudR   Hudson Review
HuR   Human Relations

IA   International Affairs
IC   International Conciliation
ICLQ   International and Comparative Law
                            Quarterly
Idea   Idea: The Patent Trademark and Copy-
                            right Journal of Research and
                            Education
IFMC   International Folk Music Council
IIJ   Indo-Iranian Journal
IJ   International Journal
IJAL   International Journal of American
                            Linguistics

IJCS	International Journal of Comparative Sociology
IJSLP	International Journal of Slavic Linguistics and Poetics
ILabR	International Labor Review
ILJ	Indiana Law Journal
ILRev	Iowa Law Review
ILRR	Industrial and Labor Relations Review
IMFSP	International Monetary Fund Staff Papers
InsCounselJ	Insurance Counsel Journal
Intercom Internationales	Jahrbuch für Geschichte-und Geographie Unterricht
IntJPoliSci	International Journal of Political Science
IO	International Organization
IPQ	International Philosophical Quarterly
IR	International Relations
IRE	International Review of Education
IRSH	International Review of Social History
IS	International Studies (India)
IS1St	Indiana Slavic Studies
ISSJ	International Social Science Journal (Revue Internationale des Sciences Sociales-Paris)
JAAC	Journal of Aesthetics and Art Criticism
JAOS	Journal of the American Oriental Society
JAirL	Journal of Air Law and Commerce
JAS	Journal of Asian Studies
JASA	Journal of Acoustical Society of America
JCLCPS	Journal of Criminal Law, Criminology and Political Science
JCR	Journal of Conflict Resolution
JCS	Journal of Croatian Studies

JDA	Journal of Developing Areas
JEGP	Journal of English and Germanic Philology
JEH	Journal of Economic History
Jewish Quarterly Review	
JFI	Journal of the Folklore Institute
JG	Journal of Geography
JGai	Jauna Gaita
JGLS	Journal of the Gypsy Lore Society
JGO	Jahrbücher für Geschichte Osteuropas
JHI	Journal of the History of Ideas
JHP	Journal of the History of Philosophy
JHR	Journal of Human Relations
JIA	Journal of International Affairs
JLing	Journal of Linguistics
JMF	Journal of Marriage and the Family
JMH	Journal of Modern History
JO	Jewish Observer and Middle East Review
The Journal of the Royal Institute of Philosophy	
JP	The Journal of Philosophy
JPE	The Journal of Political Economy
JPol	Journal of Politics
JPOS	Journal of the Patent Office Society
JR	Journal of Religion
JRME	Journal of Research in Music Education
JSE	Journal of Secondary Education
JSHR	Journal of Speech and Hearing Research
JSI	Journal of Social Issues
JSP	Journal of Social Psychology
JSS	Jewish Social Studies

Kalevalaseuran Vuosikirja	
Kul	Kultura (Paris)
KR	Kenyon Review
Kritika	Kritika: A Review of Current Soviet Books on Russian History

Latvijas vesture	
LCP	Law and Contemporary Problems
LDA	Labor Developments Abroad

LE   Land Economics
LEE   Law in Eastern Europe (Netherlands)
Lg   Language
LgL   Language Learning
Lg&S   Language and Speech
Ling   Linguistics (Netherlands)
Lingua   Lingua: International Review of
                    General Linguistics
LitR   Literary Review
Lituanus
LJ   Library Journal
LQ   Library Quarterly
LT   Library Trends

M   Minerva:Review of Science Learning and
                    Policy
MA   Medium Aevum
McGill Law Journal
MD   Modern Drama
MEJ   Middle East Journal
MEJrn   Music Educator's Journal
Metmenys
MFS   Modern Fiction Studies
MH   Medievalia et Humanistica
Midway
MilA   Military Affairs
MilR   Military Review
Mizan
MJ   Music Journal
MJPS   Midwest Journal of Political Science
MLabR   Monthly Labor Review
MLJ   Modern Language Journal
MLQ   Modern Language Quarterly
MLR   Modern Language Review
M&L   Musica and Letters
MM   Mariner's Mirror
ModA   Modern Age
Moderne Welt
Modern World
Monthly Review
MP   Modern Philology

MQ   The Musical Quarterly
Ms   Midstream
MSM   Michigan Slavic Materials
MTe   Mathematics Teacher
MTh   Journal of Music Theory
MW   Muslim World

Narodno stvaralistvo
Nation (U.S.)
NATO-Brief
NGM   National Geographic Magazine
NL   New Leader
NLR   New Left Review
NMHR   New Mexico Historical Review
NR   New Review
NRep   New Republic
NRev   National Review (U.S.)
NRJ   Natural Resources Journal
NWR   New World Review
NYR   New York Review of Books
NYULRev   New York University Law Review
NŽ   Novyj Žurnal

Oe-W   Österuropa-Wirtschaft
ON   Opera News
Opera (England)
Orbis (Louvain)
Orientalia
Österuropäische Rundschau

P   Philosophy
PacA   Pacific Affairs
Pamiętnik Literacki

PAPhS   Proceedings of the American Philosoph-
                    ical Society
Paris Review
Past and Present
PB   Psychological Bulletin
PDK   Phi Delta Kappan

PennBAQ   Pennsylvania Bar Association Quarterly
Personalist
PG   Professional Geographer
P&G   Poland and Germany
PHR   Pacific Historical Review
PhR   Philosophical Review
Phonetica (Switzerland)
PLL   Papers on Language and Literature
PMLA   Publications of the Modern Language
                    Association
PoC   Problems of Communism
PolR   The Polish Review
Population Bulletin
POQ   Public Opinion Quarterly
PoQ   Political Quarterly
PP   Personnel Psychology
PPJ   Prilozi proučavanju jezika
PPR   Philosophy and Phenomenological
                    Research
PQ   Philological Quarterly
PR   The Partisan Review
PSc   Political Scientist
PSci   Philosophy of Science
PSQ   Political Science Quarterly
PSt   Political Studies
Psychiatry and Social Science Review

QJE   Quarterly Journal of Economics
QJLC   Quarterly Journal of the Library of
                    Congress
QJS   Quarterly Journal of Speech
QQ   Queens Quarterly
QR   Quarterly Review

Reporter   The Reporter: The Magazine of Facts
                    and Ideas
RES   Review of Economics and Statistics
Research Studies
RESl   Revue des études slaves

Review   Review [Published by the Study Centre
                        of Jugoslav Affairs, London]
Review of International Affairs
RH   Revue Historique
Ricerche slavistiche
RLJ   Russian Language Journal
RM   Review of Metaphysics
RMSSJ   Rocky Mountain Social Science Journal
Roczslaw   Rocznik Slawistyczny
RPh   Romance Philology
RPol   Review of Politics
RR   Romanic Review
RusR   Russian Review

SAIS Review
SAQ   South Atlantic Quarterly
SatR   Saturday Review
The School Counselor
ScSl   Scando-Slavica
Science
Scientific American
SEd   Science Education
SE   Sociology of Education
SEEJ   Slavic and East European Journal
SEER   Slavonic and East European Review
SEJ   Southern Economic Journal
SJA   Southwestern Journal of Anthropology
SlavR   Slavic Review
SocA   Sociological Analysis
SocE   Social Education
SocF   Social Forces
SoQ   Southern Quarterly
Soviet Studies in Philosophy
SovS   Soviet Studies
SS   School and Society
SSF   Studies in Short Fiction
SST   Studies in Soviet Thought
SStD   Soviet Statutes and Decisions
SSU   Studies on the Soviet Union

StudLEconDev   Studies in Law and Economic Development
Survey   Survey: A Journal of Soviet and East
                    European Affairs
Symposium

T&C   Technology and Culture
TDR   Tulane Drama Review
Technology Review
TFSB   Tennessee Folklore Society Bulletin
TSLL   Texas Studies in Literature and Lan-
                    guage
Tulimuld
TV   Treji Varty
Twentieth Century Literature

UAJ   Ural-Altaische Jahrbücher
UCPL   University of California Publications
                    in Linguistics
UCPMP   University of California Publications
                    in Modern Philology
University of Denver Magazine
UQ   The Ukrainian Quarterly
UR   Ukrainian Review (England)
USNIP   United States Naval Institute Proceed-
                    ings
UTQ   University of Toronto Quarterly

VandLRev   Vanderbilt Law Review
Ventures
Virginia Quarterly Review
Vista
VJa   Voprosy Jazykoznanija (Moscow)

WAr   Weltwirtschaftliches Archiv
War/Peace Report
WAUS   World Affairs (U.S.)
WEJ   Western Economic Journal
WJ   World Justice
WLR   Wisconsin Law Review
Word   Word: Journal of the Linguistic Circle
                    of New York

The World Year Book of Education 1967: Education
                    Planning
WP   World Politics
WPQ   The Western Political Quarterly
WSCL   Wisconsin Studies in Contemporary
                    Literature
WSl   Die Welt der Slaven
WSlJ   Wiener slavistiches Jahrbuch
WT   World Today (England)

YCGL   Yearbook of Comparative and General
                    Literature
YELS   The Yearbook of the Estonian Learned
                    Society in America
YEE   Yale Economic Essays
YICA   Yearbook on International Communist
                    Affairs
YLJ   Yale Law Journal
YR   Yale Review
YULG   Yale University Library Gazette

Zapysky Naukovoho Tovarystva imeny Ševčenka
Zapysky Naukovoho Tovarystva imeny Ševčenka: Ivan
                    Franko
ZB   Zeitschrift für Balkanologie
Zbornik Radova Vizantološkog Instituta
ZFL   Zbornik za filologiju i lingvistiku
ZPSK   Zeitschrift fï Phonetik, Sprachwis-
                    senschaft und Kommunications-
                    forschung
ZSP   Zeitschrift für slavische Philologie

ANALYZED COLLECTIONS

1. [Arseniev, N.S., et al., ed.] Zapiski russkoj akademičeskoj gruppy v S.Š.A.:1967g. /Transactions of the Association of the Russian-American Scholars in the USA of the Year 1967. Richmond Hill, New York. (216). Rev. 1a. Puskarev, S. NŽ 90(1968):286-290.

2. Braham, Randolph L. and Hendel, Samuel, eds. The U.S.S.R. After Fifty Years: Promise and Reality. New York: Knopf (viii,299,viii). Rev. 2a. Chamberlin, William H. RusR 27(1968):231-236.

3. Byrnes, Robert F., ed. The United States and Eastern Europe. Englewood Cliffs: Prentice Hall (ix, 176). Rev. 3a. Fischer, Gabriel. IJ 23,i:169. 3b. Vardy, Stevan B. DR 14,i:89-91. 3c. Zacek, Joseph F. PolR 13,iii(1968):85-86. 3d. Zinner, Paul. SlavR 28 (1969):157-158.

4. Hamm, Josef, ed. Phonologie der Gegenwart. Hermann Böhlaus Nachf: Graz-Wien-Koln (392).

5. Karcz, Jerzy F., ed. Soviet and East European Agriculture. [Preface by J.F. Karcz] Berkeley and Los Angeles: U of California P (xxc,445). Rev. 5a. Bandera, Vladimir N. JEH 28(1968):139-140. 5b. Domar, Evsey, D. SlavR 27(1968):674-675. 5c. Klatt, W. SEER 46(1968):264-265. 5d. Laird, Roy D. APSR 62(1968): 290-291; RusR 26(1968):418. 5e. Matley, Ian M. GR 58 (1968):326-327. 5f. Mallor, R.E.H. GJ 134(1968):94.

[Analyzed Collections for the year 1967 have been placed at the beginning of the Bibliography, "F" numbers in brackets following a title in the body refer to these items.]

5g.   Spulber, Nicolas.   EDCC 17(1969):287-291.   5h.
Thornton, Judith.   AER 58(1968)293-294.   5i. Zauberman, Alfred.   IA 44(1968):123-124.

6.   Sarratt, Reed, Foust, Clifford M. and Lerner,
Warren, eds.   The Soviet World in Flux: Six Essays.
Atlanta, Georgia: Southern Regional Education Board
(173).

7.   To Honor Roman Jakobson: Essays on the Occasion
of his Seventieth Birthday 11 October 1966.   Vol. I-
III.   The Hague-Paris: Mouton (xxxiii,2464).

I. General

BIBLIOGRAPHY AND SOURCES

8.   Anon. "Selected Bibliography of Nabokov's
Work," WSCL 8:310-311.

9.   Berton, Peter, Rubinstein, Alvin Z. and Allot,
Anna. Soviet Works on Southeast Asia: A Bibliography
of Non-Periodical Literature, 1946-65. Los Angeles:
U of Southern California P (201).

10.   Bochanski, J.M.   "Bibliography of Soviet Philosophy," SST 7:256-267;351-360.

11.   Bridge, R. The Hapsburg Monarchy 1804-1918:
Books and Pamphlets Published in the United Kingdom
between 1818 and 1967: A Critical Bibliography.   London: U of London.

12.   Carlton, Robert G. and Horecky, Paul L.   The
USSR and Eastern Europe: Periodicals in Western Lan-
guages. [3rd ed.,rev.,enl.] Washington: Library of
Congress (89).

13.   Chary, Fred B.   "A Bibliography of Bulgarian
Archaeology, Anthropology and Sociology," CSlStB 1,
iv:87-88.

14.   Chary, Fred B.   "A Bibliography of Bulgarian
Economics," CSlStB 1,iv:91-99.

15.   Chary, Fred B.   "A Bibliography of Bulgarian
Geography," CSlStB 1,iv:102.

16.   Chary, Fred B.   "A Bibliography of Bulgarian
Government and Politics," CSlStB 1,iv:73-76.

17. Chary, Fred B. "A Bibliography of Bulgarian History," CS1StB 1,iv:52-59.

18. Chary, Fred B. "A Bibliography of Bulgarian International Relations," CS1StB 1,iv:84.

19. Chary, Fred B. "A Bibliography of Bulgarian Philosophy," CS1StB 1,iv:84-87.

20. Dewey, Horace W. "A Bibliography of Medieval Russian History," CS1StB 1,iv:34.

21. Dewey, Horace W. "A Bibliography of Medieval Russian Literature," CS1StB 1,iv:14-15.

22. Dossick, Jesse J. "Doctoral Dissertations on Russia, The Soviet Union, and Eastern Europe Accepted by American, Canadian and British Universities 1966-1967," SlavR 26:705-712.

23. Gibian, George. Soviet Russian Literature in English: A Checklist Bibliography. Ithaca: Center for International Studies, Cornell U (vi,118). Rev. 23a. Struve, Gleb. SlavR 27(1968):681-683.

24. Goy, Peter A. and Miller, Laurence H. A Biographical Directory of Librarians in the Field of Slavic and East European Studies. Chicago: American Library Association (xv,80).

25. Hotinsky, C.M. "A Bibliography of Library Science in the USSR," CS1StB 1,iv:1-14.

26. Howard, Richard C. "Bibliography of Asian Studies 1967," JAS 27,v:1-398.

27. Kanet, Roger E. "International Relations-Soviet Union," CS1StB 1,iii:45-54;1,iv:76-84.

28. Kramer, Karl D. "A Bibliography of Imperial Russian Literature," CS1StB 1,iv:15-16.

29. Lachs, John. Marxist Philosophy: A Bibliographical Guide. Chapel Hill: U of North Carolina P
(xiv,166). Rev. 29a. Blakeley, T.J. WJ 11(1969):80.

30. Lewanski, R.C., and Lewanski, L.G. The Liter-
atures of the World in English Translation: A Bibliog-
raphy. Vol. II: The Slavic Literatures. New York:
New York Public Library and Ungar (xiv,630). Rev. 30a.
Mihailovich, Vasa D. SlavR 27(1968):690-691. 30b.
Simmons, Robert W.,Jr. SEEJ 12(1968):119.

31. Long, John. "A Bibliography of Soviet Russian
History," CSlStB 1,iv:38-42.

32. Medwidsky, B. "A Bibliography of Ukrainian
Language and Linguistics," CSlStB 1,iv:27-32.

33. Miller, Laurence H. "East European History,"
LT 15:730-744.

34. Munby, Lionel M. and Wangermann, Ernst. Marxism and History: A Bibliography of English Language
Works. London: Lawrence and Wishart (62).

35. Orton, Lawrence D. "A Bibliography of Czechoslovak History," CSlStB 1,iv:49-52.

36. Papacosma, Victor. "A Bibliography of Greek
History," CSlStB 1,iv:61-64.

37. Robbins, Richard G. "A Bibliography of Imperial Russian History," CSlStB 1,iv:35-38.

38. Rudnyc'kyj, Jaroslav B., comp. Slavica Canadi-
ana A.D. 1966, Winnepeg: Canadian Assoc. of Slavists,
Polish Research Inst. in Canada, and Ukrainian Free
Academy of Sciences (48). Rev. 38a. Žyla, W.T.
SEEJ 13(1969):273.

39. Sakmyster, Thomas L. "A Bibliography of Hungarian History," CSlStB 1,iv:59-61.

40. Salter, Francis. "Bibliography of Bulgarian Language and Linguistics," CSlStB 1,iv:34.

41. Salter, Francis. "Bibliography of Czech Language and Linguistics," CSlStB 1,iv:32-33.

42. Salter, Francis. "Bibliography of Hungarian Language and Linguistics," CSlStB 1,iv:34.

43. Salter, Francis. "Bibliography of Polish Language and Linguistics," CSlStB 1,iv:32.

44. Salter, Francis. "Bibliography of Russian Language and Linguistics," CSlStB 1,iv:25-27.

45. Salter, Francis. "Bibliography of Yugoslavian Languages and Linguistics," CSlStB 1,iv:33.

46. Schlacks, Charles. "A Bibliography of Rumanian History," CSlStB 1,iv:67-73.

47. Smith, Edward. "The Okhrana"; The Russian Department of Police: A Bibliography. [With the collaboration of Rudolf Lednicky] Stanford: Hoover Institution (280). Rev. 47a. Jones, David R. CSlStB 3 (1969):597-598.

48. Struk, D. "A Bibliography of Ukrainian Literature," CSlStB 1,iv:16-24.

49. Sturm, Rudolf. Czechoslovakia: A Bibliographic Guide. Washington: Library of Congress (xii,157). Rev. 50a. Meyerstein, Zlata, P. SEEJ 13(1969):280-281.

50. Thompson, Lawrence S. "Continental European Literature," LT 15:573-588.

51. Timberlake, Charles E. "Source Materials on Russian and American History in the Alexander Petrunkevich Collection," YULG 41,iii:120-130. [Footnote to article in YULG 42,iv:110-111.]

52. Villmow, Jack R. "A Bibliography of Czech Geography," CS1StB 1,iv:101.

53. Villmow, Jack R. "A Bibliography of Hungarian Geography," CS1StB 1,iv:103.

54. Villmow, Jack R. "A Bibliography of Polish Geography," CS1StB 1,iv:99-101.

55. Villmow, Jack R. "A Bibliography of Rumanian Geography," CS1StB 1,iv:103.

56. Villmow, Jack R. "A Bibliography of Soviet Union Geography," CS1StB 1,iv:99.

57. Villmow, Jack R. "A Bibliography of Yugoslav Geography," CS1StB 1,iv:102.

58. Welsh, David J. "A Bibliography of Polish Literature," CS1StB 1,iv:24-25.

59. Wynot, Edward D. "A Bibliography of Polish History," CS1StB 1,iv:42-49.

See also 378, 2029.

REFERENCE WORKS

60. Chew, Allen F. An Atlas of Russian History: Eleven Centuries of Changing Borders. New Haven: Yale U P (x,111).

61. Maichel, Karol. Guide to Russian Reference Books. Vol. V: Science, Technology and Medicine. [With the assistance of B.J. Pooler and Rudolf Lednicky] Stanford: Hoover Institution (304).

62. Zimmerman, Mikhail G. Russian-English Translators Dictionary: A Guide to Scientific and Technical Usage. NY:PP (293). Rev. 62a. Smeaton, B. Hunter. LJ 92:2553-2554.

See also 716, 1780, 1782, 1921.

LIBRARIES AND ARCHIVES

63. Buist, Eleanor. "Soviet Centralized Catalog-
ing: A View From Abroad," LT 16,i:127-142.

64. Grinberg, R.N., ed. Vozdušnye puti: Al'manax,
Vol. V. New York: Grinberg (314). Rev. 64a. Krzyzanowski, Jerzy R. BA 42(1968):465. 64b. Sheldon, Richard. SlavR 27(1968):683-684.

65. Little, Arthur D.,Inc. Directory of Selected
Research Institutes in Eastern Europe. New York: Columbia U P (x,445). Rev. 65a. Kister, Kenneth F. LJ
92:102.

66. Timberlake, Charles E. "The Leningrad Collection of Zemstvo Publications," SlavR 26:474-478.

See also 25, 1921.

BIOGRAPHY, AUTOBIOGRAPHY, AND MEMOIRS

67. Alliluyeva, Svetlana. "To Boris Leonidovich
Pasternak," AM 219,vi:133-140. [Russian version New
York (15).] Rev. 67a. Gul', R. NŽ 88:273-274.

68. Alliluyeva, Svetlana. Dvadcat' pisem k drugu.
New York and Evanston: Harper and Row (vii,216); London: Hutchinson (222).

69. Alliluyeva, Svetlana. Twenty Letters to a
Friend. [Tr. by Priscilla Johnson McMillan] New York
and Evanston: Harper and Row (ix,246). Rev. 69a. Barman, Thomas. IA 44(1968):345-347. 69b. Campbell,
Alex. NRep 157,xvi:25-26. 69c. Douglas, A. Vibert.

QQ 75:364-365. 69d. Hardwick, Elizabeth. NYR 9(12 Oct):3-4. 69e. Latey, Maurice. HT 17:787. 69f. MacIntyre, Alasdair. YLJ 70:1032-1036. 69g. Salisbury, Harrison E. SatR 50,xl:33-34,70. 69h. Werth, Alexander. Nation(U.S.) 205:469-470. 69i. Wilkinson, Paul. ConR 211(Nov):272-273.

70. Arseniev, N.S. "Moi vosponimanija o Moskovskom universitete (1906-1910 g.g.)," Zapiski [Fl]:7-22. [Synopsis in English: "Moscow University 1906-1910 (Personal Recollections)."]

71. Baylen, Joseph O. "Bishop Strossmayer and Mme. Olga Novikov: Two Unpublished Letters, 1879," SlavR 26:468-473.

72. Beerman, R. "Comment on 'Who was the Soviet Kulak?'," SovS 18:371-375.

73. Berberova, Nina. "Kursiv moj," NŽ 87:30-53.

74. Brock, Peter. "A Pacifist in Wartime: Wojcieck Bogumil Jastraębowski," PolR 12,ii:68-77.

75. Broido, Eva, ed. and tr. Memoirs of a Revolutionary. New York, Toronto and London: Oxford U P (150). Rev. 75a. Ascher, Abraham. PoC 16,vi:94-95. 75b. Basil, John D. CSlSt 2(1968):132-133. 75c. Lichtheim, George. NYR 9(9 Nov):10-15. 75d. Poor, Harold. AHR 74(1969):1328-1329.

76. Brown, Harold O.J. "John Laski, A Theological Biography: A Polish Contribution to the Protestant Reformation," Harvard [PhD diss] 1967.

77. Clardy, Jesse V. G.R. Derzhavin: A Political Biography. The Hague-Paris: Mouton (227). Rev. 77a. Cross, A.G. SEER 46,cvii(1968):498-500.

78. Deutscher, Isaac. <u>Stalin: A Political Biogra</u>-<u>phy</u> [2d ed.] New York: Oxford U P (xix,661). Rev. 78a. Barman, Thomas. <u>IA</u> 44(1968):345-347. 78b. Wilkinson, Paul. <u>ConR</u> 211(Nov):272-273.

79. Dygat, Stanislaw. "Impressions - A Polish Report," <u>Atlas</u> 13,iv:45-46.

80. Ehrenburg, Ilya. "Ilya Ehrenburg: What I Have Learned," <u>SatR</u> 50,xxxviii:38-31.

81. Ehrenburg, Ilya. <u>Post-War Years, 1945-1954</u>. [Tr. by Tatiana Shebunina in collaboration with Yvonne Kapp] Cleveland and New York: World (349). Rev. 81a. Gersh, Gabriel. <u>RusR</u> 27(1968):244-245. 81b. Kalb, Marvin. <u>SatR</u> 50,xlvi:53-54. 81c. Taylor, A.J.P. <u>NYR</u> 9(9 Nov):6-8.

82. Ehrenburg, Ilya. "The Climate of Our Time," <u>NWR</u> 35,vi:35-40.

83. Ellison, Herbert J. "The Socialist Revolution-aries," <u>PoC</u> 16,vi:2-14.

84. Epstein, Fritz T. "Hamburg und Osteuropa: Zum Gedächtnis von Professor Richard Salomon (1884-1966)," <u>JGO</u> 15:59-98.

85. Farnsworth, Beatrice. <u>William C. Bullitt and</u> <u>the Soviet Union</u>. Bloomington and London: Indiana U P (x,244). Rev. 85a. Accinelli, R.D. <u>IJ</u> 23,iii:495-496. 85b. Ferrell, Robert H. <u>SlavR</u> 27(1968):657. 85c. Schwarz, R.W. <u>LJ</u> 92:2557. 85d. Trani, Eugene P. <u>RusR</u> 27(1968):256-257.

86. Findlay, Dorothy and John. "Letters from Vla-divostok," <u>SEER</u> 45,cv:497-530.

87. Frankland, Mark. <u>Khrushchev</u>. [Intr. by Harry Schwartz] New York: Stein and Day (vii,213). Rev. 87a.

Fischer, Louis. SatR 50,xxxv:36. 87b. G.R.R. EE 16,
ix:54-55. 87c. Leinbach, Philip E. LJ 92:2394-2395.
87d. Rush, Myron. SlavR 27(1968):492-494. 87e. Werth,
Alexander. Nation (U.S.) 204:790-792.

88. Getzler, Israel. Martov: A Political Biography of a Russian Social Democrat. New York: Cambridge
U P (viii,246). Rev. 88a. Basil, John D. RusR 27
(1968):485-486. 88b. Daniels, Robert V. AHR 73(1968):
1585-1586. 88c. Giffin, Frederick C. Historian 30
(1968):465-466. 88d. Lichtheim, George. NYR 9(9 Nov):
10-15. 88e. Mendelsohn, Ezra. PoC 16,vi:95. 88f.
Treadgold, Donald W. SlavR 27(1968):490-491.

89. Getzler, Israel. "The Mensheviks," PoC 16,vi:
15-29.

90. Gibbons, Robert E. "Christopher Caudwell,
Marxist Apologist and Critic," Bowling Green State U
[PhD diss] 1967. DA 28:1076A.

91. Ginzburg, Eugenia. Journey into the Whirl-
wind. [Tr. by Paul Stevenson and Max Hayward] New
York: Harcourt, Brace and World (418). Rev. 91a.
Bailey, James. SEEJ 13(1969):387-388. 91b. Muchnic,
Helen. NYR 9(4 Jan 1968):15-16. 91c. Schmidt, Albert
C. Reporter 38,i(1968):44-47.

92. Gordey, Michel. "Svetlana," NRep 157:17-21.

93. Grossman, Kurt. "Letter from Czechoslovakia,"
Ms 13,ix:46-55.

94. Gruber, Ruth. "The Heroism of Staszek Jac-
kowski," SatR 50,xv:19-21.

95. Gul', R. "Kniga Svetlany," NŽ 88:251-252.

96. Harasowski, Adam. The Skein of Legends around
Chopin. [Foreword by Arthur Hedley] Glasgow: William
MacLellan Publ. (383).

97. Hayter, Sir William. The Kremlin and the Embassy. Macmillan (160). Rev. 97a. Eubank, Keith. LJ 92:1839.

98. Heitman, Sidney. "Nikolai Ivanovich Bukharin," PoC 16,vi:41-50.

99. Hodin, Josef P. Ruszkowski (Zdzislaw): Life and Work. London: Cory, Adams, and Mackay (72).

100. Izboldin, B. "K jubileju prof. M.A. Bunjatjana,"NZ 89:272-274.

101. Jelavich, Barbara, ed. "L'Ambassade russe à Paris, 1881-1898: Les Memoires de Nicolas Giers," CSlSt 1:1-23,212-237,379-403,587-617.

102. Kennan, George F. Memoirs: 1925-1950. Boston and Toronto: Little, Brown (vii,583). Rev. 102a. Holmes, John W. IJ 23:477-478. 102b. Kovacs, Imre. EE 17,iii(1968):52-54. 102c. von Mohrenschildt, Dimitri. RusR 27(1968):237-239. 102d. Steel, Ronald. NYR 9(4 Jan 1968):8-14. 102e. Woodward, David. HT 18(1968):289-290.

103. Korey, William. "Grigori Yevseevich Zinoviev" PoC 16,vi:51-61.

104. Kosteckyj, I. Myroslaw Radyš. New York: Ukrainian Academy of Arts and Sciences (176). Rev. 104a. Starow, Simon. BA 42(1968):496.

105. Kuznecova, Galina. Grasski Dnevnik. Washington: Kamkin (316). Rev. 105a. Gul', R. NZ 92(1968): 290-291.

106. Lunarcharsky, Anatoly V. Revolutionary Silhouettes, [Tr. and ed. by Michael Glenny, intro by Isaac Deutscher] London: Penguin; New York: Hill and Wang (155). Rev. 106a. Latey, Maurice. HT 17:787.

107. Malinowski, Bronislaw. <u>A Diary in the Strict Sense of the Term</u>· [Tr. by Norbert Guterman, preface by Valetta Malinowski, intr. by Raymond Firth, index of native terms by Mario Bick] New York: Harcourt, Brace and World (xxii,315). Rev. 107a. Middleton, John. <u>SatR</u> 50,xiv:65. 107b. Symmons-Symonolewicz, Konstantin. <u>PolR</u> 12,iii:67-72.

108. Manuxin, I.I. "S. Botkin, I. Mečnikov, M. Gor'kij," <u>NŽ</u> 86:139-158.

109. McErlean, John M. "The Formative Years of a Russian Diplomat: Charles Andre Pozzo Di Borgo in Corsica 1789-96," Washington, Seattle [PhD diss] 1967. <u>DA</u> 29(1968):215A.

110. Miliukov, Paul. <u>Political Memoirs, 1905-1917</u>. [Ed. by Arthur P. Mendel, tr. by Carl Goldberg], Ann Arbor: U of Michigan P (xv,508). Rev. 110a. Bushkoff, Leonard. <u>CSlSt</u> 2(1968):576-580. 110b. Miller, David B. <u>SlavR</u> 27(1968):326-327. 110c. Pushkarev, Sergei G. <u>RusR</u> 27(1968):358-259. 110d. Anon. <u>JMH</u> 41(1969): 415-416.

111. Naglovskij, A.D. "Lenin," <u>NŽ</u> 88:170-184.

112. Odoevceva, Irina. <u>Na beregax Nevy</u>. Washington: Kamkin (491). Rev. 112a. Gul', R. <u>NŽ</u> 92(1968): 288-289.

113. Pawelek, Anne J. <u>An American in Poland</u>. [Ed. by Joseph A. Wytrwal] Detroit: Endurance Press (285).

114. Pines, Herman. "Ipatieff: Man and Scientist," <u>Science</u> 157:166-170.

115. Poltoratsky, M.A. [Poltorackaja] "Sovetskaja aspirantura.(Iz perežitogo)," <u>Zapiski</u> [Fl]:23-46. [Synopsis in English: "Memoirs of My Academic Life."]

116. Pribić, Nikola R. "George Šagić-Fisher: Patriot of Two Worlds," FSUSP 1:35-47.

117. Pundeff, Marvin V. "Sources for Bulgarian Biography," QJLC April:98-102.

118. Raditsa, Bogdan. "David Sarnoff's Memories of Pupin and Tesla," JCS 7-8:164-166.

119. Reddaway, Peter and Schapiro, Leonard, eds. Lenin: The Man, the Theorist, the Leader. New York: Praeger (317). Rev. 119a. Conolly, Violet. IA 44 (1968):342-344. 119b. Gregor, Richard. IJ 23:642-643. 119c. Hofstetter, Eleanore O. LJ 92:3049.

120. Sanuelli, Annie. The Wall Between. Washington: Luce (237). Rev. 120a. Anon. EE 17,vi(1968):56.

121. Schlesinger, Arthur, Jr. "Twenty Letters to a Father," AM 220,v:90-95.

122. Serge, Victor. Memoirs of a Revolutionary 1901-1941. London and New York: Oxford U P (401).

123. Simmonds, George W., ed. Soviet Leaders. New York: Cromwell (405). Rev. 123a. Leinbach, Philip E. LJ 92:1917. 123b. Petrov, Vladimir. PoC 17,i (1968):39. 123c. Rubinstein, Alvin Z. CH 55(1968): 299.

124. Smith, Edward E. The Young Stalin: The Early Years of an Elusive Revolutionary. New York: Farrar, Straus, Giroux (470). Rev. 124a. Schwartz, Harry. SatR 50,xlix:32. 124b. Warth, Robert D. SlavR 27 (1968):328-329.

125. Švebe, Irina. "V. A. Lednickij," NZ 89:263-266.

126. Trotsky, Leon. Stalin. New York: Stein and

Day (xxv,516). Rev. 126a. Schwartz, Harry. SatR 50, xlix:32.

127. Tsuzuki, Chushichi. The Life of Eleanor Marx 1855-1898. Oxford: Clarendon P (354).

128. Urbański, Edmund S. "Dr. Józef Leonard and His Cultural-Political Activities in Spain Between 1868 and 1881," PolR 12,iii:18-27.

129. Walker, Franklin A. "Constantine Pavlovich: An Appraisal," SlavR 26:445-452.

130. Wirth, Andrzej. "A Discovery of Tragedy (The Incomplete Account of Tadeusz Borowski)," PolR 12,iii: 43-52.

131. Wolfenstein, E. Victor. The Revolutionary Personality: Lenin, Trotsky, Gandhi. Princeton: Princeton U P (x,330). Rev. 131a. Toma, Peter A. WPQ 20:761.

132. Anon. "G. V. Vernadskij," NŽ 88:263-266.

See also 332, 519, 1570, 2212, 2372, 2374, 2376.

TRAVEL AND DESCRIPTIONS

133. Beer, Ethel S. Marvelous Greece: An Appreciation of the Country and Its People. Walker (320). Rev. 133a. Willis, Katherine T. LJ 92:1833.

134. Birnbaum, Norman. "A Journey to Eastern Europe," Dissent(US) (May-Jun):322-344.

135. Boldizsar, Ivan, ed. Hungary: A Comprehensive Guidebook for Visitors and Armchair Travelers. Hastings House (401). Rev. 135a. Newman, Vivian D. LJ 92:2408.

136. Botting, Douglas. One Chilly Siberian Morn-
ing. [Photographs by John Bayliss and author, drawings
by Leslie W. Botting] New York: Macmillan (192). Rev.
136a. Ivsky, Oleg. LJ 92:1833. 136b. Rosenfeld,
Stephen S. PoC 17,iii(1968):66.

137. Fiene, Donald. "Up Mt. Elbrus by Motorcycle,"
NWR 35,vii:34-40.

138. Johnston, William M. "William Kingslake's 'A
Summer in Russia': A Neglected Memoir of St. Peters-
bury in 1845," TSLL 9:103-115.

139. Kalb, Marvin. "Is Russia a Tourist Country?"
SatR 50,i:51-52,102-105.

140. Michael, Henry N., ed. Lieutenant Zagoskin's
Travels in Russian America 1842-1844: The First Ethno-
graphic and Geographic Investigations in the Yukon and
Kuskokwim Valleys of Alaska. Toronto: U of Toronto P
[publ. for Arctic Institute of North America, Anthropology of the North] (xiv,358). Rev. 140a. Dvoichen-
ko-Markov, Demetrius. CSlSt 1:510-513.

141. Nearing, Helen K. "Winter Pleasures: Leningrad and Moscow in the Snows of Winter," NWR 35,ii:
30-33.

142. Olearius, Adam. The Travels of Olearius in
Seventeenth-Century Russia. [Tr. and ed. by Samuel H.
Baron] Stanford: Stanford U P (xviii,349). Rev. 142a.
Hegarty, Thomas J. CSlSt 2(1968):597-599. 142b.
O'Brien, C. Bickford. SlavR 28(1969):127-128.

143. Parsons, Helen B. "Dunaujvaros: Peace City
in Socialist Hungary," NWR 35,v:35-38.

144. Petrow, Richard. Across the Top of Russia.
New York: David McKay (374). Rev. 144a. Hayward,
Edward B. LJ 92:2572.

145. Plastrik, Stanley. "In the Land Without Soviets," Dissent(US) (Jan-Feb):54-64.

146. Rosenfeld, Stephen and Barbara. Return from
Red Square. Washington: Luce (236). Rev. 146a. Ro-
bothan, John S. LJ 92:1827.

147. Staples, Eugene S. "The Eagles of Kazakhstan," AM 219,i:92-95.

148. Urness, Carol, ed. A Naturalist in Russia:
Letters from Peter Simon Pallas to Thomas Pennant.
[Publication from the James Ford Bell Collection in
the U of Minnesota Library], Minneapolis: U of Minnesota P (189). Rev. 148a. Menon, P.K. CS1St 2(1968):
611-612. 148b. Vucinich, Alexander. SlavR 27(1968):
360-361.

ÉMIGRÉS AND REFUGEES

149. Kelley, John P., and Timberlake, Charles E.
"Impressions of Russian Pioneers in the West," NMHR
42,ii:145-150.

150. Kirschbaum, Joseph M. Slovaks in Canada.
Toronto: Canadian Ethnic Press Assoc. of Ontario (xvi,
468). Rev.. 150a. Čuješ, Rudolf. ESEE 13(1968):90-
91. 150b. Taborsky, Edward. SlavR 29(1970):344-345.
150c. Anon. CS1P 11(1969):140-141.

151. Kul'man, M.M. "Russkie podvižnicy za rube-
žom," NŽ 87:178-197.

152. Lasocki, Stanislas G. "Participation in
Nation Building (Polish Immigration to Brazil),"
Claremont [PhD diss] 1967. DA 29(1968):948A.

153. Lovrich, Frank M. "Croatians in Louisiana,"
JCS 7-8:31-163.

154. Makowski, William B. History and Intergration of Poles in Canada. Niagara Peninsula, Canada: The Canadian Polish Congress (274). Rev. 154a. Kaye, V.J. CSlP 11(1969):142-144.

155. Prpic, George J. "Croatians in the U.S.," New Catholic Encyclopedia 4:467-468.

156. Rodney, William. "Broken Journey: Trotsky in Canada, 1917," QQ 74:649-665.

157. Starczewska, Maria. "The Historical Geography of the Oldest Polish Settlement in the United States," PolR 12,ii:11-40.

158. Turek, Victor. Poles in Manitoba. [Foreword by William J. Rose, ed. and intr. by Benedict Heydenkorn] Toronto: Canadian Polish Congress (xiv,339).

159. Woycenko, Ol'ha. The Ukrainians in Canada. Winnipeg: Trident (xv,271). Rev. 159a. MacGregor, J.G. CSlP 11(1969):140-141.

160. Yuzyk, Paul. Les Canadiens-Ukrainiens - leur place et leur rôle dans la vie canadienne. Winnipeg: Prosvita (99).

161. Yuzyk, Paul. "75th Anniversary of Ukrainian Settlement in Canada," UQ 23,iii:247-254.

162. Yuzyk, Paul. Ukrainian Canadians: Their Place and Role in Canadian Life. Toronto: Ukrainian Canadian Business and Professional Federation (viii, 104). Rev. 162a. Tesla, J.I. CSlP 10(1968):109-110.

See also 677.

II. Anthropology and Archaeology

GENERAL

163. Burks, R.V. "Social Forces and Cultural Change," US and EEur [F3]:81-100.

164. Cheney, George A. "Culture Change and Revolution in Outer Mongolia," Washington, Seattle [PhD diss] 1966. DA 27(1966):296B.

165. Feinstein, C.H., ed. Socialism, Capitalism, and Economic Growth: Essays Presented to Maurice Dobb. Cambridge U P (x,367).

166. Gerber, Stanford N. "Russkoye Celo: The Ethnography of a Russian-American Community," U of Missouri, Kansas City [PhD diss] 1967. DA 28:773B.

167. Lockwood, William G., ed. Essays in Balkan Ethnology. Berkeley: Kroeber Anthropological Society (iii,126).

168. Pirožkova, V. "Čelovek v totalitarnom gosudarstve," NŽ 87:260-293.

169. Quitta, Hans. "The C14 Chronology of the Central and Southeast European Neolithic," Antiquity 41:263-270.

170. Renkiewicz, Frank A. "The Polish Settlement of St. Joseph County, Indiana: 1855-1935," Notre Dame [PhD diss] 1967. DA 28(1968):4102A.

171. Stafford, Peter. Sexual Behavior in the Communist World. New York: Julian (287).

172. Stearns, Peter N. European Society in Up-
heaval: Social History Since 1800. New York: Macmillan; London: Collier-Macmillan (xix,425).

173. Stoianovich, Traian. A Study of Balkan Civilization. New York: Knopf (x,215). Rev. 173a.
Banks, E. Pendleton. AA 70(1968):989-990.

174. Suliminski, T. "First International Congress
of Slavonic Archeology (Warsaw, Sept 1965)," SEER 45:
212-215.

175. Tomes, Igor. "Basic Features of Sickness
Insurance: European Socialist Countries," ILabR (Mar):
202-214.

176. Wenzel, Marian. "The Dioscuri in the Balkans," SlavR 26:363-381.

        See also 250, 268, 1163.

                        BALTIC STATES

177. Babris, Peter J. Baltic Youth Under Communism. Arlington Heights, Ill.: Research Publishers
(vi,351). Rev. 177a. Pradès, A. WJ 10(1968):390.

178. Suliminski, Tadeusz. "Ancient Southern
Neighbors of the Baltic Tribes," Acta Balto-Slavica,
5:1-17.

                        BULGARIA

        See 12.

                        CZECHOSLOVAKIA

179. Pech, Stanley Z. "The Czech Working Class
in 1848," CSlP 9:60-73.

180. Ulč, Otto. "Class Struggle and Socialist Justice: The Case of Czechoslovakia," APSR 61:727-743.

181. Anon. "Some Questions for Social Scientists [from Rudé Pravo 5 July 1967]," EE 16,x:23-25.

See also 1320.

GREECE

182. Rodman, Hyman. "Marital Power in France, Greece, Yugoslavia, and the United States," JMF 29: 320-324.

183. Safilios-Rothschild, Constantina. "A Comparison of Power: Structure and Marital Satisfaction in Urban Greek and French Families," JMF 29:345-352.

HUNGARY

184. Anon. "Jews, Atheists, Gypsies [from Valosog, April]," EE 16,vii:31-33.

POLAND

185. Ostrowski, Krzysztof and Przewarski, Adam. "Preliminary Inquiry into the Nature of Social Change: The Case of the Polish Countrysides," IJCS 8:25-43.

186. Schulman, Elias. "The Economic Life of the Jews in Poland as Reflected in Yiddish Literature," Jewish Quarterly Review 57:333-336.

187. Szczepanski, Jan. "The Social Science Press in Poland," ISSJ 19:227-235.

RUSSIA AND THE SOVIET UNION

188. Aspaturian, Vernon V. "Armenia," Encyclopedia Americana 2:337-338.

189. Dodge, Norton T. and Feshbach, Murray. "The
Role of Women in Soviet Agriculture," SEEA [F5]:265-
302. Rev. 189a. Murphy, George S. SEEA [F5]:303-305.

190. Dunn, Stephen P. and Ethel. The Peasants of
Central Russia. [Foreword by George and Louise Spind-
ler and Alexander Vucinich] New York: Holt, Rinehart
and Winston (xiv,139). Rev. 190a. Krader, Lawrence.
SlavR 27(1968):337-338. 190b. Legters, Lyman H. CS1St
2(1968):278-279.

191. Dunn, Stephen P. and Ethel. "Soviet Regime
and Native Culture in Central Asia and Kazakhstan: The
Major Peoples," CA 8:147-208.

192. Field, Mark G. "An Assessment of the New
Society," SSU 7,ii:1-21.

193. Field, Mark G. "New Values and Old Problems,"
[Rev. of Howard S. Becker, ed., Social Problems: A
Modern Approach]. Psychiatry and Social Science Review
1,xi:18-21.

194. Fischer, George, ed. Science and Ideology in
Soviet Society. New York: Atherton (xii,176). Rev.
194a. Blakeley, T.J. WJ 11:501-502. 194b. Sauer, Warren L. ASR 33(1968):1019-1020.

195. Fischer, J.L. "On Soviet Views of Totemism,"
[Comments on "The Problem of Totemism as Seen by Soviet Scholars," CA 7(1966):185-188]. CA 8:257-260.

196. Fletcher, William C. and Strover, Anthony J.,
eds. Religion and the Search for New Ideals in the
USSR. New York, Washington, and London: Praeger (vii,

135).   Rev. 196a. Bociurkiw, Bohdan R.   IJ 23:166-167.
196b. Leinbach, Philip E.   LJ 92:2162.   196c. Sylvester, Anthony.   IA 44(1968):563-564. 196d. Zernov,
Nicholas.   JR 47:362-363.

197.   Hindus, Maurice.   The Kremlin's Human Dilemma: Russia After Half a Century of Revolution.   New
York: Doubleday (x,395).   Rev. 197a. Juviler, Peter.
APSR 62(1968):286-288.   197b. Robotham, John S.   LJ
92:231.   197c. Schwartz, Harry.   SatR 50,vii:33-34.
197d. Simmonds, George.   CSlSt 1:692-693.

198.   Hulicka, Karel and Irene M.   Soviet Institutions, The Individual and Society.   Boston: Christopher Publishing House (xviii,680).   Rev. 198a. Mickiewicz, Ellen.   APSR 62(1968):657-658.

199.   King, Beatrice.   "Women in the USSR: Fifty
Years of Emancipation," NWR 35,viii:44-49.

200.   Kurganov, I.A.   Sem'ja v SSSR, 1917-1967. New
York: Posev (330).   Rev. 200a. Ivanov, A.   NŽ 89:296-
299.

201.   Lee, Priscilla T.   "The Ket: A Contribution
to the Ethnography of a Central Siberian Tribe," Stanford [PhD diss] 1966.   DA 28:2703B.

202.   Makarenko, A.S.   The Collective Family: A
Handbook for Russian Parents.   [Intr. by Urie Bronfer-
brenner, tr. by Robert Daglish] Garden City: Doubleday (xxi,368).   Rev. 202a. Elliott, Mabel A.   AAAPSS
374:217-218.   202b. Nichols, Elizabeth P.   LJ 92:788.

203.   Mandel, William M.   "Reflections on the Soviet System: Toward a More Human and Equal Society,"
USSR after 50 Yrs [F2]:159-204.

204.   Murvar, V.   "Max Weber's Urban Typology and
Russia," Sociological Quarterly 8:481-494.

205. Nove, Alec. "Peasants and Officials," SEEA
[F5]:57-72. Rev. 205a. Kerblay, Basile. SEEA [F5]:
73-76.

206. Parsons, Howard L. "Soviet Young People:What
Are They Like?" NWR 35,viii:27-33.

207. Schlesinger, Ina. "The Pioneer Organization:
The Evolution of Citizenship Education in the Soviet
Union," Columbia [PhD diss] 1967. DA 28:1873A.

208. Simmons, Ernest J. "The 'New Soviet Man',"
SWIF [F6]:19-40.

209. Stavrianos, L. S. Soviet Union: A Cultural
Area in Perspective. Boston: Allyn and Bacon (80).

210. Thompson, M.W. Novgorod the Great: Excava-
tions at the Medieval City Directed by A.V. Artsikhov-
sky and B.A. Kolchin. New York and Washington: Praeger (xvii,104). Rev. 210a. Gimbutas, Marija. SlavR
29(1970):99-100.

211. Trousdale, William B. "The Long Sword and
Scabbard Slide in Asia [with] Volume II: Catalogue and
Plates," Michigan [PhD diss] 1967. DA 28:4077A.

212. Wagman, James. "Modern Science, Communist
Faith and Soviet Society," Colorado [PhD diss] 1966.
DA 28:111A.

213. Watters, Francis M. "Land Tenure and the
Financial Burdens of the Russian Peasant, 1861-1905,"
California, Berkeley [PhD diss] 1966. DA 27:3596A.

214. Zekulin, Gleb. "Aspects of Peasant Life as
Portrayed in Contemporary Soviet Literature," CSlSt 1:
552-565.

See also 166, 409, 437, 1190, 1405, 1725,
1726, 1727, 1728.

YUGOSLAVIA

215. Buila, T. "An Analysis of Yugoslav Communes Based on Communications and Agricultural Land Quality," Rural Sociology 32:302-309.

216. Halpern, Joel M. A Serbian Village. Santa Fe: Gammon.

217. Kreider, Paul E. "The Social-Psychological Nature and Determinants of Attitudes Toward Education and Toward Physically Disabled Persons in Belgium, Denmark, England, France, the Netherlands, and Yugoslavia," Michigan [PhD diss] 1966. DA 28:1679A.

218. Winner, Irene. "Zerovnica, A. Slovenian Village," North Carolina, Chapel Hill [PhD diss] 1967. DA 28(1968):3144B

See also 156.

III. Geography and Demography

GENERAL

219. Hoffman, George W. "The Problem of the Un-
derdeveloped Regions in Southern Europe: A Comparative
Analysis of Rumania, Yugoslavia, and Greece," AAAG 57:
637-666.

220. Osborne, R. H. East-Central Europe: An Introductory Geography. New York: Praeger (384). Rev.
220a. Hamilton, F. E. Ian. SEER 46,cvii(1968):551-
552. 220b. Hoffman, George W. GR 59(1968):303-305.
220c. Ivsky, Oleg. LJ 92:2923. 220d. Pounds, Norman
J.G. SlavR 27(1968):497-498. 220e. Steers, Harriet.
GJ 133:517.

BALTIC STATES

221. Rutkis, J., ed. Latvia: Country and People.
Stockholm: Latvian National Foundation (683).

222. Remeikis, Thomas. "The Impact of Industrialization on the Ethnic Demography of the Baltic Countries," Lituanus 13,i:29-41.

223. Stewart, John M. "Life in a Baltic Capital,"
GM 40:247-253.

BULGARIA

See 14.

CZECHOSLOVAKIA

224. Harris, Lement. "'Let There Be Light':Socialist Farming in Czechoslovakia," NWR 35,vi:41-43.

See also 52.

FINLAND

225. Mead, W.R., and Smeds, Helmer. Winter in Finland: A Study in Human Geography. New York and Washington: Praeger (144). Rev. 225a. Rice, John. SlavR 27(1968):692.

POLAND

226. Hamilton, F.E. Ian. "Ancient Road Through Modern Poland," GM 40:200-208.

227. Tomlinson, A.K. "Poland's Demographic and Territorial Status," P&G 11:40-48.

228. Anon. "The Future of Farming. Excerpts from Zycie Warszawy (9 Jun 1967)" EE 16,viii:25-26.

229. Wieckowski, Michal. "Applied Geography in the Polish Geographic Society," Proceedings of the Two International Meetings of the Commission on Applied Geography. [A.A. Michel, ed] Kingston, R.I.: U of Rhode Island:33-34.

See also 56.

RUMANIA

230. Helin, Ronald A. "The Volatile Administrative Map of Rumania," AAAG 57:481-502.

231. Rugg, Dean S. "A Socialist Landscape - The
Case of Rumania," AAAG 57:190.

See also 55.

RUSSIA AND THE SOVIET UNION

232. Anderson, Jeremy. "A Historical-Geographical
Perspective on Khrushchev's Corn Program," SEEA [F5]:
104-128. Rev. 232a. Waedekin, Karl E. SEEA [F5]:129-
134.

233. Cole, John. A Geography of the U.S.S.R. Baltimore: Penguin (326).

234. Conger, Dean. "Siberia: Russia's Frozen
Frontier," NGM 131:297-347.

235. Demko, George J. "Agrarian Structure and
Peasant Discontent in the Russian Revolution of 1905,"
ELG(Oct):3-20.

236. Gibson, James R. "The Geography of Provi-
sionment of the Fur Trade of the Okhotsk Seaboard and
Kamchatka, 1639-1856: Overland Supply and Local Agriculture," Wisconsin [PhD diss] 1967. DA 28:5074B.

237. Groves, Robert G. "Arctic Ports of the Ye-
nisey," GM 39:744-749.

238. Hewsen, Robert H. "Introductions to the
Study of Armenian Historical Geography: The Seventh
Century Geography of Ananias of Shirak with Translation and Commentary," Georgetown [PhD diss] 1967. DA
28:3098A.

239. Hooson, David. "Plan for the Ob' River," GM
39:977-979.

240. Hultquist, Warren E. "Soviet Sugar-Beet Production: Some Geographical Aspects of Agro-Industrial Coordination," SEEA [F5]:135-151. Rev. 240a. Romanowski, Jacek. SEEA [F5]:152-155.

241. Jensen, Robert G. "The Soviet Concept of Agricultural Regionalization and Its Development," SEEA [F5]:77-98. Rev. 241a. Jackson, W.A. Douglas. SEEA [F5]:99-103.

242. McKee, Jesse O. "Soviet Transportation: A Geographical Analysis," SoQ 5:197-222.

243. Mazur, D. Peter. Fertility Among Ethnic Groups in the U.S.S.R. Berkeley: International Population and Urban Research Institute of International Studies and Dept. of Demography [U of California](24).

244. Mazur, D. Peter. "Reconstruction of Fertility Trends for the Female Population of the USSR," Population Studies 21,i:33-52.

245. Melezin, Abraham. "A View of Soviet Regionalization," AAAG 57:183.

246. Ojala, Carl F. and Steila, Donald. "Location and Depth Zones of Major Geologic Coal Reserves in the U.S.S.R.," JG 66:507-509.

247. Shabad, Theodore. "A Directory of Soviet Geographers," PG 19,iv:210-211.

248. Stebelsky, Ihor. "Land Tenure and Farm Holdings in European Russia on the Eve of Collectivization," Washington, Seattle [PhD diss] 1967. DA 29 (1969):242B.

249. Thomas, C. "Population Trends in the Soviet Union: 1959-1964," Geo 52(Apr):193-196.

250.   Wolfe, Dael.   "Soviet Population Theory,"
Science 158:999.

See also 56, 60, 144, 148, 1010.

YUGOSLAVIA

251.   Alexander, Paul B.   Land Utilization in the
Karst Region of Zgornja Pivka, Slovenia.   New York and
Washington: Studia Slovenica (xi,132).   Rev. 251a.
Baxevanis, John J.   GR 59(1969):466-467.

252.   Kostanick, Huey.   "Population Trends and Mi-
grations in Yugoslavia," AAAG 57:793.

253.   Singleton, F.B.   "Macedonia on the Move," GM
40:537-547.

254.   Singleton, F.B.   "Peace on a Redrawn Frontier," GM 39:821-829.

255.   Velikonja, Joseph.   "Territorial Identification and Functional Relationships in Yugoslavia," AAAG
57:193.

See also 57.

IV. History

GENERAL

256. Boba, Imre. "The Episcopacy of St. Methodi-
us," SlavR 26:85-93.

257. Drachkovitch, Milorad M., ed. The Revolutionary Internationals 1864-1943. Stanford: Stanford
U P (256).

258. Fay, Sidney B. The Origins of the World War.
Vol. I: Before Sarajevo; Vol. II: After Sarajevo. [2nd
ed., revised] New York: Free Press; London: Collier-
Macmillan (xxiii,583; xxiii,583).

259. Jelinek, Yeshayahu. "That Some Might Survive," [The Jewish Resistance During the Second World
War] U of Denver Magazine (Sep):20-23.

260. Keck, Daniel. "Designs for the Postwar
World: Anglo-American Diplomacy, 1941-1945," Connecticut [PhD diss] 1967. DA 28:3746A.

261. Mandelstam, Osip. "An Interview with Ho Chi
Minh - 1923," Com 44,ii:80-81.

262. Markiewicz, Z. "Charles Edmond intermédiaire
entre le monde slave et la France," CSlP 9:122-130.

263. Plekhanov, George. The Role of the Individual in History. New York: International Publishers
(62).

264. Prpic, George J. Fifty Years of World Communism [1917-1967]. Cleveland: [John Carroll U] Institute for Soviet and East European Studies (180).

265. Sherwood, Morgan B., ed. Alaska and Its History. Seattle and London: U of Washington P (xx,475).

266. Vryonis, Speros, Jr. Byzantium and Europe.
New York: Harcourt, Brace and World (216). Rev. 266a.
Miller, Dean A. SlavR 27(1968):131-132.

See also 173.

EAST EUROPE

267. Boba, Imre. Nomads, Northmen and Slavs: Eastern Europe in the Ninth Century. The Hague: Mouton;
Wiesbaden: Harrassowitz (138). Rev. 267a. Stokes, A.D.
SlavR 29(1970):98-99.

268. Dawidowicz, Lucy S., ed. The Golden Tradition: Jewish Life and Thought in Eastern Europe. New
York: Holt, Rinehart and Winston (502). Rev. 268a.
Friedberg, Maurice. SlavR 26:518. 268b. Sanders,
Ronald. Ms 13,v:78-80.

269. Fine, John V.A.,Jr. "The Dead Man's Hand
and the Hand of Glory," Narodno Stvaralištvo 6,xxi:23-
25.

270. Fischer, Fritz. Germany's Aims in the First
World War. [Intro. by Hajo Holborn and James Joll]
New York: Norton (xxviii,652).

271. Hussey, J.M., Nicol, D.M., and Cowan, G.,eds.
The Cambridge Medieval History. Vol. IV: The Byzantine
Empire. Part II: Government, Church and Civilisation.
Cambridge: Cambridge U P (xlii,517). Rev. 271a. Terras, Victor. SEEJ 12(1968):261-262.

272. Kertesz, Stephen D. "The Land and Peoples in
History," US and EEur [F3]:5-27.

273. Király, Bela K. "Prussian Diplomatic Adventure with Poland and the Feudal Revolt in Hungary in 1790," PolR 12,i:3-11.

274. Lendvai, Paul. "The New Austria and the Old Nazis," Com 44,iii:81-88.

275. Macartney, C.A. and Palmer, A.W. Independent Eastern Europe: A History. New York: St. Martin's (vii,499).

276. Petrov, Vladimir. Money and Conquest: Allied Occupation Currencies in World War II. Baltimore: Johns Hopkins P (282).

277. Pois, Robert A. "Friedrich Meinecke and Eastern Europe: A Study of the World War I Period," EEQ 1:249-260.

278. Ryder, A.J. The German Revolution of 1918: A Study of German Socialism in War and Revolt. Cambridge: Cambridge U P (xv,304). Rev. 278a. Ascher, Abraham. SlavR 27(1968):654-655.

279. Triska, Jan F. "Social Democracy in Interwar East-Central Europe," EEQ 1:231-248.

See also 33, 71, 172, 381, 692, 1326.

THE BALKANS

280. Fine, John V.A.,Jr. "Aristodios and Rastudije--A Re-examination of the Question," Godišnjak Društva Istoričara Bosne i Hercegovine 16:223-229.

281. Fine, John V.A.,Jr. "Two Contributions on the Demes and Factions in Byzantium in the Sixth and Seventh Century," Zbornik Radova Vizantološkog Instituta 10:29-37.

282.   Fine, John V.A.,Jr.   "Was the Bosnian Banate
Subjected to Hungary in the Second Half of the Thirteenth Century?" EEQ 3:167-177.

283.   Gewehr, Wesley M.   The Rise of Nationalism in
the Balkans, 1800-1930. Hamden, Conn.: Archon (xi,137).

284.   Macesich, George.   "Theory of Economic Integration and Experience of the Balkans and Danubian
Countries before 1914," FSUSP 1:11-18.

285.   Skendi, Stavro.   "Crypto-Christianity in the
Balkan Area Under the Ottomans," SlavR 26:227-246.

286.   Taylor, Alan J.P.   From Sarajevo to Potsdam.
New York: Harcourt, Brace and World (216).

287.   Živojinović, Dragan R.   "The Emergence of
American Policy in the Adriatic: December 1917-April
1919," EEQ 1:173-215.

See also 1336.

HAPSBURG EMPIRE

288.   Deak, Istvan.   "Amerikai történészek az
Ostrák-Magyar Monarchiárol," [American Historians on
the Austro-Hungarian Monarchy] Századok vi:1401-1412.

289.   Deak, Istvan.   "The Ruling Nationalities of
Austria-Hungary," AHY 3:303-308.

290.   Edmondson, Clifton E.   "The Heimwehr and Austrian Politics, 1918-1934," Duke [PhD diss] 1966. DA
27(1966):2982A.

291.   Elrod, Richard B.   "The Venetian Question in
Austrian Foreign Relations 1860-1866," Illinois [PhD
diss] 1967. DA 28(1968):3106A.

292. Fick, George H. "The Austrian Lands in Imperial Politics, 1198-1250," Harvard [PhD diss] 1967.

293. Heacock, Roger L.,Jr. "Diplomatic Relations between the Austro-Hungarian Empire and the German Reich in World War I, 1916-1918: A Study Based on Documents from the Austrian State Archives," Denver [PhD diss] 1967. DA 28:4572A.

294. Ionescu, Ghita. "The Austrian State Treaty and Neutrality in Eastern Europe," IJ 23:408-420.

295. Kramer, Zoltan. "The Road to Compromise, 1849-1867: A Study of the Hapsburg-Hungarian Constitutional Struggle in Its Terminal Phase," Nebraska [PhD diss] 1966. DA 27(1966):3401A.

296. Morley, Charles. "The Poles in the Hapsburg Monarchy," AHY 3:321-327.

297. O'Brien, Charles H. "Ideas of Religious Toleration at the Time of Joseph II," Columbia [PhD diss] 1967. DA 28:2181A.

298. Pauley, Bruce F. "Hahnenschwanz and Swastika: The Styrian Heimatschutz and Austrian National Socialism, 1918-1934," Rochester [PhD diss] 1967. DA 28:179A.

299. Schlesinger, Thomas O. "Austrian Neutrality in Postwar Europe," American [PhD diss] 1967. DA 28: 1500A.

300. Shapiro, Sheldon. "The Relations Between Louis XIV and Leopold of Austria from the Treaty of Nymegen to the Truce of Ratisbon," California, Los Angeles [PhD diss] 1966. DA 27:1771A.

301. Sugar, Peter F. "Report on the International Historical Congress Commemorating the Hundredth Anniversary of the Austro-Hungarian Compromise of 1867," CEF 15,ii:45-46.

302. Sugar, Peter F. "The Rise of Nationalism in
the Habsburg Empire," AHY 3:91-120.

ALBANIA

303. Skendi, Stavro. The Albanian National Awak-
ening, 1878-1912. Princeton: Princeton U P (xvi,498).
Rev. 303a. Boucek, J.A. IJ 23:169-170. 303b. Jela-
vich, Barbara. JMH 40(1968):684-685. 303c. Pundeff,
Marin. SlavR 26:680-682. 303d. Stoianovich, Traian.
AHR 73:537-538.

BALTIC STATES

304. Anderson, Edgar. Latvijas vēsture. Stockholm: Daugava (755).

305. Anderson, Edgar. "Toward the Baltic Union,
1927-1934," Lituanus 13,i:5-28.

306. Anderson, Edgar. "Through the Baltic Gate:
Impact of the First World War on the Baltic Area," BR
33:3-22.

307. Balodis, Agnis. "Ğenerāļa Dankera atmiņas,"
JGai 61:55-56.

308. Balodis, Agnis. "Par rusifikāciju no nepa-
rasta viedokļa," JGai 66:53-55.

309. Campion, Loren K. "Behind the Modern Drang
Nach Osten: Baltic Emigrés and Russophobia in Nineteenth Century Germany," Indiana [PhD diss] 1966. DA
28 (1966):581A.

310. Dardzāns, Pēteris. "Diplomātiskas atmiņas,"
JGai 64:62-64.

311. Ezergailis, Andrew. "The Bolshevization of
the Latvian Social Democratic Party," CSlSt 1:238-252.

312. Ezergailis, Andrievs. "1917 gada marta revo-
lūcija Rīgā," JGai 65:37-41.

313. Ezergailis, Andrievs. "Politikas romantika,"
JGai 63:54-56.

314. Gērmanis, Uldis. "Latvijas neatkarības
idejas attīstība," JGai 61:38-47;62:26-37.

315. Gērmanis, Uldis. "Pa baltu pēdām," JGai 62:
53-54.

316. Lelis, Jāzeps. "Daudzpusīgs rakstu krājums,"
JGai 64:59-61.

317. Lemberg, Adelaïda. "Russification in the
Baltic States," BR 33:32-41.

318. Maldutis, Julius, Jr. "Lithuanian Land Reforms, 1919-1939," Columbia [PhD diss] 1967. DA 31
(1970):885A.

319. Senn, Alfred E. "Garlawa: A Study in Emigré
Intrigue, 1915-1917," SEER 45,cv:411-424.

320. Švābe, Lidija. "Richarda fon der Harta pētī-
jumi Zviedrijas Valsts archīvā," JGai 66:38-40.

321. Urban, William L. "The Baltic Crusade of the
Thirteenth Century," Texas [PhD diss] 1967. DA 27:
4186A.

322. Vardys, V. Stanley. "The Baltic Peoples,"
PoC 16,v:55-64.

323. Vasariņš, P. "Latviešu gara aristokratija un
tās citadele," JGai 61:56-58.

See also 221.

BULGARIA

324. Drake, Edson J. "Bulgaria at the Paris Peace
Conference: A Diplomatic History of Neuilly-sur-Seine,"
Georgetown [PhD diss] 1967. DA 28:4087A.

325. Petrovich, Michael B. "The Russian Image in
Renascence Bulgaria (1760-1878)," EEQ 1:87-105.

See also 16.

CZECHOSLOVAKIA

326. Campbell, Fenton G.,Jr. "Czechoslovak-German
Relations During the Weimer Republic, 1918-1933," Yale
[PhD diss] 1967. DA 28(1968):4084A.

327. Jelinek, Yeshayahu A. "Hlinka's Slovak
People's Party, 1939-1945," Indiana [PhD diss] 1966.
DA 27:4193A.

328. Jelinek, Yeshayahu. "The Role of the Jews in
Slovakian Resistance," JGO 15:415-422.

329. Kaminsky, Howard. A History of the Hussite
Revolution. Berkeley and Los Angeles: U of California P (xv,580). Rev. 329a. Fousek, Marianka. SlavR
29 (1970):502-503.

330. O'Neill, John R. "The Functional Genesis of
a National Communist Party: Czechoslovakia, 1945-1948,"
Claremont [PhD diss] 1967. DA 29(1968):652A.

331. Ullman, Walter. "Czechoslovakia's Crucial
Years, 1945-1948: An American View," EEQ 1:217-230.

332. Vnuk, František. Dr. Josef Tiso, President of the Slovak Republic: In Commemoration of the Twentieth Anniversary of His Death at the Hands of the Enemies of Slovak Independence. Sydney: Association of Australian Slovaks (49).

333. Wiskemann, Elizabeth. Czechs and Germans: A Study of the Struggle in the Historic Provinces of Bohemia and Moravia. New York: St. Martin's (xi,299).

334. Slovak Studies V: Historica 3. Cleveland and Rome: Slovak Institute (268). Rev. 334a. Kirschbaum, Joseph M. CSlP 11(1969):124-127.

See also 35, 179, 362.

FINLAND

335. Hodgson, John H. Communism in Finland: A History and Interpretation. Princeton: Princeton U P (xi,261). Rev. 335a. Carsten, F.L. SEER 46,cvii (1968):545. 335b. Futrell, Michael. RusR 26:417. 335c. Pesonen, Pertti. PoC 17,iii(1968):67-68. 335d. Smith, C. Jay. SlavR 27(1968):141-142.

GREECE

336. Goldbloom, Maurice. "What Happened in Greece," Com 44,vi:68-74.

337. Xydis, Stephen G. Cyprus: Conflict and Conciliation, 1954-1958. Columbus: Ohio State U P (704). Rev. 337a. Woodhouse, C.M. IJ 23:636-637.

338. Zotos, Stephanos. Greece: The Struggle for Freedom. New York: Crowell (xi,194). Rev. 338a. Leinbach, Philip E. LJ 92:2571.

See also 36, 1370.

HUNGARY

339. Aczel, Tamas, ed. Ten Years After: The Hun-
garian Revolution in the Perspective of History. New
York: Holt, Rinehart and Winston (253). Rev. 339a.
Kecskemeti, Paul. SlavR 27(1968):324-325. 339b.
Leinbach, Philip E. LJ 92:1618. 339c. Reid, A.L.
PSt 16(1968):128-129. 339d. Tikos, Laszlo M. EEQ 2
(1968):185-189.

340. Eddie, Scott M. "The Changing Pattern of
Landownership in Hungary, 1867-1914," EcHR 20:293-310.

341. Eddie, Scott M. "Role of Agriculture in the
Economic Development of Hungary, 1867-1913," Massachusetts Institute of Technology [PhD diss] 1967.

342. Gáspár, Steven. "Four Nineteenth Century
Hungarian Travelers in America," Southern California
[PhD diss] 1967. DA 27:3810A.

343. Kessler, Joseph A. "Turanism and Pan-Turan-
ism in Hungary: 1890-1945," California, Berkeley [PhD
diss] 1967. DA 28(1968):4575A.

344. Kovacs, Imre. "Hungarians Who Helped the
Bolsheviks," EE 16,xi:9-13.

345. Lenz, Henry. "The German Cultural Influence
in Hungary before the Eighteenth Century," Ohio State
[PhD diss] 1967. DA 28:2083A.

346. Paster, Leslie P. "Young Széchenyi: The
Shaping of a Conservative Reformer, 1791-1832," Columbia [PhD diss] 1967. DA 31(1970:1734A.

347. Sólyom-Fekete, William. "The Hungarian Constitutional Compact of 1867," QJLC 24:286-308.

348. Spira, Thomas. "The Origins of Hungarian
Nationalism in the History Books of the Vormärz,"
Internationales Jahrbuch für Geschichte-und Geographie-
Unterricht, 11.

349. Stein, Arthur. India's Reaction to the Hungarian Revolution: An Appraisal. Kingston: U of Rhode
Island (13).

350. Stone, Norman. "Constitutional Crises in
Hungary, 1903-1906," SEER 45,civ:163-182.

351. Tökés, Rudolf L. Béla Kun and the Hungarian
Soviet Republic: The Origins and Role of the Communist
Party of Hungary in the Revolutions of 1918-1919. New
York and Washington: Praeger (xiii,292). Rev. 351a.
Peter, L. IA 44(1968):511-512. 351b. Volgyes, Ivan.
EEQ 2(1968):180-184.

352. Várdy, Steven B. "Baron Joseph Eötvös: The
Political Profile of a Liberal Hungarian Thinker and
Statesman," Indiana [PhD diss] 1967. DA 28:2616A.

353. Vermes, Gabor P. "Count István Tisza, A.
Political Biography," Stanford [PhD diss] 1966. DA 27:
2126A.

354. Wagner, Francis S., ed. The Hungarian Revolution in Perspective. Washington: F.F. Memorial
Foundation (350).

See also 39, 275, 294, 692.

POLAND

355. Bromke, Adam. Poland's Politics: Idealism vs
Realism 1689-1775. Cambridge: Harvard U P (x,316).
Rev. 355a. Beneš, Václav L. MJPS 12(1968):291-292.
355b. Blit, Lucjan. SEER 46,cvi(1968):258-259. 355c.
Bregman, Alexander. EE 16,vi:49-52. 355d. Chrypin-
ski, Vincent. CSlP 11(1969):137-140. 355e. Dziewan-
owski, M.K. JGO 16(1968):305-306. 355f. Griffith,
William E. EEQ 1:290-293. 355g. Rubinstein, Alvin Z.
CH 53:239. 355h. Symmons-Symonolewicz, K. PolR 13
(1968):102-104. 355i. Wagner, W.J. ESEE 12:128-131.

356. Bujarski, George T. "Polish Liberalism, 1815-
1831: The Misplaced Discourse," Harvard [PhD diss]
1967.

357. Charnock, Joan (Thomson). The Land and
People of Poland. New York: Macmillan; London: Adam
and Charles Black (96).

358. Ciencala, Anna. "The Significance of the
Declaration of Nonaggression of January 26, 1934, in
Polish-German and International Relations: A Reap-
praisal," EEQ 1:1-30.

359. Drzewieniecki, Walter M. "The Knowledge of
China in XVII Century Poland as Reflected in the Cor-
respondence between Leibniz and Kochański," PolR 12,
iii:53-66.

360. Gömöri, George. "East European Federation:
Worcell's Forgotten Plan," PolR 12,iv:37-43.

361. Gromada, Thaddeus V. "The Slovak Question in
Polish Foreign Policy (1934-1939)," Fordham [PhD diss]
1966. DA 27(1966):1755A.

362. Halecki, Oscar. "Problems of Ecumenism in
Poland's Millennium," CHR 52:477-493.

363. Halecki, Oscar. "The Place of Czestochowa in Poland's Millennium," CHR 52:494-508.

364. Hunczak, Taras. "Polish Colonial Ambitions in the Inter-War Period," SlavR 26:648-656.

365. Johnpoll, Bernard K. The Politics of Futility: The General Jewish Workers Bund of Poland, 1917-1943. Ithaca: Cornell U P (xix,298). Rev. 365a. Dunner, Joseph. APSR 62(1968):667-668. 365b. Gitelman, Zvi. EEQ 2(1968):335-338. 365c. Zelnik, Reginald E. AAAPSS 376(1968):162-163.

366. Kieniewicz, Stefan. "Polish Society and the Insurrection of 1863," Past and Present 37:130-148.

367. Knoll, Paul W. "The Stabilization of the Polish Western Frontier under Casimir the Great, 1333-1370," PolR 12,iv:3-29.

368. Korbonski, Andrzej. "Peasant Agriculture in Socialist Poland since 1956: An Alternative to Collectivization," SEEA [F5]:411-431. Rev. 368a. Romanowski, Jacek. SEEA [F5]:432-435.

369. Korbonski, Andrzej. "The Polish Communist Party 1938-1942," SlavR 26:430-444.

370. Kruszewski, Anthony Z. "Industrialization and Changing Society: A Case Study of the History and Effects of the Post World War II Population and Boundary Shifts on the Structure of the Newly Created Society in the Polish Western Territories," Chicago [PhD diss] 1967.

371. Lang, Henry. "Notions of Liberty and Freedom Presented by the Polish Delegation at the Council of Constance," Indiana [PhD diss] 1966. DA 28:177A.

372.   Mamatey, Victor S.   "Wilson and the Restoration of Poland: New Documents," FSUSP 1:1-10.

373.   Oleś, Marian.   "Casimir the Great and the Armenian Privileges, 1333-1370," ESEE 11,iii-iv:67-90.

374.   Rosenthal, Harry K.   "German-Polish Relations in the Caprivi Era," Columbia [PhD diss] 1967.   DA 28:1774A.

375.   Shewchuk, Serge M.   "The Russo-Polish War of 1920," Maryland [PhD diss] 1966.   DA 27(1966):2988A.

376.   Sokol, Irene M.   "The American Revolution and Poland: A Bibliographical Essay," PolR 12,iii:3-17.

377.   Staar, Richard F.   "The Hard Line in Poland," CH 52:208-213.

378.   Starzewski, J.   "De Gaulle's State Visit to Poland," P&G 11,iii/iv:21-28.

379.   Szczesniak, Boleslaw.   "The Turkish Chapter of the Thirty Years War," ESEE 12:226-231. [Partnership of the Polish and Imperial Forces as Documented in the Unique Pamphlet of 1621.]

380.   Thompson, Larry V.   "Nazi Administrative Conflict: The Struggle for Executive Power in the General Government of Poland 1939-1943," Wisconsin [PhD diss] 1967.   DA 28(1968):5001A.

381.   Trzeciakowski, Lech.   "The Prussian State and the Catholic Church in Prussian Poland 1871-1914," SlavR 26:618-637.

382.   Von Riekhoff, Harald.   "Pilsudski's Conciliatory Overtures to Stressman," CSlP 9:74-85.

383.   Weisser, Henry G.   "Polonophilism and the British Working Class, 1830-1845," PolR 12,ii:78-96.

384. de Weydenthal, J.B. "Paris: The Habitual
Émigrés," EE 16,vii:20-22.

385. Wieczerzak, Joseph W. A Polish Chapter in
Civil War America. The Effects of the January Insur-
rection on American Opinion and Diplomacy. New York:
Twayne Publishers (264). Rev. 385a. Kutolowski, John
F. PolR 13,i(1968):104.

386. Wrobel, Alfred J. "The American Revolution
and the Poland of Stanislaus Augustus Poniatowski
(1763-1795)," Southern California [PhD diss] 1967. DA
28(1968):3096A.

      See also 59, 76, 152, 273, 296, 698, 700.

                        RUMANIA

387. Fischer-Galati, Stephen. The New Rumania:
From People's Democracy to Socialist Republic. Cam-
bridge and London: M.I.T. P (ix,126). Rev. 387a.
Burks, R.V. AHR 73(1968):859. 387b. Stavrianos, H.S.
AAAPSS 379(1968):173-174.

388. Florescu, Radu R. "The Uniate Church: Cata-
lyst of Rumanian National Consciousness," SEER 45,cv:
324-342.

      See also 46.

                RUSSIA AND THE SOVIET UNION

GENERAL

389. Adams, Arthur E., Matley, Ian M., and McCagg,
W.O. An Atlas of Russian and East European History.
New York and Washington: Praeger (xi,204). Rev. 389a.
Backus, Oswald P.,III. SEEJ 12(1968):263. 389b.
Dreijmanis, John. Historian 30(1968):265. 389c.
Tvaruzka, Joseph J. SlavR 29:246-247.

390. Chirovsky, Nicholas L. *An Introduction to Russian History*. New York: Philosophical Library (xiii,229). Rev. 390a. von Gronicka, André. SEEJ 14 (1970):503-509. 390b. Ruud, Charles. CS1St 2(1968): 612-613. 390c. Veryha, Wasyl. CS1P 11(1969):134-135.

391. Hoetzsch, Otto. *The Evolution of Russia*. New York: Harcourt, Brace and World (213). Rev. 391a. Schwarz, R.W. LJ 92:237.

392. Jackson, George D.,Jr. "Toward a New Style in Surveys," SlavR 26:119-127.

393. Kirchner, Walther. *Commercial Relations Between Russia and Europe 1400-1800: Collected Essays*. Bloomington: Indiana U P (xiii,322). Rev. 393a. Esper, Thomas. SlavR 27(1968):132.

394. Kristof, Ladis K.D. "The Geopolitical Image of the Fatherland: The Case of Russia," WPQ 20:941-954.

395. Lavrov, Peter. *Historical Letters*. [Tr. with intr. and notes by James P. Scanlan] Berkeley and Los Angeles: U of California P (x,371). Rev. 395a. Pomper, Philip. SlavR 27(1968):648-649. 395b. Rainey, Thomas B. SEEJ 12:(1968):486-487.

396. Manning, Clarence A. "Moscow's Traditional Interest in the Orient," UQ 23:238-246.

397. Payne, Robert. *The Fortress*. New York: Simon and Schuster (448). Rev. 397a. Nomad, Max. SatR (13 May):38-39.

398. van der Post, Laurens. *A Portrait of All the Russias*. New York: Morrow (175).

399. Rosenberg, Arthur. *A History of Bolshevism from Marx to the First Five Years' Plan*. New York: Doubleday (282).

400. Wallace, Robert, and eds. of Time-Life Books. Rise of Russia.. New York: Time Inc. (184).

401. Wines, Roger, ed. Enlightened Despotism. Boston: Heath (81).

402. Yaney, George L. "War and the Evolution of the Russian State," SAQ 66:291-306.

See also 51, 60, 695, 826, 1092, 2056.

MEDIEVAL AND PRE-PETRINE

403. Alef, Gustave. "Reflections on the Boyar Duma in the Reign of Ivan III," SEER 45:76-123.

404. Andreev, Nikolaj. "Literatura i ikonopis': K istorii idej v Moskovskoj Rusi," THRJ [F7]:63-81.

405. Dewey, Horace W. "Defamation and False Accusation (Jabedničestvo) in Old Muscovite Society," ESEE 11:109-120.

406. Dmytryshyn, Basil, ed. Medieval Russia: A Source Book, 900-1700. New York: Holt, Rinehart and Winston (viii,312). Rev. 406a. Backus, Oswald P., III. SEEJ 12(1968):119-120. 406b. Huttenbach, Henry R. CSlSt 1:679-681.

407. Eaton, Henry L. "Cadasters and Censuses of Muscovy," SlavR 26:54-69.

408. Esper, Thomas. "A Sixteenth-Century Anti-Russian Arms Embargo," JGO 15:180-196.

409. Hellie, Richard, tr. Readings for Introduction to Russian Civilization: Muscovite Society. Chicago: Syllabus Division, The College, U of Chicago (iii,320). Rev. 409a. Szeftel, Marc. SlavR 29(1970): 302-303.

410. Howes, Robert C., tr. and ed. The Testaments of the Grand Princes of Moscow. Ithaca: Cornell U P (xvii,445). Rev. 410a. Orchard, G.E. CS1St 2(1968): 432-433.

411. Mackiw, Theodore. Prince Mazepa, Hetman of Ukraine in Contemporary English Publications, 1687-1709. Chicago: Ukrainian Research and Information Institute (126). Rev. 411a. Ellersieck, Heinz E. AHR 73(1968):1579. 411b. Kaye, V.J. CS1P 10(1968):233-234. 411c. Kuchar, Roman V. UQ 23:278-279.

412. Meyendorff, John. "Alexis and Roman: A Study in Byzantino-Russian Relations (1352-1354)," B-S 2: 278-288.

413. Miller, David B. "The Coronation of Ivan IV of Moscow," JGO 15:559-574.

414. Miller, David B. "The Literary Activities of Metropolitan Macarius: A Study of Muscovite Political Ideology in the Time of Ivan IV," Columbia [PhD diss] 1967. DA 31(1970):1176A.

415. Orchard, George E. "Economic and Social Conditions in Muscovy During the Reign of Ivan III," McGill [PhD diss] 1967.

416. Orchard, George E. "The Town of Medieval Muscovy," NR 7,i-ii:34-43.

417. Ostrogorskij, G. "Vizantija i kievskaja knjaginja Ol'ga," THRJ [F7]:1458-1473.

418. Puškarev, S.G. "Russkaja zemlja v 'Bezgosu-darnoe vremja' (1606-1613 g.g.)," Zapiski [F1]:67-86. [Synopsis in English: "Russia Without a Sovereign: 1606-1613."]

419. Raba, Joel. "The Fate of the Novgorodian Republic," SEER 45,cv:307-323.

420. Raba, Joel. "Novgorod in the Fifteenth Century: A Re-examination," CS1St 1:348-364.

421. Ševčenko, Ihor. "Muscovy's Conquest of
Kazan: Two Views Reconciled," SlavR 26:541-547.

422. Velde, Sister M. Richard Ann. "Muscovy in
the Sixteenth Century: The Accounts of Sigismund Von
Herberstein and Antonio Possevina," Indiana [PhD diss]
1966. DA 28:170A.

423. Von Staden, Heinrich. The Land and Government of Muscovy: A Sixteenth-Century Account. [Tr. and
ed. by Thomas Esper.] Stanford: Stanford U P (xxvi,
142). Rev. 423a. Backus, Oswald P., III. JMH 41(1969):
372-373. 423b. Hegarty, Thomas J. CS1St 2 (1968):
412-414. 423c. Ivsky, Oleg. LJ 92:2773. 423d.
O'Brien, C. Bickford. SlavR 28(1969):127-128. 423e.
Zenkovsky, Serge A. RusR 27(1968):375-376.

See also 19, 142, 210, 2051, 2056.

IMPERIAL RUSSIA

424. Adler, Charles C.,Jr. "The Promulgation of
Serf Emancipation in Saint Petersburg 5/17 March 1861:
An Eyewitness Account," CS1St 1:271-275.

425. Afferica, Joan M. "The Political and Social
Thought of Prince M.M. Shcherbatov (1733-1790)," Harvard [PhD diss] 1967.

426. Alef, Gustave. "The Origin and Early Development of the Muscovite Postal Service," JGO 15:1-15.

427. Alexander, John T. "The Russian Government
and Pugachev's Revolt," Indiana [PhD diss] 1966. DA
28:170A.

428. Backor, Joseph. "M. N. Katkov: Introduction

to His Life and His Russian National Policy Program, 1818–1870," Indiana [PhD diss] 1966. $\underline{DA}$ 27(1966): 3388A.

429. Bohachevsky-Chomiak, Martha. The Spring of a Nation: The Ukrainians in Eastern Galicia in 1848. Philadelphia: Shevchenko Scientific Society (80). Rev. 429a. Kohut, Zenon E. and Rudnytsky, Ivan L. CSlSt 2 (1968):75-76.

430. Braunthal, Julius. History of the International 1864-1914. [Tr. by Henry Collins and Kenneth Mitchell] New York: Praeger (631). Rev. 430a. Lichtheim, George. NYR 9(9 Nov):10-15.

431. Chamberlin, William H. "The First Russian Revolution," RusR 26:4-12.

432. Costello, D.P. "Griboedov as a Diplomat," ISlSt 4:52-73.

433. Czap, Peter, Jr. "P.A. Valuyev's Proposal for a Vyt Administration, 1864," SEER 45,cv:391-410.

434. Delderfield, R.F. The Retreat From Moscow. New York: Antheneum (257). Rev. 434a. Britt, Albert S. SlavR 28(1969):130-132. 434b. Ragsdale, Hugh. RusR 27(1968):492-493.

435. Dukes, Paul. Catherine the Great and the Russian Nobility: A Study Based on the Materials of the Legislative Commission of 1767. Cambridge: Cambridge U P (xi,269). Rev. 435a. Augustine, Wilson R. SlavR 27(1968):645-646. 435b. Bushkoff, Leonard. CSlSt 3(1969):121-127. 435c. Drew, R.F. Historian 30 (1968):658-659.

436. Dmytryshyn, Basil, ed. Imperial Russia: A Source Book, 1700-1917. New York: Holt, Rinehart & Winston (x,435). Rev. 436a. Terras, Victor. SEEJ 13

(1969):279.   436b. Williams, D.S.M.   SEER 46,cvii (1968):525-526.

437.   Emmons, Terrence.   "The Russian Landed Gentry and the Peasant Emancipation of 1861," Calif., Berkeley [PhD diss] 1966.   DA 27(1966):1317A.

438.   Esper, Thomas.   "The Odnodvortsy and the Russian Nobility," SEER 45,civ:124-134.

439.   Fisher, Alan W.   "Sahin Girey, the Reformer Khan, and the Russian Annexation of the Crimea," JGO 15:341-364.

440.   Fisher, Alan W.   "The Russian Annexation of the Crimea, 1774-1783," Columbia [PhD diss] 1967.   DA 31(1970):1169A.

441.   Florovskij, A.V.   "Carevič Aleksej Petrovič v 1710 godu: Zapiska Gr. G.V. Velčeka," THRJ [F7]: 672-677.

442.   Foust, Clifford M.   Muscovite and Mandarin: Russia's Trade with China and Its Setting, 1727-1805. Chapel Hill: U of North Carolina P (424).

443.   Fox, Frank.   "French-Russian Commercial Relations in the Eighteenth Century and the French-Russian Commercial Treaty of 1787," Delaware [PhD diss] 1966.   DA 28(1966):4988A.

444.   Giffin, Frederick C.   "In Quest of an Effective Program of Factory Legislation in Russia: The Years of Preparation, 1859-1880," Historian 29:175-185.

445.   Griffiths, David M.   "Russian Court Politics and the Questions of an Expansionist Foreign Policy under Catherine II, 1762-1783," Cornell [PhD diss]. DA 28(1968):4090A.

446.   Hassell, James E.   "The Vicissitudes of Russian Administrative Reform 1762-1801," Cornell [PhD diss] 1967. DA 28:1371A

447.   Haywood, Richard M. "The Beginnings of Railway Development in Russia in the Reign of Nicholas I: 1835-1842," Columbia [PhD diss] 1966. DA 30(1970): 4372A.

448.   Keenan, Edward L.,Jr.   "Muscovy and Kazan: Some Introductory Remarks on the Patterns of Steppe Diplomacy," SlavR 26:548-558.

449.   Kleber, Louis C.   "Alaska . . . Russia's Folly," HT 17:229-235.

450.   Kohls, Winfried A.   "The State-Sponsored Russian Secondary School in the Reign of Alexander II, The First Phase: Search for a New Formula, 1855-1864," California, Berkeley [PhD diss] 1967. DA 28:4460A.

451.   Lauber, Jack M.   "The Merchant-Gentry Conflict in Eighteenth Century Russia," Iowa [PhD diss] 1967. DA 28:597A.

452.   Lensen, George A. The Russo-Chinese War. Tallahassee: Diplomatic (315). Rev. 452a. Miller, Forrest A. RusR 27(1968):483-484. 452b. White, John A. JAS 27:623-624.

453.   Lincoln, William B.   "Nicholas Alekseevich Milyutin and Problems of State Reform in Nicholaevan Russia," Chicago [PhD diss] 1966.

454.   Liu, Hsien-Tung. "Border Disputes Between Imperial China and Tsarist Russia," Claremont [PhD diss] 1967. DA 29:1267A.

455.   MacKenzie, David. The Serbs and Russian Pan-Slavism 1875-1878. Ithaca: Cornell U P (xxii,365).

Rev. 455a. Hitchins, Keith. SlavR 27(1968):489-490.
455b. Jelavich, Barbara. JMH 40(1968):682-683. 455c.
Kellog, Frederick. CSlSt 3(1969):433. 455d. Petrovich, Michael B. RusR 27(1968):239-241. 455e. Rothenberg, Gunther E. EEQ 2:94-96. 455f. Roucek, Joseph
S. AAAPSS 376(1968):161-162.

456. Massie, Robert K. Nicholas and Alexandra.
New York: Atheneum (xvii,584). Rev. 456a. Heitman,
Sidney. SatR 50,xl:34-35. 456b. Kohn, Marjorie R.
LJ 92:2558-2559. 456c. Poltoratzky, Nikolai P. RusR
27(1968):246-249. 456d. Ritchie, Galen B. SlavR 27
(1968):652-653. 456e. Von Laue, Theodore H. AHR 73
(1968):1204-1205.

457. Miller, Mary R. "The Crimean War in British
Periodical Literature, 1854-1859," Duke [PhD diss]
1966. DA 27(1966):3055A.

458. Mills, James C., Jr. "Dmitrii Tolstoi as
Minister of Education in Russia, 1866-1880," Indiana
[PhD diss] 1967. DA 28:3612A.

459. Morley, Charles. "Peter the Great," Brison
Gooch, ed. Interpreting European History, 227-258.
Homewood, Illinois: Dorsey.

460. Netting, Anthony G. "Russian Liberalism: The
Years of Promise, 1842-1855," Columbia [PhD diss] 1967.
DA 20:2101A.

461. Neuhauser, Rudolf. "Notes on Early Russian-
American Cultural Relations," CSlSt 1:461-473.

462. Nichols, Irby C., Jr. "The Russian Ukase and
the Monroe Doctrine: A Reevaluation," PHR 36,i:13-26.

463. Olivier, Daria. The Burning of Moscow, 1812.
[Tr. from French by Michael Heron]. New York: Crowell
(221). Rev. 463a. Britt, Albert S. SlavR 28:130-132.

464. Palmer, Alan. Napoleon in Russia. New York: Simon and Schuster (318). Rev. 464a. Ragsdale, Hugh. RusR 27(1968):492-493.

465. Papazian, Dennis. "Nicholas Ivanovich Kostomarov: Russian Historian, Ukrainian Nationalist, Slavic Federalist," Michigan [PhD diss] 1967. DA 28: 178A.

466. Pelenski, Jaroslaw. "Muscovite Imperial Claims to the Kazan Khanate," SlavR 26:559-576.

467. Perry, John. The State of Russia Under the Present Czar. [Reprint, 1st edition, London, 1716] London: Frank Cass (280). Rev. 467a. Keep, John. SEER 46,cvii(1968):523-524.

468. Pierce, Richard A. "Alaska in 1867 as Viewed from Victoria," QQ 74:666-673.

469. Pintner, Walter M. Russian Economic Policy Under Nicholas I. Ithaca: Cornell U P (xvii,291). Rev. 469a. Curtiss, John S. AHR 73(1968):1580-1581. 469b. Kirchner, Walther. JGO 15:576-577. 469c. Monas, Sidney. RusR 27(1968):472-474. 469d. Riasanovsky, Nicholas V. JMH 41(1969):411-412. 469e. Rudolph, Richard L. JEH 28(1968):496-497. 469f. Sinel, Allen. CSlSt 2(1968):603-604. 469g. Watters, Francis M. SlavR 28(1969):132-133.

470. Pritsak, Omeljan. "Moscow, the Golden Horde and the Kazan Khanate from a Polycultural Point of View," SlavR 26:577-583.

471. Pyziur, Eugene. "Mikhail N. Katkov: Advocate of English Liberalism in Russia, 1856-1863," SEER 45, cv:439-456.

472. Raeff, Marc. "La jeunesse russe à l'aube du XIXe siècle:André Turgenev et ses amis," CMRS 8:560-586.

473. Riasanovsky, Nicholas V. Nicholas I and Official Nationality in Russia, 1825-1855. Berkeley and Los Angeles: U of California P (xii, 296).

474. Robinson, Geroid T. Rural Russia Under the Old Regime. Berkeley and Los Angeles: U of California P (342).

475. Rollins, Patrick J. "Russia's Ethiopian Adventure, 1888-1905," Syracuse, [PhD diss] 1967. DA 28:1379A.

476. Rosgosin, Boris I. "The Politics of Mikhail P. Dragomanov: Ukrainian Federalism and the Question of Political Freedom in Russia," Harvard [PhD diss] 1967.

477. Russell, William H. Russell's Despatches from the Crimea 1854-1856. [Ed. and intr. by Nicolas Bentley] New York: Hill and Wang (287). Rev. 477a. Saul, Norman E. SlavR 27(1968):149.

478. Ryu, In-Ho Lee. "Freemasonry under Catherine the Great: A Reinterpretation," Harvard [PhD diss] 1967.

479. Seton-Watson, Hugh. The Russian Empire: 1801-1917. Oxford: Clarendon; New York: Oxford U P (xx,813). Rev. 479a. Barghoorn, Frederick C. APSR 62 (1968):1276-1278. 479b. Brown, A.H. PSt 16(1968): 480-481. 479c. Clarkson, Jesse D. SlavR 27(1968): 646-647. 479d. Curtiss, John S. JMH 40(1968):676-677. 479e. Latey, Maurice. HT 17:709. 479f. Mosse, W.E. SEER 46,cvii(1968):526-528. 479g. Pierce, Richard A. QQ 75(1968):378-380. 479h. Treadgold, Donald W. AHR 73(1968):1201-1202. 479i. Zacek, Judith C. CSlSt 1.691 699. 479j. Anon. DD 17,iii(1968.54-55.

480. Smith, Irving. "Am English View of Russia in the Early Eighteenth Century," CSlSt 1:276-283.

481.   Squire, P.S.   "Metternich and Benckendorff, 1807-1834," SEER 45,civ:135-162.

482.   Squire, P.S.   "The Metternich-Benckendorff Letters, 1835-1842," SEER 45,cv:368-390.

483.   Swiętochowski, Tadeusz.   "Czartoryski and Russia's Turkish Policy, 1804-1806," PolR 12,iv:30-36.

484.   Vernadskij, G.V.   "Ivan Groznyj i Simeon Bekbulatovič," THRJ [F7]:2133-2151.

485.   Von Wahlde, Peter.   "Military Thought in Imperial Russia," Indiana [PhD diss] 1966. DA 28(1966): 183A.

486.   Wortman, Richard. The Crisis of Russian Populism. Cambridge: Cambridge U P (xii,211). Rev. 486a. Balmuth, Daniel. CSlSt 3(1969):415-422. 486b. Baron, Samuel H. AHR 73(1968):1581. 486c. Cross, Truman B. RusR 27(1968):482-483. 486d. Duran, James A.,Jr. SlavR 27(1968):649-650. 486e. Footman, David. SEER 46,cvii(1968):531-532. 486f. Rieber, Alfred. JMH 41 (1969):278-280.

487.   Zacek, Judith C.   "A Case Study in Russian Philanthropy: The Prison Reform Movement in the Reign of Alexander I," CSlSt 1:196-211.

488.   Zelnik, Reginald E.   "Factory Labor and the Labor Question in Tsarist St. Petersburg: 1856-1871," Stanford [PhD diss] 1966. DA 27(1966):3416A.

        See also 37, 47, 77, 101, 129, 213, 309, 325, 589, 645, 670, 826, 1309, 1579, 1623, 2126.

WAR, REVOLUTION, AND CIVIL WAR

489.   Alexander, Hunter.   "The Kronstadt Revolt of 1921 and Stefan Petrichenko," UQ 23:255-263.

490. Andreyev, Vladimir. "The First Days of the War," ModA 11:236-246.

491. Anin, David. "K 50-letiju oktjabrja," NŽ 89: 170-182.

492. Anin, David. "The February Revolution: A Note on the Causes of its Defect," SovS 18:265-266.

493. Ascher, Abraham. "Axelrod and Kautsky," SlavR 26:94-112.

494. Asher, Harvey. "The Kornilov Affair: A History and an Interpretation," Indiana [PhD diss] 1967. DA 28:3593A.

495. Avrich, Paul. "The Anarchists in the Russian Revolution," RusR 26:341-350.

496. Avrich, Paul. The Russian Anarchists. Princeton: Princeton U P (ix,303). Rev. 496a. Ascher, Abraham. SlavR 27(1968):137. 496b. Fedenko, P. BISUSSR 15,vi(1968):40-44. 496c. Footman, David. SEER 46,cvi(1968):254-255. 496d. Ivsky, Oleg. LJ 92: 1939. 496e. MacMaster, Robert E. JMH 40(1968):687-689. 496f. Wade, Rex A. CSISt 3(1969):601-602. 496g. Yaney, George L. AHR 73:184-185.

497. Basil, John D. "Political Decisions Made by the Menshevik Leaders in Petrograd during the Revolution of 1917," Washington, Seattle [PhD diss] 1966. DA 27(1966):2975A.

498. Bernal, J.D. "1917 and World Science," NWR 35,ix:153-156.

499. Bohon, John W. "Reactionary Politics in Russia: 1905-1909," North Carolina [PhD diss] 1967. DA 28: 2169A.

500. Burns, Paul E. "Liberalism Without Hope: The

Constitutional Democratic Party in the Russian Revolution, February-July, 1917," Indiana [PhD diss] 1967.
DA 28:2169A.

501. Buzinkai, Donald I. "The Bolsheviks, the
League of Nations, and the Paris Peace Conference,"
SovS 19:257-263.

502. Carr, E.H. The Bolshevik Revolution 1917-
1923. New Orleans: Pelican.

503. Chamberlin, William H. "Fifty Years of Communist Power." ModA 11:364-373.

504. Cherniavsky, Michael, ed. Prologue to the
Revolution. Notes of A.N. Iakhontov on the Secret
Meetings of the Council of Ministers, 1915. Englewood
Cliffs: Prentice-Hall (vi,249). Rev. 504a. Anon. NWR
35,vi:64.

505. Chmielewski, Edward. "Stolypin and the Russian Ministerial Crisis of 1909." CalSlSt 4:1-38.

506. Cross, Truman B. "Purposes of Revolution:
Victor Chernov and 1917," RusR 26:351-360.

507. Daniels, Robert V. "The Bolshevik Gamble,"
RusR 26:331-340.

508. Daniels, Robert V. Red October: The Bolshevik Revolution of 1971. New York: Scribner's (269).
Rev. 508a. Avrich, Paul. RusR 27(1968):225-230. 508b.
Leinbach, Philip E. LJ 92:3039. 508c. Pierce, Richard A. QQ 75(1968):378-380. 508d. Radkey, Oliver H.
SlavR 29(1970):518-519. 508e. Wade, Rex. JMH 41(1969):
116.

509. Davies, David A. "V.A. Maklakov and the
Problems of Russia's Westernization," Washington, Seattle [PhD diss] 1967. DA 29:209A

510. Dushnyck, Walter. "The Kerensky Provisional
Government and the Ukrainian Central Rada," UQ 23,ii:
109-129.

511. Feldman, Robert S. "Between War and Revolution: The Russian General Staff, February-July 1917,"
Indiana [PhD diss] 1967. DA 28:3602A.

512. Filene, Peter G. Americans and the Soviet
Experiment 1917-1933. Harvard U P (viii,389). Rev.
512a. Bennett, Edward M. Historian 30(1968):301-302.
512b. Mott, H. Wilmarth. LJ 92:236. 512c. Skotheim,
Robert A. AQ 20(1968):119-129.

513. Foner, Philip S. The Bolshevik Revolution:
Its Impact on American Radicals, Liberals and Labor.
[A Documentary Study] New York: International Publish-
ers (304).

514. Gak, Alexander. "Lenin and the Americans,"
NWR 35,ix:37-43.

515. Gapanovič, I.I. "Revoljucija na severe:
Oxotskokamčatskij kraj v 1917-1922 g.g.," NŽ 89:132-
145.

516. Gard, William G. "The Party and the Proletariat in Ivanovo-Voznesensk 1892-1906," Illinois [PhD
diss] 1967. DA 28:4989A.

517. Garvi, P. "1917 god," NŽ 87:166-177.

518. Gins, G. "Vremennoe pravitel'stvo i bol'-
ševizm," NŽ 88:222-238.

519. Gleason, Abbott. "The Emigration and Apos-
tasy of Lev Tikhomirov," SlavR 26:414-429.

520. Goldston, Robert. The Russian Revolution.
London: Dent (224).

521. Grant, Natalie. "The 'Zinoviev Letter'
Case," SovS 19:264-277.

522. Guins, George C. "The Fateful Day of 1917,"
RusR 26:286-295.

523. Hoffman, Jerry H. "The Ukrainian Adventure
of the Central Powers, 1914-1918," Pittsburgh [PhD
diss] 1967. DA 28:4092A.

524. Hook, Sidney. "The Human Cost," NL 50,xxii:
16-20.

525. Hookham, Maurice. "Reflections on the Russian Revolution," IA 43:643-654.

526. Hovannisian, Richard G. "Armenia on the Road
to Independence, 1918," California, Los Angeles [PhD
diss] 1966. DA 27(1966):792A.

527. Hovannisian, Richard G. Armenia on the Road
to Independence, 1918. Berkeley and Los Angeles: U
of California P (xi,364). Rev. 527a. Footman, David.
SEER 46,cvii(1968):541-542. 527b. Garsoïan, Nina G.
SlavR 27(1968):320-321.

528. Jagan, Cheddi. "The Russian Revolution and
Colonial Freedom," NWR 35,ix:32-33.

529. Johnston, Robert H. "Continuity versus Rev-
olution: The Russian Provisional Government and the
Balkans, March-November, 1917," Yale [PhD diss] 1966.
DA 27:2480A-2481A.

530. Karal, Halil I. "Turkish Relations with
Soviet Russia during the National Liberation War of
Turkey, 1918-1922: A Study in the Diplomacy of the
Kemalist Revolution," California, Los Angeles [PhD
diss] 1967. DA 28:2316A.

531. Katkov, George. Russia 1917: The February
Revolution. New York: Harper and Row (xxviii,489).
Rev. 531a. Curtiss, John S. JMH 41(1969):630-634.
531b. Hanak, Harry. EHR 83(1968):577-580. 531c.
Hookham, M. IA 43:756-758. 531d. Hutchinson, John.
CS1St 1:482-489. 531e. Ivsky, Oleg. LJ 92:1620.
531f. Laqueur, Walter. NYR 9(15 Jun):23-26. 531g.
Rabinowitch, Alexander. PSQ 84(1968):127-129. 531h.
Treadgold, Donald. RusR 26:404-406.

532. Kelley, Rita M.C. "The Role of Vera Ivanova
Zasulich in the Development of the Russian Revolutionary Movement," Indiana [PhD diss] 1967. DA 28:4678A.

533. Kennan, George F. "The Russian Revolution--
Fifty Years After: Its Nature and Consequences," FA
46:1-21.

534. Kenz, Peter. "The First Year of the Volun-
teer Army: Civil War in South Russia, 1918," Harvard
[PhD diss] 1967.

535. Kimball, Robert A. "The Early Political
Career of Peter Lavrovich Lavrov, 1823-1873: A Study
in the Failure of Liberalism and the Formation of Revolutionary Socialism in Russia," Washington, Seattle
[PhD diss] 1967. DA 28:4994A.

536. Kochan, Lionel. "Kadet Policy in 1917 and
the Constituent Assembly," SEER 45,civ:183-192.

537. Kochan, Lionel. Russia in Revolution 1890-
1918. New York: NAL (352). 537a. Laqueur, Walter.
NYR 9(15 Jun):23-26. 537b. Latey, Maurice. HT 17:
209. 537c. Robotham, John S. LJ 92:2155.

538. Laqueur, Walter. The Fate of the Revolution:
Interpretations of Soviet History. New York: Macmillan (viii,216). Rev. 538a. Byrnes, Robert F. JMH 40

(1968):689-690.   538b. Fisher, Harold H.   AAAPSS 379
(1968):171-172.   538c. Jacobs, Walter D.   WAUS 130,iv
(1968):262-264.   538d. Latey, Maurice.   HT 17,viii:
559.   538e. Mazour, Anatole G.   SlavR 27(1968):321.
538f. Pethybridge, Roger.   PSt 16(1968):314-315.   538g.
Pethybridge, Roger.   SEER 46,cvii(1968):546-547. 538h.
Thompson, John M.   RusR 27(1968):356-357.   538i. Ulam,
Adam B.   Com 45,ii(1968):91-93.   538j. Anon.   EE 17,
iii(1968):54-55.   538k. Wolfe, Bertram.   APSR 63(1969):
227-228.

539.   Lecar, Helene.   The Russian Revolution: A
Concise History and Interpretation. [Foreword by Ells-
worth Raymond] New York: Ardmore (149).

540.   Levitin, Anatolij and Šavrov, Vadim. "Očerki
po istorii russkoj cerkovnoj smuty," NŽ 86:159-220;
87:198-244.

541.   Lockhart, R.H. Bruce.   The Two Revolutions:
An Eye-Witness Account of Russia, 1917.   London:
Bodley Head (144).   Rev. 541a. Avrich, Paul.   RusR 27
(1968):225-230.   541b. Gretton, George.   HT 17:345.

542.   von Loewe, Karl F.   "Challenge to Ideology:
The Petrograd Soviet, February 27-March 3, 1917,"
RusR 26:164-175.

543.   Lowenthal, Richard.   "'1917': An After-
thought," Encounter 29,v:60-65.

544.   Lowenthal, Richard.   "1917, and After,"
Encounter 29,iv:21-31.

545.   Lubomirski, S.   "Lenin and Germany," P&G 11,
i/ii:14-20.

546.   Manning, Clarence A.   "The American and
Ukrainian Revolutions," UQ 23:65-74.

547. Masaryk, Thomas Garrigue. The Spirit of Russia, Vol. III. [Ed. by George Gibian, tr. by Robert Bass] New York: Barnes and Noble (331). Rev. 547a. Rabinowitch, Janet. SovS 21(1969):110-111.

548. Meaker, Gerald H. "Spanish Anarcho-Syndicalism and the Russian Revolution, 1917-1922," Southern California [PhD diss] 1967. DA 28:4995A.

549. Menashe, Louis. "'A Liberal With Spurs': Alexander Guchkov, A Russian Bourgeois in Politics," RusR 26:38-53.

550. Mieli, Renato. "Lenin and the Revolution," PoC 16,vi:71-75.

551. Miller, J. "Questions on 1917," SovS 19:255-256.

552. Morgenthau, Hans J. "The Political Cost," NL 50,xxii:13-16.

553. Mosse, W.E. "The February Regime: Prerequisettes of Success," SovS 19:100-108.

554. Nash, Roderick. "Woodrow Wilson, The Russian Embassy, and Siberian Intervention," PHR 36:423-434.

555. Neumann, William L. After Victory: Churchill, Roosevelt, Stalin and the Making of the Peace. New York: Harper and Row (xii,212). Rev.555a. Eubank, Keith. LJ 92:2166. 555b. Wolfe, James H. WAUS 131 (1969):250.

556. Oppel, Bernard F. "Russo-German Relations, 1904-1906," Duke [PhD diss] 1966. DA 27(1966):1766A.

557. Parsons, William H. "Soviet Historians and 'Bourgeois' Interpretations of the Russian Revolu-

tion," Indiana [PhD diss] 1966. DA 27(1966):4200A.

558. Pearlstien, Edward W. Revolution in Russia!:
As Reported by the New York Tribune and the New York
Herald, 1894-1921. New York: Viking (297). Rev.
558a. Avrich, Paul. RusR 27(1968):225-230. 558b.
Jacobs, Walter D. WAUS 130:186-187.

559. Peck, Ira. Russian Revolution. Scholastic
(126).

560. Pethybridge, Roger. "The Significance of
Communications in 1917," SovS 19:109-114.

561. Procko, Bohdan P. "American Ukrainian Catholic Church: Humanitarian and Patriotic Activities,
World War I," UQ 23:161-169.

562. Pushkarev, Sergei. "1917--A Memoir," RusR
26:54-67.

563. Puškarev, S. "Oktjabr'skij perevorot 1917
goda bez legend," NŽ 89:146-169.

564. Putnam, George. "P.B. Struve's View of the
Russian Revolution of 1905," SEER 45,cv:457-473.

565. Riha, Thomas. "1917-A Year of Illusions,"
SovS 19:115-121.

566. Rosenburg, William G. "Constitutional Democracy and the Russian Civil War," Harvard [PhD diss]
1967.

567. Royal Institute of International Affairs.
The Impact of the Russian Revolution 1917-1967: The
Influence of Bolshevism on the World Outside. London
and New York: Oxford U P (vi,357). Rev. 567a. Hanak,
Henry. IA 44(1968):344-345. 567b. London, Kurt L.
Orbis 12 (1968):906-909. 567c. Rubinstein, Alvin Z.

CH 54:106. 567d. Triska, Jan F. RusR 27(1968):243-244.

568. Sanders, Ronald. "Fifty Years After the Messiah," Ms 13,vii:13-20.

569. Schakovskoy, Zinaida. "The February Revolution as Seen by a Child," RusR 26:68-73.

570. Schwarz, Solomon M. The Russian Revolution of 1905: The Workers' Movement and the Formation of Bolshevism and Menshivism. [Tr. by Gertrude Vakar, intr. by Leopold Haimson. Vol. I in the History of Menshivism series.] Chicago and London: U of Chicago P (xix,245 with 109 pp. of appendices). Rev. 570a. Curtiss, John S. RusR 26:406-407. 570b. Jacobs, Dan N. CSlSt 2(1968):422-424. 570c. Keep, John. SlavR 27(1968):319-320. 570d. Lane, D.S. SEER 46,cvii (1968):532-534. 570e. Leinbach, Philip E. LJ 92:774-775. 570f. Pipes, Richard. NL 50,xi:9-12. 570g. Riasanovsky, Nicholas V. PSQ 84(1968):126-127.

571. Seton-Watson, Hugh. "Russia's February Revolution," Encounter 28,vi:75-80.

572. Shukman, Harold. Lenin and the Russian Revolution. New York: Putnam (224). Rev. 572a. Fishman, W.J. HT 17:491-493. 572b. Hookham, M. IA 43:756-758. 572c. Ivsky, Oleg. LJ 92:2406. 572d. Laqueur, Walter. NYR 9(15 Jun):23-26. 572e. Schapiro, Leonard. Survey 67(1968):142-144.

573. Smal-Stocki, Roman. "Beginning of Fight for Rebirth of Ukrainian Statehood," UQ 23:12-26.

574. Sontag, John P. "Russian Diplomacy, The Balkans and Europe, 1908-1912," Harvard [PhD diss] 1967.

575. Souvarine, Boris. "The 'Durability' of October," PoC 16,ii:80-81.

576. Srečinskij, Ju. "Kompartija i krest'janstvo,"
NŽ 89:198-214.

577. Stachiw, Matthew. Ukraine and Russia: An
Outline of History of Political and Military Relations
(December 1917-1918). [Tr. by Walter Dushnyck, preface
by Clarence Manning] New York: Schevchenko Scientific
Society (215). Rev. 577a. Smal-Stocki, Roman. UQ 23:
373-375.

578. Stachiw, Matthew. "The Ukrainian Revolution
and Russian Democracy," UQ 23:212-225.

579. Šub, D. "Kupec revoljucii," NŽ 87:294-322.

580. Swettenham, John. Allied Intervention in
Russia 1918-1919 and the Part Played by Canada. London: Allen and Unwin (315). Rev. 580a. Ullman, Richard. IJ 24(1968):388-389.

581. Synn, Seung K. "The Russo-Japanese Struggle
for Control of Korea 1894-1904," Harvard [PhD diss]
1967.

582. Thompson, John M. Russia, Bolshevism, and
the Versaille Treaty. Princeton: Princeton U P (vii,
429). Rev. 582a. Degras, Jane. SlavR 27(1968):149-
151. 582b. Laqueur, Walter. NYR 8(15 Jun):23-26.
582c. Polner, Murray. RusR 26:298-300. 582d. Spencer, Frank. IA 44(1968):290-291.

583. Tompkins, Stuart R. The Triumph of Bolshevism: Revolution or Reaction? Norman: U of Oklahoma P
(xi,331). Rev. 583a. Bernt, H.H. LJ 92:1019. 583b.
Elwood, Ralph C. SlavR 27(1968):653-654. 583c. Hookham, M. IA 43:756-758. 583d. Laqueur, Walter. NYR 8
(15 Jun):23-26. 583e. McNeill, Charles L. MilR 47:
109. 583f. Pierce, Richard A. QQ 75(1968):378-380.
583g. Wilkinson, Paul. ConR 211(July):49-50.

584. Toynbee, Arnold,Jr., et al. The Impact of the Russian Revolution, 1917-1967: The Influence on the World Outside Russia. [Richard Lowenthal, Neil McInnis, Hugh Seton-Watson and Peter Wiles] New York: Oxford U P (357). Rev. 584a. Hanak, Harry. IA 44 (1968):344-345. 584b. McLane, Charles B. IJ 23:643-645.

585. Ulam, Adam B. "Reflections on the Revolution," Survey 64:3-13.

586. Von Laue, T.H. "Westernization, Revolution and the Search for a Basis of Authority--Russia in 1917," SovS 19:155-180.

587. Wade, Rex A. "Argonauts of Peace: The Soviet Delegation to Western Europe in the Summer of 1917," SlavR 26:453-467.

588. Wade, Rex A. "Irakli Tsereteli and Siberian Zimmerwaldism," JMH 39:425-431.

589. Wade, Rex A. "1917: Three Studies," CSlSt 2:559-570.

590. Wade, Rex A. "The Triumph of Siberian Zimmerwaldism: (Mar-May,1917)," CSlSt 1,i:253-270.

591. Walz, John D. "State Defense and Russian Politics under the Last Tsar," Syracuse [PhD diss] 1967. DA 28:1383A.

592. Weeks, Albert L. "The First Bolshevik," PoC 16,vi:96-102.

593. Wildman, Allan K. The Making of a Workers' Revolution: Russian Social Democracy, 1891-1903. Chicago: U of Chicago P (xxvi,271). Rev. 593a. Avrich, Paul. RusR 27(1968):354-355. 593b. Baron, Samuel H.

JMH 41(1969):283-284.   593c. Brennan, James F.   CS1St
3(1969):602-603.   593d. Keep, John.   SlavR 28(1969):
135-136.   593e. Legters, Lyman H.   AAAPSS 389(1968):
183-184.

594.   Williams, Albert R.   "The Russian Revolution," NWR 35,iv:26-31.

595.   Williams, Albert R.   Through the Russian Revolution. Moscow: Progress Publishers (238).

596.   Williams, Robert C.   "Russian War Prisoners
and Soviet-German Relations: 1918-1921," CS1P 9:270-
295.

597.   Zimmerman, Judith E.   "Between Revolution and
Reaction: The Russian Constitutional Democratic Party,
October, 1905 to June, 1907," Columbia [PhD diss]
1967.   DA 28:2194A.

598.   The Russian Revolution: A CBS Legacy Book.
New York: Macmillan (248).   Rev. 598a. Avrich, Paul.
RusR 27(1968):225-230.

599.   "Ukrainian Independence: Prime Antithesis to
Fraudulent Russian Bolshevik Revolution." [A Congressional reprint] [49th Anniversary of Ukraine's Inde-
pendence] Washington: Government Printing Office.

See also 89, 110,. 131, 248, 379, 526, 699,
714, 780, 817, 2390.

THE SOVIET PERIOD

600.   Baird, Jay W.   "German Home Propaganda, 1941-
1945, and the Russian Front," Columbia [PhD diss]
1966.   DA 28:2165A.

601.   Beitzell, Robert E.   "Major Strategic Confer-

ences of the Allies, 1941-1943: Quadrant, Moscow, Sex-
tant and Eureka," North Carolina [PhD diss] 1967. DA
28:3594A.

602. Bentwich, Norman. "The Paris Peace Conference—Part II: The Russian Battle," HT 17:799-804.

603. Bloembergen, Samuel. "The Union Republics:
How Much Money?" PoC 16,v:27-35.

604. Bradley, J.F.N. "L'intervention alliée dans
les états Baltes," ESEE 12:71-83;201-218.

605. Bunyan, James. The Origin of Forced Labor
in the Soviet State 1917-1921. [Documents and Materials Stanford: Hoover Institution] Baltimore: Johns
Hopkins P (xi,276). Rev. 605a. Bernt, H.H. LJ 92:
2919. 605b. Herman, Leon M. RusR 27(1968):360. 605c.
Smith, Nathan. AAAPSS 379(1968):175.

606. Chester, Lewis, Fay, Stephen and Young,
Hugo. The Zinoviev Letter: A Political Intrigue.
Philadelphia: Lippincott (xix,219) [12 plates].

607. Clemens, Diane. "Soviet Diplomacy at Yalta,"
California, Santa Barbara [PhD diss] 1967.

608. Daniels, Robert V. "The Left Communists,"
PoC 16,vi:62-70.

609. Demaitre, Edmund. "Stalin and the Era of
Rational Irrationality," PoC 16,vi:76-85.

610. Deutscher, Isaac. The Unfinished Revolution:
Russia 1917-1967. New York: Oxford U P (vii,115).
Rev. 610a. Barry, Donald D. APSR 62(1968):662-663.
610b. Clarkson, Jesse D. RusR 27(1968):355-356. 610c.
Dobriansky, Lev E. UQ 23:378-380. 610d. Jacobs,
Walter D. WAUS 130:186-187. 610e. Latey, Maurice.
HT 17:559. 610f. Lichtheim, George. NYR 9(9 Nov):

10-15. 610g. Nomad, Max. SatR 50,xlix:32-35. 610h.
Pethybridge, Roger. PST 16(1968):314-315. 610i.
Pierce, Richard A. QQ 75(1968):378-380. 610j. Rubin-
stein, Alvin Z. CH 53:240.

611. Dobriansky, Lev E. "Russia, Ukraine and the
World: 50 Years of Conflict," UQ 23:203-211.

612. Eissner, Albin. "Soviet Territorial Gains in
Europe: 1939-1946," CEJ/SB 15:159-165.

613. Fleming, D.F. "The Western Inverventions,"
NWR 35,ix:45-57.

614. Fothergill, Garland W. "Stalinist Communism
and Facism: A Study in the Ambivalences of New Republic Liberalism," Minnesota [PhD diss] 1966. DA 27
(1966):2569A.

615. Grey, Ian. The First Fifty Years: Soviet
Russia 1916-67. New York: Coward-McCann (588). Rev.
615a. Chamberlin, William H. RusR 27(1968):231-236.
615b. Keep, John. IA 44(1968):560-561. 615c. Latey,
Maurice. HT 17:857.

616. Hawkes, James R. "Stalin's Diplomatic Offensive: The Politics of the Second Front, 1941-1943,"
Illinois [PhD diss] 1966. DA 27(1966):4192A.

617. Hendel, Samuel, ed. The Soviet Crucible,
1917-1967. Princeton: Van Nostrand (xlii,458). Rev.
617a. Chamberlin, William H. RusR 27(1968):231-236.

618. Holter, Howard R. "A.V. Lunacharskii and the
Formulation of a Policy Toward the Arts in the RSFSR,
1921-1927," Wisconsin [PhD diss] 1967. DA 28:1031A.

619. Hook, Sidney. "Whither Russia? Fifty Years
After," PoC 16,ii:76-79.

620.   Hoska, Lukas E.,Jr.   "Summit Diplomacy During World War II: The Conferences at Teheran, Yalta and Potsdam," Maryland [PhD diss] 1966. DA 27(1966):3108A.

621.   Khoshbafe Farshi, K.   "Sir Winston S. Churchill's Attitude Toward Communism," Illinois [PhD diss] 1967. DA 28:3730A.

622.   Klimenko, V.   "Settlers of the Soviet East," EW 21,xi-xii:24.

623.   Larson, Thomas B.   "What Happened to Stalin," PoC 16,ii:82-90.

624.   Lensen, George A.   The Soviet Union: An Introduction. New York: Appleton-Century-Crofts (ix, 181).   Rev. 624a. Gerus, Oleh W.   CSlSt 2:608-610.

625.   Leonhard, Wolfgang.   "The Day Stalin Died," PoC 16,iv:76-82.

626.   Linden, Carl A.   Khrushchev and the Soviet Leadership, 1957-1964. London: Oxford U P (270). Rev. 626a. Conolly, Violet.   SEER 46,cvi(1968):261-262. 626b. Hanak, Harry.   IA 43:759-760.

627.   Nelson, Robert C. and Rieber, Alfred A.   A Study of the U.S.S.R. and Communism: An Historical Approach. Chicago: Scott, Foresman (272).

628.   Nettl, J.P.   The Soviet Achievement 1917-1967. New York: Harcourt, Brace and World (288).   Rev. 628a. Pethybridge, Roger W.   IA 44(1968):349.

629.   Oppenheim, Samuel A.   "Rehabilitation in the Post-Stalinist Soviet Union," WPQ 20:97-115.

630.   Pundeff, Marin, ed. and comp.   History in the USSR, Selected Readings. San Francisco: Chandler

(x,313). Rev. 630a. Orchard, G.E. RMSSJ 6(Apr 1969):
202. 630b. Webb, William H. CS1St 3(1969):156.

631. Salisbury, Harrison E.,ed. The Soviet Union:
The Fifty Years. New York: Harcourt, Brace and World
(xxii,484). Rev. 631a. Chamberlin, William H. RusR
27(1968):231-236. 631b. Davis, Saville R. NRep 57,
xxii:29-30.

632. Seth, Ronald. The Executioners: The Story of
SMERSH. London: Cassell.

633. Sullivant, Robert S. "The Ukrainians," PoC
16,v:46-54.

634. Toews, John B. Lost Fatherland: The Story of
the Mennonite Emigration from Soviet Russia, 1921-1927.
Scottdale, Pa.: Herald P (262). Rev. 634a. Kaufman,
Edward G. AHR 74(1969):954-955.

635. Tuchak, William. "Nikita S. Khrushchev:
Yezhov's Collaborator," SoQ 5:433-469.

636. Urban, Joan B. "The Italian Communist Party
and Moscow, 1926-1945," Harvard [PhD diss] 1967.

637. Werth, Alexander. "The Soviet People in the
Second World War," NWR 35,ix:58-65.

638. Werth, Alexander. "Year of Jubilee: The USSR
at Fifty," Nation(U.S.) 205:424-430.

639. Wilczynski, J. "Strategic Embargo in Perspective," SovS 19:74-86.

640. Anon. "The Deported Nationalities . . . An
Unsavory Story," PoC 16,v:102-104.

641. Anon. "The Personality Cult in Russia and
China," [Discussion of a draft volume of the history

of the CPSU and of A.M. Nekrich's work on the opening
events of Soviet participation in World War II] Survey
63:159-194.

        See also 31, 78, 81, 87, 123, 126, 197, 687,
802, 1038, 1450, 1672.

THE CAUCASUS AND CENTRAL ASIA

    642. Allworth, Edward, ed. Central Asia: A Cen-
tury of Russian Rule. New York and London: Columbia
U P (xiv,552). Rev. 642a. Emerson, John. IA 44(1968):
124-125. 642b. Entner, Marvin L. JAS 27:154-155.
642c. Hostler, Charles W. MEJ 22(1968):221-222. 642d.
Lattimore, Owen. GJ 133:538. 642e. Needham, Lucien
and Orchard, G.E. CS1St 2(1968):584-586. 642f.
Peirce, Richard A. SlavR 26:486-487. 642g. Zenkovsky,
Serge A. RusR 27(1968):344-350.

    643. Caroe, Olaf. Soviet Empire: The Turks of
Central Asia and Stalinism. [2d ed] London, Melbourne
and Toronto: Macmillan; New York: St. Martin's (xxxv,
308). Rev. 643a. Carlisle, Donald S. PoC 16,v:132-
134. 643b. LeCompte, Gare. CS1St 1:677-679. 643c.
Rosser, Richard F. APSR 62(1968):661-662.

    644. Conolly, Violet. "The Yakuts," PoC 16,v:81-
91.

    645. Curzon, George N. Russia in Central Asia in
1889 and the Anglo-Russian Question. New York: Barnes
and Noble (xxiii,477). Rev. 645a. Williams, D.S.M.
SEER 46,cviii(1968):528-529.

    646. Jauksch-Orlovski, C. "Les Récits historiques
Sibériens," ESEE 12:219-226.

    647. Mackenzie, David. "Kaufman of Turkestan: An
Assessment of his Administration (1867-1881)," SlavR
26:265-285.

648.   Matossian, Mary.   "The Armenians," <u>PoC</u> 16,v:
65-71.

649.   Nelbandian, Louise.   <u>The Armenian Revolution-</u>
<u>ary Movement</u>.   Berkeley and Los Angeles: U of Califor-
nia P (247).   Rev. 649a. Rothenberg, Gunther E.   <u>CS1St</u>
2(1968):277-278.

650.   Rubel, Paula G.   <u>The Kalmysk Mongols: A Study</u>
<u>in Continuity and Change</u>.   Bloomington: Indiana U (xiv,
282).

651.   Shimkin, Demitri B.   "Pre-Islamic Central
Asia," <u>CS1St</u> 1:618-639.

652.   Tillet, Lowell R.   "Nationalism and History,"
<u>PoC</u> 16,v:36-45.

653.   Vaidyanath, R.   <u>The Formation of the Soviet</u>
<u>Central Asian Republics (A Study in Soviet Nationali-</u>
<u>ties Policy) 1917-1936</u>.   New Delhi: Peoples Pub. House
(xiii,297).

654.   Wheeler, Geoffrey. "The Muslims of Central
Asia," <u>PoC</u> 16,v:72-81.

655.   Wilber, Charles K.   "The Soviet Model of
Economic Development: A Historical Approach with a
Case Study of Soviet Central Asia," Maryland [PhD
diss] 1966.   <u>DA</u> 27:3566A.

<u>TURKEY</u>

656.   Bahrampour, Firouz.   <u>Turkey: Political and</u>
<u>Social Transformation</u>.   New York: Gaus (100).

657.   Daniel, Robert L. "The United States and the

Turkish Republic Before World War II: The Cultural
Dimension," MEJ 21:52-63.

658. Karpat, Kemal H. "Socialism and the Labor
Party of Turkey," MEJ 21:157-172.

659. Mango, Andrew. Turkey. London: Thames and
Hudson (192). Rev. 659a. Purcell, H.D. IA 44(1968):
844.

660. Sayilgan, Aclan. Rifts Within the Turkish
Left (1927-66). [2nd ed] Washington: Joint Publications Research Service (ii,112).

661. Shorter, Trederic C., ed. Four Studies on
the Development of Turkey. London: Cass; New York:
Augustus Kelley (xi,145). Rev. 661a. Robinson, Richard D. MEJ 22(1968):513-515.

See also 530, 938.

YUGOSLAVIA

662. Atanacković, Žarko, Donlagić, Ahmet and
Plenča, Dušan. Yugoslavia in the Second World War.
[Tr. by Lovett F. Edwards] Belgrade: Medjunarodna
Štampa--Interpress (245).

663. Djordjević, Dimitrije. "Contemporary Yugoslav Historiography," EEQ 1:75-86.

664. Fuyet, Hervé. "Histoire des relations entre
la Serbie et la France pendant la periode d'insurrection serbe (1802-1813)," Montreal [PhD diss] 1966.

665. Prpic, George J. "The South Slavs," The Im-
migrants' Influence on Wilson's Peace Policies, ed. by
Joseph P. O'Grady. Lexington: U of Kentucky P:173-203.

666. Ružičić, Gojko. "The Birth Year of Stephan Nemanya," THRJ [F7]:1704-1708.

667. Živojinović, Dragoljub R. "The United States and Italy, April 1917-April 1919, with Special Reference to the Creation of the Yugoslav State," Pennsylvania [PhD diss] 1966. DA 27(1966):1329A.

See also 179, 455.

INTELLECTUAL HISTORY

668. Anderson, Thornton. Russian Political Thought: An Introduction. Ithaca: Cornell U P (xiii, 444). Rev. 668a. Daniels, R.V. APSR 62(1968):612-613. 668b. von Gronicka, André. SEEJ 14(1970):503-509. 668c. Hutchinson, J. CS1St 2(1968):601-602. 668d. Mazour, Anatole G. RusR 27(1968):250-251. 668e. Rabinowitch, Janet. PSQ 84(1968):111-112. 668f. Raeff, Marc. AHR 73:541.

669. Kline, George L. "Kareyev, Nicholas Ivanovich (1850-1931)," Encyclopedia of Philosophy 4:325.

670. Raeff, Marc. "Filling the Gap Between Radishchev and the Decembrists," SlavR 26:395-413.

671. Raeff, Marc. "Les Slaves, les allemands et les 'lumières'," CS1St 1:521-551.

672. Schapiro, Leonard. Rationalism and Nationalism in Russian Nineteenth-Century Political Thought. New Haven and London: Yale U P (173). Rev. 672a. Black, J.L. CS1St 2(1968):594-596. 672b. Emmons, Terrence. RusR 27(1968):360-361.

673. Szamuely, Tibor. "The Intellectual Revolt in Poland," Reporter 36,xi:32-34.

674.   Zernov, V. "Iz glubiny," NŽ 88:239-250.

See also 329, 1207, 1266, 1672, 1696.

INTELLIGENTSIA

675.   Avineri, Shlomo. "Marx and the Intellectuals," JHI 28:269-278.

676.   Brower, Daniel R. "The Problem of the Russian Intelligentsia," SlavR 26:638-647.

677.   Lednicki, Wacław. "The Role of the Polish
Intellectual in America," PolR 12,ii:3-10.

678.   Lesnoj, Sergej. "Kul'tura i poluintelligen-
cija," NŽ 86:238-243.

679.   Poltoratsky, Nikolai P. "The Vekhi Dispute
and the Significance of Vekhi," CSlP 9:86-106.

680.   Raeff, Marc. Origins of the Russian Intel-
ligentsia: The Eighteenth-Century Nobility. New York:
Harcourt, Brace and World (vii,248). Rev. 680a.
Bushkoff, Leonard. CSlSt 3(1969):121-127. 680b. Per-
vushin, Nicholas. ESEE 12:138-139. 680c. Simmonds,
George W. SlavR 27(1968):317-318.

681.   Raina, P.K. "Poland: Intellectuals vs. the
Party, A Report on the Kolakowski Case." Dissent(U.S.)
(Sep-Oct):576-589.

682.   Shatz, Marshall. "Jan Waclaw Machajski: The
'Conspiracy' of the Intellectuals," Survey 62:45-57.

683.   Wortman, Richard. "The New Soviet Intelligentsia and Russia's Past," Midway 8,iii:21-38.

See also 2081.

HISTORIOGRAPHY

684. Bloomfield, Edith. "Soviet Historiography of 1905 as Reflected in Party Histories of the 1920's," Washington, Seattle [PhD diss] 1966. DA 27(1966): 2977A.

685. Bromke, Adam. "Polish Communism: The Historians Look Again," EE 16,xii:20-27.

686. Byrnes, Robert F. "Pobedonostsev on the Role of Change in History," RusR 26:231-250.

687. Daniels, Robert V. "Soviet Historians Prepare for the Fiftieth," SlavR 26:113-118.

688. Eissenstat, Bernard W. "M.N. Pokrovsky and Soviet Historiography," Kansas [PhD diss] 1967. DA 28:3602A.

689. Fleming, D.F. "The USSR and World War II," NWR 35,ii:13-18.

690. Gefter, M.J. and Malkov, V.L. "Reply to a Questionnaire on Russian Historiography," H&T 6:180-207.

691. Genchev, Nikolay. "The Quest for Identity," EE 16,i:20-22.

692. Hanak, Peter. "Problems of East European History in Recent Hungarian Historiography," EEQ 1: 123-142.

693. Nove, A. "A Brief Reply to Critics," SovS 19:130-132.

694. Poltoratskij, Nikolaj P. <u>Berdjaev i Rossija</u>
(<u>Filosofija istorii Rossii u N. A. Berdjaeva</u>). New
York: Obščestvo Druzej Russkoj Kul'tury (vi,270).
Rev. 694a. Story, J.C. <u>SlavR</u> 29(1970):515-517.

695. Poltoratsky, Nikolaj P. "Nikolay Berdyayev's
Interpretation of Russia's Historical Mission," <u>SEER</u>
45,civ:193-206.

696. Schapiro, Leonard. "Out of the Dustbin of
History," <u>PoC</u> 16,vi:86-91.

697. Szporluk, Roman. "Pokrovskii's View of the
Russian Revolution," <u>SlavR</u> 26:70-84.

698. Troscianko, Wiktor. "Polish Historians: A
New Day?" <u>EE</u> 16,viii:10-15.

699. Warth, Robert D. "On the Historiography of
the Russian Revolution," <u>SlavR</u> 26:247-264.

700. Wereszycki, Henryk. "Polish Insurrections as
a Controversial Problem in Polish Historiography,"
<u>CSlP</u> 9:107-121.

701. Wolfe, Bertram D. "Backwardness and Industrialization in Russian History and Thought," <u>SlavR</u>
26:177-203.

See also 663, 1651.

V. International Relations and Politics

INTERNAL COMMUNIST BLOC

702. Abrahams, Roger D. and Wukasch, Charles. "Political Jokes of East Germany," TFSB 33:7-10.

703. Armstrong, John A. "Comparative Politics and Communist Systems: Introductory Remarks," SlavR 26: 1-2.

704. Aspaturian, Vernon V. "The Soviet Union and International Communism," in Roy C. Macridis, ed., Foreign Policy in World Politics, 216-245. Englewood Cliffs: Prentice-Hall. [3rd ed.]

705. Bakotic, B., Csabafi, I. and Kopal, V. "Space Law in the Socialist Countries of Eastern Europe: Czechoslovakia, Hungary, and Yugoslavia," CSlSt 1:60-78.

706. Bennett, E.M., ed. Polycentrism: Growing Dissidence in the Communist Bloc? Pullman: Washington State U P (63).

707. Bloemer, Klaus. "East European Politics and Reunification," ACQ 5:219-222.

708. Braham, Randolph L. "The 'Socialist Commonwealth': An Appraisal," USSR After 50 Years [F2]:263-294.

709. Bregman, Alexander. "The USSR and Eastern Europe," PoC 16,iii:50-54.

710. Brzezinski, Zbigniew K. "Communism is Dead," NL 50,xv:10-13.

711.   Brzezinski, Zbigniew K.   "Communist State Relations: The Effect on Ideology," EEQ 16:2-7.

712.   Brzezinski, Zbigniew K.   The Soviet Bloc: Unity and Conflict.   Cambridge: Harvard U P (xvii,599). Rev. 712a. Bregman, Alexander.   PoC 16,vi:92-94. 712b. Ionescu Ghita.   IA 44(1968):341-342.   712c. Ra'anan, Uri.   NL 50,xiii:21-23.   712d. Rubinstein, Alvin Z. CH 53:239.

713.   Brzezinski, Zbigniew K.   "Staaliche Beziehungen und Ideologie," Österopäische Rundschau 12, iv:3-8.

714.   Ciolkosz, Adam.   "The Bolshevik Revolution: Its Impact in Eastern Europe," EE 16,xi:3-8.

715.   Dallin, Alexander.   "International Communism in Flux," SWIF [F6]:141-163.

716.   Drachkovitch, Milorad M.,ed.   Yearbook on International Communist Affairs 1966.   Stanford: Stanford U P (xx,766).   Rev. 716a. Gyorgy, Andrew.   CSlSt 2(1968):425-426

717.   Egbert, Donald D.   "Politics and the Arts in Communist Bulgaria," SlavR 26:204-216.

718.   Farrell, R. Barry.   "Foreign Policy Formation in the Communist Countries of Eastern Europe," EEQ 1: 39-74.

719.   Grodnis, Jāzeps.   "Domas par Latvijas valsti," JGai 64:45-46.

720.   Gyorgy, Andrew.   "Diversity in Eastern Europe: Cohesion and Disunity," CSlSt 1:24-43.

721.   Hopmann, P. Terry.   "International Conflict and Cohesion in the Communist System," IS 11:212-236.

722. Ionescu, Ghita. The Politics of the European Communist States. New York and Washington: Praeger (ix,303). Rev. 722a. Croan, Melvin. Survey 67(1968): 156-158. 722b. Fischer-Galati, Stephen. AAAPSS 379 (1968):174-175. 722c. Gömöri, George. SovS 20(1968): 144-146. 722d. Hanak, Harry. IA 44(1968):117-118. 722e. Macfarlane, L.J. PSt 16(1968):481-483. 722f. Prybyla, Jan S. EE 17,iii(1968):55-56. 722g. Rupen, Robert A. APSR 62(1968):663-666. 722h. Skilling, H. Gordon. EEQ 2(1968):347-350.

723. Kaser, Michael. COMEON: Integration Problems of the Planned Economies. New York: Oxford U P (279). Rev. 723a. Kronsten, Joseph A. IA 44(1968):566-567. 723b. Pick, Otto. IJ 23:641.

724. Kaser, Michael. "The East European Economic Reforms and Foreign Trade," WT 23:512-522.

725. Lichtheim, George. "What is Left of Communism?" FA 46:78-94.

726. London, Kurt L. "Eastern Europe in the Communist World," US and EEur [F3]:101-123.

727. London, Kurt. The Permanent Crisis: Communism in World Politics. Waltham: Blaisdell (246).

728. McNeal, Robert H., ed. International Relations Among Communists. Englewood Cliffs: Prentice-Hall (x,181). Rev. 728a. Fischer, Gabriel. IJ 23: 484-486. 728b. Leinbach, Philip E. LJ 92:1500. 728c. Toma, Peter A. CSlSt 1:323-325.

729. Meyer, Alfred G. "The Comparative Study of Communist Political Systems," SlavR 26:3-12.

730. Pertot, V. "Yugoslavia's Economic Relations with Eastern European Countries," Coexistence 4:7-13.

731. Pick, O. "Soviet Alliance Policies in Retrospect," IJ 22:576-592.

732. Pounds, Norman J.G. "Fissures in the Eastern European Bloc," AAAPSS 372:40-58.

733. Robinson, William F. "Hungary's Turn to Revisionism," EE 16,ix:14-17.

734. Rubinstein, Alvin Z. "Politics and Political Change," US and EEur [F3]:29-55.

735. Sanness, J. "Eastern Europe--Integration, Hegemony, Empire," Cooperation and Conflict 2,i:47-53.

736. Shaffer, Harry G., ed. The Communist World: Marxist and Non-Marxist Views. New York: Appleton-Century-Crofts (xv,558). Rev. 736a. Hinton, Harold C. ChQ 34(1968):152-153. 736b. Kerschner, Lee R. JDA 2 (1968):431-432. 736c. Novosel, Pavle. JDA 2(1968): 432-433.

737. Sharlet, Robert S. "Systematic Political Science and Communist Systems," SlavR 26:22-26.

738. Smolansky, Oles. "Moscow and the Problem of National Socialism: An Ideological Approach," CSlSt 1: 196-211.

739. Sorensen, Theodore C. "Report from Rumania," SatR 50,lii:14-15.

740. Spilners, Ilgvars. "Domas par Latvijas valsti," JGai 61:33-34.

741. Staar, Richard F. "Osteuropa im Wandel: Eine Bestandsaufnahme," Moderne Welt 8:258-278.

742. Staar, Richard F. The Communist Regimes in

Eastern Europe: An Introduction. Stanford: Stanford
U P (xix,387). Rev. 742a. Anderson, Stephen. CH 56
(1969):230. 742b. Barman, Thomas. IA 44(1968):798.
742c. Potichnyj, Peter J. CSlSt 2(1968):610-611.

  743. Stolte, Stefan C. "Economic Developments in
the Soviet Bloc," BISUSSR 14,x:29-34.

  744. Stolte, Stefan C. "Three Problems Facing the
Soviet Bloc," BISUSSR 14,cii:20-28.

  745. Streips, Laimonis. "Domas par Larvijas valsti," JGai 62:41-44.

  746. Sylvester, Anthony. "Revisionists and Stal-
inists in the Balkans," EE 16,i:2-8. [German Version:
Osteuropäische Rundschau 13,iv:9-14.]

  747. Taborsky, Edward. "Where is Czechoslovakia
Going?" EE 16,ii:2-12.

  748. Tarrow, Sidney G. "Political Dualism and
Italian Communism," APSR 61:39-53.

  749. Viktorov, Felix. "Economic Association of
Countries of Socialism," EEQ 1:261-276.

  750. Volgyes, Ivan. "Eastern Europe Twenty Years
After," WAUS 130:95-106.

  751. Winston, Henry. "Unity of Soviet Nations,"
NWR 35,ix:35-36,57.

  752. Anon. "The Warsaw Pact," MilR 47,x:18-21.

       See also 1173, 1149.

THE SOVIET UNION

POLITICS

753. Aldridge, James. "A Half Century of Soviet Diplomacy," NWR 35,vii:47-50.

754. Anderson, Stephen S. "Soviet Russia and the Two Europes," CH 52:203-207,241-242.

755. Aron, Raymond. Peace and War: A Theory of International Relations. New York: Praeger (xviii, 820).

756. Aspaturian, Vernon V. "Moscow's Foreign Policy," Survey 65:35-60.

757. Aspaturian, Vernon V. "Soviet Foreign Policy," in Roy C. Macridis, ed., Foreign Policy in World Politics, Englewood Cliffs: Prentice-Hall (156-215).

758. Berzins, Alfreds. The Two Faces of Coexistence. New York: Speller (xii,335). Rev. 758a. Anderson, Edgar. AHR 73:550-551. 758b. Korbel, Pavel. EE 16:59-60. 758c. Kulski, W.W. APSR 62(1968):312-313. 758d. Low, Alfred D. RusR 27(1968):249-250.

759. Bilinsky, Yaroslav. "The Rulers and the Ruled," PoC 16,v:16-26.

760. Blackwood, George D. and Gyorgy, Andrew. Ideologies in World Affairs. Waltham: Blaisdell (262).

761. Bromke, Adam. "Ideology and National Interest in Soviet Foreign Policy," IJ 22:547-562.

762. Brzezinski, Zbigniew K. Ideology and Power in Soviet Politics. New York: Praeger (291).

763.   Campbell, John C.   "The Soviet Union in the International Environment," Allen Kassof, ed.   Prospects for Soviet Society, 473-496.   New York: Praeger.

764.   Chamberlain, William H.   "The Short Life of Russian Liberalism," RusR 26:144-152.

765.   Clark, Joseph.   "Evolution and Detente," PoC 16,i:49-51.

766.   Combs, Richard E.,Jr.   "The Role of Ideology in Postwar Soviet Policy Determinations," California, Berkeley [PhD diss] 1966.   DA 28:1106A.

767.   Conquest, Robert, ed.   The Politics of Ideas in the U.S.S.R.   New York: Praeger (175).   Rev. 767a. Amann, R.   IA 44(1968):347-348.   767b. Jacobs, Walter D.   WAUS 130(1968):262-264.   767c. Leinbach, Philip E.   LJ 92:3046.

768.   Conquest, Robert.   The Soviet Political System Conquest.   New York: Praeger (144).

769.   Erickson, John.   "A Framework for Soviet Foreign Policy," SSU 6:108-128.

770.   Eudin, Xenia J. and Slusser, Robert M. Soviet Foreign Policy, 1928-1934: Documents and Materials, Vol. II.   University Park and London: Pennsylvania State U P (xi,423).   Rev. 770a. Degras, Jane. SlavR 28(1969):149.   770b. Hanak, Henry.   IA 44(1968): 564-566.

771.   Finley, David D.   "Soviet Foreign Policy Decision Making," Stanford [PhD diss] 1966.   DA 27 (1966):805A.

772.   Frankel, Joseph.   "Theory of State, Cybernetics and Political Science in the Soviet Union," PSt 15,i:59-62.

773. Galay, Nikolai, "The Record of Soviet Diplomacy," SSU 6:91-107.

774. Gehlen, Michael P. The Politics of Coexistence: Soviet Methods and Motives. Bloomington and London: Indiana U P (xi,334). Rev. 774a. Griffiths, Franklyn. SlavR 28(1969):154-156. 774b. Lanyi, George A. EE 17,i(1968):55-56. 774c. Mitrany, David. AAAPSS 374:228-229. 774d. Rintala, Marvin. RusR 26:409-410. 774e. Robotham, John S. LJ 92:1166. 774f. Willenz, Eric. WAUS 132,i(1969):70-72.

775. Gibson, John S. Ideology and World Affairs. Boston: Houghton Mifflin (372).

776. Gilbert, Carl L.,Jr. "The Hirota Ministries: An Appraisal, Japan's Relations with China and the U.S.S.R., 1933-1938," Georgetown [PhD diss] 1967. DA 28:3108A.

777. Goldberg, B.Z. "Some Soviet Policies - Fact and Fiction," Ms 13,vi:39-56.

778. Gregor, R. "Lenin, Revolution, and Foreign Policy," IJ 22:563-575.

779. Gripp, Richard C. Patterns of Soviet Politics. Homewood: Dorsey (xi,386).

780. Gruber, Helmut,ed. International Communism in the Era of Lenin. Greenwich: Fawcett; Ithaca: Cornell U P (512). Rev. 780a. Hubbard, William H. CS1St 2(1968):130-132. 780b. Riha, Thomas. Historian 30 (1968):465.

781. Hoeffding, Oleg. Recent Structural Changes and Balance of Payment Adjustments in Soviet Foreign Trade. Santa Monica: Rand Corporation.

782. Jacobs, Walter D. "Soviet Views of Wars of National Liberation," MilR 47,x:59-66.

783. Jaworskyj, Michael, ed. Soviet Political
Thought: An Anthology. Baltimore: Johns Hopkins P
(xii,621).

784. Juviler, Peter and Morton, Henry W., eds.
Soviet Policy-Making: Studies of Communism in Transition. New York: Praeger (xiv,274). Rev. 784a. Barman, Thomas. IA 44(1968):118-120. 784b. Butler, William E. WAUS 129,iv:275-278. 784c. Carson, George
B., Jr. AHR 73:551. 784d. Gripp, Richard C. MJPS 12
(1968):456-458. 784e. Linden, Carl A. APSR 62(1968):
288-289. 784f. Reddaway, Peter. PoC 17,ii(1968):61-
64. 784g. Roley, Paul. RusR 27(1968):357-358.

785. Kalb, Marvin. The Volga: A Political Journey
through Russia. New York: Macmillan; London: Collier-
Macmillan (xxvii,196).

786. Kaser, Michael, ed. Soviet Affairs: Number
Four. New York: Oxford U P.

787. Landis, Lincoln. "Middle East Crises and the
USSR," WAUS 130,i:13-16.

788. Macfarlane, L.J. "Hands Off Russia: British
Labour and the Russo-Polish War, 1920," Past and Present,38:126-152.

789. Ploss, Sidney I. "Studying the Domestic
Determinants of Soviet Foreign Policy," CSlSt 1:44-59.

780A. Ra'anan, Uri. "The U.S.S.R. in World Affairs: Problems of a 'Communist' Foreign Policy," USSR
after 50 Yrs [F2]:235-262.

781A. Ross, Rhomas B. and Wise, David. The Espio-
nage Establishment. New York: Random House (308).

782A. Schuman, Frederick L. "The U.S.S.R. in World
Affairs: An Historic Survey of Soviet Foreign Policy,"
USSR After 50 Yrs [F2]:205-233.

783A. Sharlet, Robert. "Concept Formation in Political Science and Communist Studies," <u>CSlSt</u> 1:640-649.

784A. Shulman, Marshall D. "The Critical Decision for Moscow," <u>NL</u> 50,xiv:3-6.

785A. Shulman, Marshall D. "Die Weltlage in sowjetischer Sicht. Eindrücke eines Amerikaners aus Gesprächen in der Sowjetunion," <u>Europa-Archiv</u> 22:168-176.

786A. Soraghan, Joseph R. "Reconnaissance Satellites: Legan Characterization and Possible Utilization for Peacekeeping," McGill Law Journal 13:458-493.

787A. Svetlov, Y. "New State in Economic Cooperation with Japan," <u>EW</u> 21,ix/x:22-23.

788A. De Toledano, Ralph. <u>Spies, Dupes, and Diplomats</u>. New Rochesse: Arlington House (258).

789A. Anon. "Fifty Years of Socialism: The Theses of the CPSU Central Committee," <u>NWR</u> 35,viii:62-64.

        See also 27, 97, 555, 567, 615, 668, 1105, 1176, 1399, 1405.

RELATIONS WITH THE UNITED STATES

790. Barnett, Frank R., Possony, Stefan T., Swearingen, Rodger and Trager, Frank R. "Communism: A Symposium," F.R. Barnett and R. Swearingen. "The United States Faces Russia and China," S.T. Possony and F.N. Trager. "Communism and Vietnam," F.R. Barnett, et al. "Communism--Practical Next Steps," <u>InsCounselJ</u> 34:625-637.

791. Bartlett, Charles and Weintal, Edward. <u>Facing the Brink: An Intimate Study of Crisis Diplomacy</u>. New York: Scribner (vi,248).

792. Bausum, Henry S. "Alternative to Pax Americana," WAUS 130:77-88.

793. Beloff, Max. The Balance of Power. Montreal:
McGill U P (73). Rev. 793a. Arnopoulos, P.J. CS1St
2(1968):606-607.

794. Benson, David V. Christianity, Communism,
and Survival. Glendale: G/L Regal Books (202).

795. Beranek, Robert E. "The Second Berlin Crisis
and the Foreign Ministers' Conference at Geneva (1959):
A Case Study of Soviet Diplomacy," Pittsburgh [PhD
diss] 1966. DA 27(1966):4307A.

796. Berman, Harold J. and Garson, John R. "The
Road to Trade," Nation(U.S.) 204,xx:626-628.

797. Bose, Tarum C. American-Soviet Relations,
1921-1933. Calcutta, London: K.L. Mukhopadhyay (228).
Rev. 797a. Donelan, Michael. IA 44(1968):756-757.

798. Brown, Neville. "The Balance Between the
Superpowers: Into Strategic Deadlock," MilR 47,iii:
71-79.

799. Brzezinski, Zbigniew K. "The Changing Char-
acter of the Challenge," CS1P 9:50-59.

800. Campbell, John C. "Soviet-American Relations:
Conflict and Cooperation," CH 53:193-202,241.

801. Dobriansky, Lev E. "Review of U.S. Policy
Toward the USSR: A Major Theme for the 1967 Captive
Nations Week," UQ 23:27-42.

802. Druks, Herbert. Harry S. Truman and the Russians 1945-1953. New York: Speller (ix,291). Rev.
802a. Fisher, Harold H. RusR 27(1968):366-368.

803. Eagles, Keith D. "Ambassador Joseph E. Davies and American-Soviet Relations 1937-1941," Washington, Seattle [PhD diss] 1966. DA 27(1966):2981A.

804. Eckhardt, William and White, Ralph K. "A
Test of the Mirror-Image Hypothesis: Kennedy and
Khrushchev," JCR 11:325-332.

805. Findley, Paul. "Neither War nor Peace,"
CEJ/SB 15:183-194.

806. Galloway, Jonathan F. "Space Communications
Technology and United States Foreign Policy: 1957-66,"
Columbia [PhD diss] 1967. DA 28:4222A.

807. Gass, Oscar. "China, Russia and the U.S."
Com 43,iii:65-73;iv:39-46.

808. Gordenker, Leon. "International Organization
and the Cold War," IJ 23:357-368.

809. Griffith, William E. "Die Vereinigten
Staaten und die Sowjetunion in Europa: Die Auswirkun-
gen des Rustungswettlaufs, der technologischen Ent-
wicklung und des Deutschlandproblems," Moderne Welt
8(Apr):362-374.

810. Griffith, William E. "The United States and
the Soviet Union in Europe: The Impact of the Arms
Race, Technology, and the German Question," Modern
World 5:37-51.

811. Halle, Louis J. The Cold War as History. New
York: Harper and Row (xiv,434). Rev. 811a. Armstrong,
Donald. WAUS 131(1968):54-55. 811b. Bregman, Alexan-
der. PoC 17,iii(1968):64-65. 811c. Frankel, Joseph
and Williams, Geoffrey. PSt 16(1968):285-292. 811d.
Soward, F.H. IJ 23:141-142. 811e. Younger, Kenneth.
IA 43:546-547.

812. Holsti, Ole R. "Cognitive Dynamics and Images of the Enemy," JIA 21:16-39.

813. Holsti, Ole R. "Cognitive Dynamics of Images of the Enemy: Dulles and Russia," Richard R. Fagen, David J. Finlay, Ole R. Holsti, Enemies in Politics. Chicago: Rand-McNally 25-96.

814. Hudson, Geoffrey F. The Hard and Bitter Peace: World Politics since 1945. New York: Praeger (319).

815. Jablon, Howard. "Cordell Hull, the State Department and the Foreign Policy of the First Roosevelt Administration, 1933-1936," Rutgers [PhD diss] 1967. DA 28:595A.

816. Kash, Don E. The Politics of Space Cooperation. Lafayette: Purdue U (xii,137).

817. Kennan, George F. Soviet-American Relations, 1917-1920. Vol. II: The Decision to Intervene. New York: Atheneum (xii,514).

818. Kertesz, Stephen D. The Quest for Peace Through Diplomacy. Englewood Cliffs: Prentice-Hall (x,182). Rev. 818a. Chace, James. EE 18,i(1969):54-56.

819. Kindleberger, Charles P. "The Marshall Plan and the Cold War," IJ 23:369-382.

820. Kintner, William R. Peace and the Strategy Conflict. New York: Praeger (xiii,264).

821. Knapp, Wilfrid. "The Cold War Revisited," IJ 23:344-356.

822. LaFeber, Walter. America, Russia, and the Cold War, 1945-1966. New York: Wiley (xi,295). Rev. 822a. Donelan, Michael. IA 44(1968):756-757.

823. Melman, Seymour. "Small Wars: The Peril Escalates," Nation (U.S.) 204,xxv:774-775.

824. Morford, Richard. "The Movement for American-Soviet Understanding," NWR 35,ix:173-183.

825. Niehbuhr, Reinhold. "The Social Myths in the 'Cold War'," JIA 21:40-56.

826. Puškarev, Sergej. "Rossija i S.Š.A.: Istoričeskij očerk ix vzaimootnošenij s konca XVIII veka do 1917 goda," NŽ 88:185-221.

827. Rees, David. The Age of Containment: The Cold War 1945-1965. London: Macmillan; New York: St. Martin's (x,156). Rev. 827a. Bregman, Alexander. PoC 17,iii(1968):64-65. 827b. Dobell, W.M. IJ 23:482-483. 827c. Frankel, Joseph and Williams, Geoffrey. PSt 16(1968):285-292.

828. Sathyamurthy, T.V. "From Containment to Interdependence," WP 20,i:142-177.

829. Scheuer, Sidney. "To Russia with Trade," CJWB 2:67-71.

830. Schlesinger, Arthur,Jr. "Origins of the Cold War," FA 46:22-52.

831. Schuman, Frederick L. The Cold War: Retrospect and Prospect. Baton Rouge: Louisiana State U P, 2nd ed. (134).

832. Schuman, Frederick L. "US-USSR Relations and the War in Vietnam," NWR 35,ix:68-72.

833. Seabury, Paul. The Rise and Decline of the Cold War. New York and London: Basic Books (171). Rev. 833a. Armstrong, Donald. WAUS 130:202-203. 833b. Northedge, F.S. IA 44(1968):302-304. 833c. Soward,

F.H. IJ 23:140-141. 833d. Spanier, John W. Orbis 7 (1968):331-335.

834. Sorensen, Theodore C. "Why We Should Trade with the Soviets," FA 46:575-583.

835. Spiegel, Steven L. "The Soviet-American Role in the Current International System: A Theoretical Analysis," Harvard [PhD diss] 1967.

836. Tabari, Keyvan. "Iran's Policies toward the United States during the Anglo-Russian Occupation, 1941-1946," Columbia [PhD diss] 1967. DA 28:1881A.

837. Tucker, Robert C. "United States-Soviet Cooperation: Incentives and Obstacles," AAAPSS 372:1-15.

838. Turgeon, Lynn. "Upgrading U.S.-Soviet Trade: The Prospects," Finance (Jun):13-16.

839. U.S. Treaties and Other International Acts Series. Cultural Relations: Exchanges in the Scientific, Technical, Educational Cultural and Other Fields in 1966-1967. Washington: Government Printing Office (66).

840. Waltz, Kenneth W. "International Structure, National Force, and the Balance of World Power," JIA 21:215-231.

841. Weems, Miner L. "The Containment Policy After Twenty Years: An Assessment," SoQ 5:177-196.

842. Weiner, Bernard. "The Truman Doctrine: Background and Presentation," Clarement [PhD diss] 1967. DA 28:4235A.

843. White, Ralph K. "Communicating with Soviet Communists," Antioch Review 27:458-476.

844. Wilson, Joan H. "The Role of the Business Community in American Relations with Russia and Europe, 1920-1933," California, Berkeley [PhD diss] 1966. DA 27(1966):2491A.

See also 85, 512, 555.

RELATIONS WITH CHINA AND ALBANIA

845. Austin, Dennis. "Russia & China in Central Asia," WT 23:89-93.

846. Boulding, K.E. "Conflict and Community in the International System," JSI 23(Jan):23-160.

847. Boulding, K.E. "The Learning and Reality-Testing Process in the International System," JIA 21, i:1-15.

848. Boychuk, Stephan. "Mongolia and Sino-Soviet Competition," UQ 23:264-272.

849. Chen, V. Sino-Russian Relations in the Seventeenth Century. The Hague: Nijhoff (x,150).

850. Chin-Yao, Yim. "Soviet Imperialism and China," Asian Outlook 2:17-22,xii:13-16.

851. Clemens, Walter C.,Jr. "The Nuclear Test Ban and Sino-Soviet Relations," Morton H. Halperin, ed. Sino-Soviet Relations and Arms Control, 145-167. Cambridge: M.I.T. Press.

852. Farrell, Robert and Rupen, Robert A., eds. Vietnam and the Sino-Soviet Dispute. New York: Praeger (120). Rev. 852a. Caldwell, Malcolm. IA 44 (1968):595-596. 852b. Croan, Melvin. PoC 17,i(1968): 34-35. 852c. Pike, Douglas. ChQ 33(1968):140.

853. Fitzgerald, C.P. "Tension on the Sino-Soviet Border," FA:683-693.

854. Gau, Claude C. "Communist Wars of National Liberation and the Sino-Soviet Dispute," Georgetown [PhD diss] 1967. DA 28:3244A.

855. Gettings, John. "The View From Moscow: The Sino-Soviet Dispute," Far Eastern Economic Review 58: 277-278.

856. Griffith, William E., ed. Communism in Europe: Continuity, Change, and the Sino-Soviet Dispute. Cambridge: M.I.T. Press, Vol. I(x,406), Vol. II (xiv, 439). Rev. 856a. Hulse, James W. Historian 29:255-256. 856b. Ionescu, Ghita. IA 44(1968):341-342.

857. Griffith, William E.,ed. Sino-Soviet Relations, 1964-1965. Cambridge: M.I.T. Press (xii,504). Rev. 857a. Shillinglaw, George. IA 44(1968):601-603. 857b. Yahuda, M.B. PSt 16(1968):502.

858. Kashin, Alexander. "A New Phase in Sino-Soviet Relations," BISUSSR 14,iv:3-14.

859. Kim, Uoong T. "Sino-Soviet Dispute and North Korea," Pennsylvania [PhD diss] 1967. DA 28:1879A.

860. Lee, Unja. "Chinese-Soviet Relations: 1956-1960: A Study of Inter-Party and Inter-State Relations," Claremont [PhD diss] 1967. DA 28:753A.

861. Michael, Franz. "Moscow and the Current Chinese Crisis," CH 53:141-147,179-180.

862. Michael, Franz. "Struggle for Power," PoC 16,iii:12-21.

863. Moseley, George. A Sino-Soviet Cultural Frontier: The Ili Kazakh Autonomous Chou. Cambridge:

East Asian Research Center, Harvard U (viii,163). Rev.
863a. Hook, Brian. ChQ 32:168-169. 863b. Nichols,
J.L. JAS 27:628-629.

864. Parry, Albert. "Communism's Great Divide,"
Reporter 36,xi:29-32.

865. Pradhan, R.C. "The Soviet-Mongolian Treaty
of Friendship, Cooperation and Mutual Assistance,"
EW 21,i-ii:20-21.

866. Prybyla, Jan S. "Recent Trends in Sino-
Soviet Economic Relations," BISUSSR 14,v:11-21.

867. Robinson, Thomas W. "A National Interest
Analysis of Sino-Soviet Relations," IS 11:135-175.

868. Romance, Francis J. "Sino-Soviet Policies
Towards the Mongolian People's Republic, 1945-1965:
A Study of the Political and Economic Factors Invol-
ved," Georgetown [PhD diss] 1967. DA 28:756A.

869. Roucek, Joseph S. "Racial Elements in the
Sino-Russian Dispute," ConR 210 (Feb):77-84.

870. Salisbury, Harrison E. "Russia vs China:
Global Conflict?" Antioch Review 27:425-439.

871. Selton, Robert W. "Sino-Soviet Conflict in
the Developing Areas," MilR 47,i:42-50.

872. Shu-kai, Chow. "Significance of the Rift
Between the Chinese Communist Regime and the Soviet
Union," AAAPSS 372:64-71.

873. Tekiner, Süleyman. "Sinkiang and the Sino-
Soviet Conflict," BISUSSR 14,viii:9-16.

874. Treadgold, Donald W., ed. Soviet and Chinese
Communism: Similarities and Differences. Seattle and

London: U of Washington P (xix,452).   Rev. 874a. Bernstein, Thomas P. SlavR 26:687-688.   874b. Ionescu,
Ghita.   IA 44(1968):530-532.   874c. Kanet, Roger E.
RMSSJ 5,ii(1968):156-157.   874d. London, Kurt L.   RusR
27(1968):87-88.   874e. Mehnert, Klaus. PoC 17,i(1968):
31-33.   874f. Rubinstein, Alvin Z. CH 53:238.   874g.
Strong, John W. CSlP 11(1969):128-129.

875.   Tucker, Frank H. "The 'Cultural Revolution'
and the Sino-Soviet Rift," Communist Affairs 5,vi:10-
17.

876.   Tucker, Frank H. "The Sino-Soviet Rivalry in
Africa, 1960-1965," RMSSJ 4,i:114-124.

877.   Wheeler, Geoffrey. "Russia and China in Central Asia," WT 23:89-92.

878.   Wu, Aitchen K. China and the Soviet Union.
Port Washington: Kennikat (434).

879.   Yin, John Y. "Sino-Soviet Dialogue on the
Nature of War 1959-1962," Southern California [PhD
diss] 1967. DA 28(1968):2757A.

880.   Anon. "The Soviet Union and 'The Great Pro-
letarian Cultural Revolution'," Survey 63:3-194.

881.   Anon. "North Korea's Independent Stance
Towards China and USSR (II)," EW 21,i/ii:31.

        See also 442, 706, 807, 901, 903, 905, 908,
959, 967, 1179, 1550.

RELATIONS WITH CUBA

882.   González, Edward. "The Cuban Revolution and
the Soviet Union: 1959-1960," California, Los Angeles
[PhD diss] 1966. DA 27(1966):3502A.

883. Losman, Donald L. "Soviet Trade with Cuba: Motives, Methods and Meaning," DR 14,ii:127-153.

884. Tretiak, D. "Cuba and the Soviet Union: Growing Accommodation," Orbis 11:439-458.

885. Yinger, Jon A. "Cuba: American and Soviet Core Interests in Conflict," DA 28:758A.

COMMUNIST BLOC RELATIONS

WITH CHINA AND ALBANIA

886. Bregman, Alexander. "Poking Fun at Mao," EE 16,iii:21-22.

887. Devlin, Kevin. "Which Side Are You On?" PoC 16,i:52-59.

888. Goldston, Robert. The Rise of Red China. Greenwich: Fawcett (233).

889. Houn, Franklin W. "The Principles and Operational Code of Communist China's International Conduct," JAS 27:21-40.

890. Lensen, George A. The Russo-Chinese War. Tallahassee: Diplomatic (315).

891. Prybyla, Jan. "Albania's Economic Vassalage," EE 16,i:9-14.

892. Prybyla, Jan S. "Chinas Handel mit Östeuropa," Östeuropäische Rundschau 12,iv:15-19.

893. Prybyla, Jan S. "The China Trade," EE 16, iii:15-20.

894. Thornton, Richard C. "The Comintern and the

Chinese Communists, 1928-1931," Washington, Seattle [PhD diss] 1966. <u>DA</u> 27(1966):2999A.

895. Varnai, Ferenc. "China Against Herself," <u>EE</u> 16,iii:23-26.

896. Anon. "Our Man in Peking," [<u>Dikobraz</u>], <u>EE</u> 16,viii:23-25.

See also 849, 868, 1347, 1348.

WITH NORTH KOREA, NORTH VIETNAM

897. George, Alexander L. <u>The Chinese Communist Army in Action: The Korean War and its Aftermath</u>. New York: Columbia U P (255).

898. Guber, Alexander. "Soviet Aid to Vietnam," <u>NWR</u> 35,iv:12-13.

899. Howard, Peter. "Soviet Policies in Southeast Asia," <u>IJ</u> 23:435-455.

900. Kun, Joseph C. "North Korea: Between Moscow and Peking," <u>ChQ</u> 31:48-58.

901. London, Kurt. "Vietnam, A Sino-Soviet Dilemma," <u>RusR</u> 26:26-37.

902. McGovern, Raymond L. "Moscow and Hanoi," <u>PoC</u> 16,iii:64-71.

903. O'Ballance, Edgar. "Sino-Soviet Influence on the War in Vietnam," <u>ConR</u> 210:176-187.

904. Parry, Albert. "Soviet Aid to Vietnam," <u>MilR</u> 47,vi:13-22.

905. Pratt, Lawrence. "North Vietnam and Sino-Soviet Tension," <u>Behind the Headlines</u> 26,vi:20.

906.   Suh, Dae Sook.   The Korean Communist Movement, 1918-1948.   Princeton: Princeton U P (xix,406).
Rev. 906a. An, Thomas S.   PoC 16,iv:73-74.

907.   Zagoria, Donald S.   Vietnam Triangle: Moscow/
Peking/Hanoi.   New York: Pegasus (xiv,286).   Rev. 907a.
Duncanson, Dennis J.   ChQ 33(1968):139.

908.   Anon.   "Vietnam and the Sino-Soviet Dispute,"
SSU 6,ii:1-118.

See also 852, 859.

WITH CUBA

909.   Suarez, Andres.   Cuba: Castroism and Communism, 1959-1966.   Cambridge: M.T.T. Press (266).

WITH THE WEST

910.   Bromke, Adam and Uren, Philip E., eds.   The
Communist States and the West.   New York and Washing-
ton: Praeger; London: Pall Mall (x,242).   Rev. 910a.
Gyorgy, Andrew.   EEQ 2(1968):419-422.   910b. Hanak,
Harry.   SEER 46,cvii(1968):549.   910c. Miller, Wright.
IA 44(1968):85-86.   910d. Robinson, William C.   LJ 92:
125.   910e. Roley, Paul.   RusR 27(1968):357-358.   910f.
Stern, Geoffrey.   SovS 19(1968):451-452.   910g. Thumm,
G.W.   SlavR 26:686.

911.   Brzezinski, Zbigniew K.   "The Framework of
East-West Reconciliation," FA 46:256-275.

912.   Campbell, John C.   "Europe, East and West,"
US and EEur [F3]:125-150.

913.   Eisenberg, Rafael.   The East-West Conflict:
Psychological Origin and Resolution.   New York: Diplomatic (231).

914. Kronsten, Joseph A. "East-West Trade: Myth and Matter," IA 43:265-281.

915. Mosely, Philip E. "Eastern Europe in World Power Politics," ModA 11:119-130.

916. Ryle, James M. "International Red Aid, 1922-1928: The Founding of a Comintern Front Organization," Emory [PhD diss] 1967. DA 28:4104A.

917. Solomon, Anthony M. "The Revival of Trade Between the Communist Bloc and the West," AAAPSS 372: 105-112.

See also 17, 339, 373, 716, 722, 1705.

Africa

918. Attwood, William. The Reds and the Blacks, New York: Harper and Row (341). Rev. 918a. Kraus, Jon. WAUS 130:132-136.

919. Gregor, A. James. "African Socialism, Socialism, and Fascism: An Appraisal," RPol 29:324-353.

920. Grundy, Kenneth W. "Africa in the World Arena: The Communist World and Africa," CH 52:132-134.

921. Kanet, Roger E. "Soviet Economic Policy in Sub-Saharan Africa," CSlSt 1:566-586.

922. Kanet, Roger E. "The Soviet Union and Sub-Saharan Africa: Communist Policy Toward Africa, 1917-1935," Princeton [PhD diss] 1966. DA 27:3915A.

923. Klinghoffer, Arthur J. "The Soviet View of Socialism in Sub-Saharan Africa, 1955-1964," Columbia [PhD diss] 1966. DA 27:2573A.

924. Kraus, Jon. "A Marxist in Ghana," PoC 16, iii:42-49.

925. Metrowich, F.R. Africa and Communism: A
Study of Successes, Setbacks, and Stooge-States.
Johannesburg-Pretoria: Voortrekkerpers (261).

926. Morison, David L. "Africa of Moscow and
Peking," AfA 46:343-347.

927. Morison, David L. "Soviet Work on African
Law: Some Initial Steps," Mizan 9:245-251.

928. Sapp, Bernard B. "Tribal Cultures and Communism," MilR 47,vi:64-71.

929. Stokke, Baard R. Soviet and East Europe
Trade and Aid in Africa. New York: Praeger (xx,326).
Rev. 929a. Kanet, Roger E. SlavR 27(1968):496-497.
929b. Montias, John M. EEQ 2(1968):191-193.

See also 876.

Middle East

930. Abdullah, Fuad A. "Soviet Economic Aid in
the Middle East: An Economic Evaluation," Economics
and Business Bulletin 19,iii:3-19.

931. Abu-Jaber, Faiz. "Egypt and the Cold War,
1952-1956: Implications for American Policy," Syracuse [PhD diss] 1966. DA 27(1966):4306A.

932. Burnett, John H.,Jr. "Soviet-Egyptian Relations during the Khrushchev Era: A Study in Soviet
Foreign Policy," Emory [PhD diss] 1966. DA 27(1966):
2187A.

933. Dekmejian, R.H. and Ulman, A.H. "Changing
Patterns in Turkish Foreign Policy, 1959-1967," Orbis
11:772-785.

934. Devlin, Kevin. "Communism in Israel: Anatomy of a Split," Survey 62:141-151.

935. El-Biali, Abdel H. "A Comparative Analysis of the Reactions of the Countries of Egypt, Iraq, and Syria to the USSR and USA Foreign Aid Programs," American [PhD diss] 1967. DA 27:3099A.

936. Garthoff, Douglas F. "The Soviet Dilemma in Yemen," SAIS Review 12:15-22.

937. Glubb, John. Middle East Crisis: A Personal Interpretation. London: Hodder Stoughton.

938. Harris, George S. The Origins of Communism in Turkey. Stanford: Stanford U P (215). Rev. 938a. Karpet, Kemal H. SlavR 29(1970:125-126). 938b. Purcell, H.D. IA 44(1968):844. 938c. Tachau, Frank. APSR 63,i(1969):234-236. 938d. Weiker, Walter F. MEJ 22(1968):517-518.

939. Harris, Jonathan. "Communist Strategy Toward the National Bourgeoisie in Asia and the Middle East: 1945-1961," Columbia [PhD diss] 1966. DA 27(1966): 1887A.

940. Kapur, Harish. Soviet Russia and Asia 1917-1927: A Study of Soviet Policy Towards Turkey, Iran and Afghanistan. New York: Humanities (265). Rev. 940a. Rywkin, Michael. SlavR 27(1968):152-153.

941. Kimche, David. "Soviet Aims in the Middle East," Ms 13,vii:55-59.

942. Lichtblau, John H. "The Politics of Petroleum," Reporter 37,i:26-28.

943. Morison, David. "Russia, Israel and the Arabs," Mizan 9:91-107.

944.   Newth, J.A. and Nove, Alex.   The Soviet Middle East: A Communist Model for Development. New York and Washington: Praeger (160).   Rev. 944a. Carlisle, Donald S.   PoC 16,v:132-134.   944b. G.,R.R.   EE 16, vii:56-57.   944c. Issawi, Charles.   SlavR 26:503-505. 944d. Morrison, J.A.   JDA 1:396-400.   944e. Stickney, Edith P.   LJ 92:770.   944f. Zafar, Imam.   IA 43:762-763.

945.   Pennar, Joan.   "The Soviet Road to Damascus," Mizan 9:23-30.

946.   Schopflin, George.   "Rumania and the Middle East Crisis," WT 23:315-316.

947.   Shwandran, Benjamin.   "Soviet Posture in the Middle East," CH 52:331-336;368-369.

948.   Shwadran, Benjamin.   "The Soviet Union in the Middle East," CH 52:72-77.

949.   Tekiner, Süleyman.   "Soviet-Turkish Relations and Kosygin's Trip to Turkey," BISUSSR 14,iii:3-13.

950.   Windsor, Philip.   "The Middle East and the World Balance," WT 23:279-284.

See also 584, 643, 1094.

Asia

951.   Clarkson, Stephen.   "Manicheism Corrupted: The Soviet View of Aid to India," IJ 22:253-264.

952.   Clarkson, Stephen.   "Soviet Theory and Indian Reality," PoC 16,i:11-20.

953.   Edwardes, Michael.   "India, Pakistan and Nuclear Weapons," IA 43:655-663.

954. Evans, Hubert. "Recent Soviet Writing on Afghanistan," CAR 15:316-330.

955. Hata, Ikuhiko. Reality and Illusion: The Hidden Crisis Between Japan and the USSR, 1932-1934. New York: East Asian Inst., Columbia U (60).

956. Kashin, Alexander. "The October Revolution and Communism in Southeast Asia," SSU 6,iii:48-72.

957. Malik, Hafeez. "The Marxist Literary Movement in India and Pakistan," JAS 26:649-664.

958. Price, Ralph B. "Ideology and Indian Planning," AJES 26:47-64. [India's Socialist Pattern of Society--Based on U.S.S.R. plus bloc observations plus writings.]

959. Simon, Sheldon W. "The Kashmir Dispute in Sino-Soviet Perspective," AsSu 7:176-187.

960. Stein, Arthur. "India and the USSR: The Post-Nehru Period," AsSu 7:165-175.

961. Svetlov, Y. "Three Asian Visitors," EW 21, xi-xii:20-21.

See also 8, 26.

Latin America

962. Dinerstein, Herbert S. "Soviet Policy in Latin America," APSR 61:80-90.

United States and Canada

963. Byrnes, Robert F. "American Opportunities and Dilemmas," US and EEur [F3]:151-168.

964. Campbell, John C. Tito's Separate Road: America and Yugoslavia in World Politics. New York and
Evanston: Harper and Row (ix,180). Rev. 964a. Cvllé,
Krsto F. IA 44(1968):122-123. 964b. Owings, W.A.
EEQ 2(1968):193-195. 964c. Raditsa, Bogdan. NL 50,xv:
21-22. 964d. Stern, Geoffrey. SovS 20(1968):146-147.
964e. Vucinich, Wayne S. SlavR 27(1968):331-332.

965. Dinerstein, Herbert S. Intervention Against
Communism. Baltimore: Johns Hopkins P (vii,53). Rev.
965a. Delaney, R.F. LJ 92:2586.

966. Dobriansky, Lev E. "Trade with the Red Empire," UQ 23:141-160.

967. Liska, George. Imperial America: The International Politics of Primacy. Baltimore: Johns Hopkins P (xi,115).

968. Melby, John F. "The Cold War--Second Phase:
China," IJ 23:421-434.

969. Morgenthau, Hans J. "Arguing About the Cold
War," Encounter 28,v:37-41.

970. Petrovich, Michael B. "United States Policy
in East Europe," CH 52:193-199,243-244.

971. Polisensky, Josef V. Canada and Czechoslovakia. [Tr. by Jessie Kocmannova] Prague: Orbis (60).

972. Pratt, Julius W. Challenge and Rejection:
The United States and World Leadership, 1900-1921. New
York: Macmillan, London: Collier Macmillian (viii,248).

973. Puhek, Ronald E. "The Rationale of American
Foreign Policy: Containment," Nebraska [PhD diss] 1967.
DA 28:756A.

974. Rupprecht, Paul. "The Image of Hungary's

International Position in American Foreign Policy-
Making, 1937-1947," Minnesota [PhD diss] 1967. <u>DA</u> 28
(1968):5128A.

975. Scowcroft, Brent. "Congress and Foreign Policy: An Examination of Congressional Attitudes Toward
the Foreign Aid Programs to Spain and Yugoslavia,"
Columbia [PhD diss] 1967. <u>DA</u> 28:2309A.

976. Skolnikoff, Eugene B. <u>Science, Technology</u>
<u>and American Foreign Policy</u>. Cambridge and London:
M.I.T. Press (vvi,330).

977. Sturner, William F. "Aid to Yugoslavia: A
Case Study of the Influence of Congress on a Foreign
Policy Implementation," Fordham [PhD diss] 1966. <u>DA</u>
27(1966):518A.

978. Van Zanten, John W. "Communist Theory and
the American Negro Question," <u>RPol</u> 29:435-456.

979. Van Zanten, John W. "The Soviet Evaluation
of the American Negro Problem; 1954-1965: A Study of
Ideology and Propaganda," Yale [PhD diss] 1966. <u>DA</u>
27:3504A.

980. Vaughn, Ralph. "Der amerikanische Östhandel,"
<u>Österreuropäische Rundschau</u> 13,iv:20-22.

981. Windsor, Philip. "NATO and European Détente,"
<u>WT</u> 23:361-368.

982. Anon. <u>American Foreign Policy: Current Docu-</u>
<u>ments, 1963</u>. Washington: Government Printing Office
(lxxii,1380).

983. Anon. <u>Foreign Relations of the United</u>
<u>States:: Diplomatic Papers 1944</u>. Vol. II: General:
<u>Economic and Social Matters</u>. Washington: Government
Printing Office (vi,1129).

See also 799, 910.

Western Europe

984. Brown, George. "Die Öst-West Beziehungen und das Europa-Problem," NATO-Brief,ii:2-5.

985. Fejtö, François. The French Communist Party and the Crisis of International Communism. Cambridge and London: M.I.T. Press (xi,225). Rev. 985a. Goldey, D.B.. PSt 16(1968):308-309. 985b. Shirk, Albert. PoC 17,ii(1968):69. 985c. Wohl, Robert. PSQ 84(1968): 692-693. 985d. Zimmerman, William. SlavR 26:690.

986. Feller, Albert. "Security and East-West Trade," BISUSSR 14,1:3-16.

987. Ferguson, Michael L. "The Soviet Union's Place in DeGaulle's Foreign Policy: An Inquiry into French-Russian Relations with Emphasis on the Period of the Fifth Republic," MAb 5,i:18.

988. Fischer-Galati, Stephen. "France and Rumania: A Changing Image," EEQ 1:107-114.

989. Griffith, William E. "What are the Attitudes of the Eastern European Countries to East-West Relations?," Hamburg: Friedrich-Naumann-Stiftung. International Collogue on NATO and the Communist World. Jan. 30 - Feb. 4,1967.

990. Hedley, John H. "Moscow's New Look in Western Europe," YR 56:390-396.

991. Hočevar, Toussaint. "The Portorož Conference: A Plea for Liberalization of Trade in the Danubian Area," FSUSP 1:19-34.

992. Kashin, Alexander. "A New Soviet Diplomatic

Offensive in Western Europe," BISUSSR 14,ii:22-26.

993. Lund, Erik. "Krushchev in Denmark: A Study
of the Soviet and East European Press Reactions,"
Cooperation and Conflict i:26-35.

994. Maisky, Ivan M. Memoirs of a Soviet Ambassador. London: Hutchinson (408).

995. McLellan, David S. "The Changing Nature of
Soviet and American Relations with Western Europe,"
AAAPSS 372:16-32.

996. Mieczkowski, Bogdan. "Brighter Prospects for
a Less Divided Europe," CEF 15,iii:34-38.

997. Roley, Paul L. "In Search of Accommodation:
Anglo-Soviet Relations, 1919-1921," California, Berkeley [PhD diss] 1966. DA 27:3821A.

998. Schwartz, Leonard E. "Perspectives on Pug-
wash," [Pugwash Conferences on Science and World Af-
fairs--East-West Meets] IA 43:498-515.

999. Shulman, Marshall D. "'Europe' versus
'Detente'?" FA 45:389-402.

1000. Staller, George J. "Patterns of Stability
in Foreign Trade: OECD and COMECON, 1950-1963," AER
57:879-888.

1001. Stein, Michael K. "Finnish-Soviet Relations
in the Khrushchev Decade 1955-1964," MAb 5,v:23.

1002. Anon. "After the DeGaulle Visit," [Excerpts
from Sprawny, Miedzynarodowe, Polityka, Tyzodnik,
Powszechny, Zolnierg Polski, Izpilki] EE 16,xi:20-24.

See also 97, 607, 754, 1508.

United Nations

1003. Bailey, Sydney D. "Veto in the Security Council," IC 566:5-66.

1004. Bose, Jadabendra L. "A Probe into the Financing of Peace-Keeping Operations of the U.N.," IntJPoliSci 28:143-153. [Soviet refusal to support monetarily and otherwise.]

1005. Hottelet, Richard C. "Soviet Strategy and the UN," NL 50,xx:3-5.

1006. Plischke, Elmer. "East Germany's Quest for United Nations Membership," WAUS 130,ii:89-94.

1007. Schwartz, Harry. "Russia's New Face at the UN [Nikolai T. Fedorenko]," Vista 2,v:35-42.

Developing Nations

1008. Ballis, William B. "Soviet Foreign Policy Towards Developing States: The Case of Egypt," SSU 7, iii::84-113.

1009. Clarkson, Stephen. "Soviet Theory and Indian Reality," PoC 16,i:11-20.

1010. Cook, Robert C. "Soviet Population Theory from Marx to Kosygin," Population Bulletin 23:85-115.

1011. Goldman, Marshall I. Soviet Foreign Aid. New York, Washington and London: Praeger (xiv,265). Rev. 1011a. Butler, William E. JDA 2:285-286. 1011b. Gripp, Richard D. MJPS 12(1968):456-458. 1011c. Herman, Leon M. APSR 62(1968):689-690. 1011d. Jamgotch, Nish, Jr. APSR 62(1968):689-691. 1011e. Kanet, Roger E. CS1St 1:500-502. 1011f. Krassowski, A. IA 44 (1968):107-108. 1011g. McAuley, Alastair N.D. SlavR

26:686-687. 1011h. Prybyla, Jan S. RusR 27(1968): 248-249.

1012. Howard, Peter. "The USSR and Indonesia," Mizan 9:108-117.

1013. Johnson, Harry G. Economic Policies Toward Less Developed Countries. Washington: Brookings Institution (279). 1013a. Stern, Robert M. JCR 11:511-517.

1014. Kovner, Milton. "Soviet Aid and Trade," CH 52:217-223,242.

1015. Van Der Kroef, Justus M. "Jakarta between Moscow and Peking," EW 21-22,i/ii:9-10,28.

1016. Mazrui, Ali. "Numerical Strength and Nuclear Status in the Politics of the Third World," JPol 29:790-820.

1017. McLane, Charles B. "Russia and the Third World," SSU 6,iii:73-90.

1018. Melady, Thomas P. Western Policy and the Third World. New York: Hawthorn (199). Rev. 1018a. O'Shaughnessy, J. WJ 10(1968):392-393.

1019. Morison, David. "Recent Soviet Interest in Population Problems of the Developing Countries," Mizan 9:181-196.

1020. Morison, David. "Soviet Influence: Prospects for 1967," Mizan 9:31-37.

1021. Mosely, Philip E. "The Kremlin and the Third World," FA 46:64-77.

1022. Muller, Kurt. The Foreign Aid Programs of the Soviet Bloc and Communist China: An Analysis. New York: Walker (xiii,331). Rev. 1022a. Delaney, Robert

F. LJ 92:1839-1840. 1022b. Goldman, Marshall I. APSR
62(1968):1021-1025. 1022c. Holbik, Karel. IJCS 9
(1968):322-323.

1023. Pincus, John. Trade, Aid and Development:
The Rich and Poor Nations. New York: McGraw Hill [for
the Council on Foreign Relations] (400). Rev. 1023a.
Stern, Robert M. JCR 11:511-517.

1024. Power, Paul F. "The Peoples' Solidarity
Movement: Evolution and Continuity," Mizan 9:10-22.

1025. Taborsky, Edward. "The Class Struggle, the
Proletariat, and the Developing Nations," RPol 29:370-
386.

1026. Taborsky, Edward. "The Communist Parties of
the 'Third World' in Soviet Strategy," Orbis 11:128-
148.

1027. Tanham, G.K. Communist Revolutionary War-
fare. New York: Praeger (166).

1028. Tansky, Leo. U.S. and U.S.S.R. Aid to Developing Countries: A Comparative Study of India, Turkey, and the U.A.R. New York, Washington and London:
Praeger (xvii,192). Rev. 1028a. Herman, Leon M. PoC
17,iii(1968):65-66. 1028b. Kanet, Roger E. SlavR 26
(1968):693-695. 1028c. Sirc, Ljubo. IA 44,ii(1968):
323-325.

1029. Walters, Robert S. "American and Soviet Aid
to Less Developed Countries: A Comparative Analysis,"
Michigan [PhD diss] 1967. DA 28:5131A.

1030. Yellon, R.A. "The Winds of Change," Mizan
9:51-57,155-173.

1031. Anon. "The Middle East: Soviet Anxieties,"
Mizan 9:145-153.

See also 871.

Germany and Berlin

1032. Burks, R.V. "Comment on the Papers of Professors Petrovich and Fischer-Galati," EEQ 1:115-121.

1033. Childs, David. "The Socialist Unity Party of East Germany," PSt 15:301-321.

1034. Czechanowski, S. "Eastern European Policy Unchanged," P&G 11,i/ii:3-6.

1035. Dulles, Eleanor L. Berlin: The Wall Is Not Forever [Foreword by Konrad Adenauer] Chapel Hill: U of North Carolina P (xv,245).

1036. Dyck, Harvey L. "German-Soviet Relations, 1926-1933: A Study in the Diplomacy of Instability," DA 28:586A.

1037. Hangen, Welles. The Muted Revolution: East Germany's Challenge to Russia and the West. London: Gollancz (241). Rev. 1037a. Ascherson, Neal. NYR 8 (9 Mar):19-23. 1037b. Jones, Treharne. IA 44(1968): 121-122.

1038. Higgins, T. Hitler and Russia: The Third Reich in a Two-Front War, 1937-1943. London: Collier-Macmillan (310).

1039. Hinterhoff, E. "German Reunification and Poland's Interests," P&G 11,i/ii:7-13.

1040. Katelbach, T. "Pragmatism in Polish-German Affairs," P&G 11,iii/iv:29-35.

1041. Korbel, Josef. "Soviet-German Relations: The Past and Prospects," Orbis 10:1046-1060.

1042. Lowenthal, Richard. "Germany's Role in East-West Relations," WT 23:240-248.

1043. Mann, F.A. "Germany's Present Legal Status Revisited," ICLQ 16:769-799.

1044. Pirožkova, V. "Germanija i Èvropa ot Urala do Atlantiki," NŽ 89:215-227.

1045. Pirožkova, V. "Germanija na Perelome," NŽ 86:286-304.

1046. Piszczkowski, T. "The German Problem," P&G 11,i/ii:21-39.

1047. Prowe, Diethelm M. "City Between Crises: The International Relations of West Berlin from the End of the Berlin Blockade in 1949 to the Khrushchev Ultimatum of 1958," Stanford [PhD diss] 1967. DA 28:4581A.

1048. Smith, Jean E. "The United States, German Unity, and the Deutsche Demokratische Republik," QQ 74:21-35.

1049. Spencer, Robert. "Berlin, the Blockade, and the Cold War," IJ 23:383-407.

1050. Spittman, Ilse. "East Germany: The Swinging Pendulum," PoC 16,iv:14-20.

1051. Wettig, Gerhard. "The SED-SPD Dialogue: Communist Political Strategy in Germany," Orbis 11:570-581.

1052. Anon. "Allies Fall Out," [Neues Deutschland Feb 3 1967] EE 16,iii:26-30.

See also 707, 795.

ARMS CONTROL AND DISARMAMENT

1053. Bargman, Abraham. "The Study of Test Ban and Disarmament Conferences: A Review," JCR 11:223-246.

1054. Beaton, Leonard. "Nuclear Fuel-for-all," FA 45:662-669. [Soviet-American position on nonproliferation of nuclear weapons.]

1055. Berman, Harold J. and Maggs, Peter B. Disarmament Inspection Under Soviet Law. Dobbs Ferry: Oceana (viii,154). Rev. 1055a. Ainsztein, R. IA 44 (1968):318-319. 1055b. Butler, William E. AJIL 62,i (1968):236. 1055c. Clemens, Walter C.,Jr. SlavR 27 (1968):667-668. 1055d. Hazard, John N. RusR 27(1968): 255. 1055e. Smith, D.D. ICLQ 17,i(1968):243-244. 1055f. Schwartz, R.W. LJ 92:2585.

1056. Carroll, Kent J. "A Second Step Toward Arms Control," MilR 47,v:77-84.

1057. Clemens, Walter C.,Jr. "Arms Control in 1975--the Utility of a Modernist Approach," Review of International Affairs 418 (5 Sep):19-20;419(20 Sep): 16-19.

1058. Clemens, Walter C.,Jr. "China's Nuclear Tests: Trends and Portents," ChQ 32:111-131.

1059. Clemens, Walter C.,Jr. "A World of Nuclear Powers?" War/Peace Report 7,iv:12-14.

1060. Clemens, Walter C.,Jr. "Multipolarization and Arms Control," Thomas B. Manton, comp. Background Papers: The United Nations in 1975, 53-62. Muscatine, Iowa: Stanley Foundation.

1061. Clemens, Walter C.,Jr. "Outer Space, Strategy, and Arms Control," BAS 23,ix:24-28; Technology Review 69,viii:18-21.

1062. Dougherty, James E. and Lehman, J.F.,Jr.,
eds. Arms Control for the Late Sixties. Princeton:
Van Nostrand (xlvii,265). Rev. 1062a. Gerberding,
William P. APSR 62(1968):678-679.

1063. Griffiths, F. "Inner Tensions in the Soviet
Approach to 'Disarmament'," IJ 22:593-617.

1064. Halperin, Morton H., ed. Sino-Soviet Relations and Arms Control. Cambridge: M.I.T. Press (vi,
342). Rev. 1064a. Larson, Thomas B. SlavR 27(1968):
153-154. 1064b. Lee, C.J. WPQ 20:745-746. 1064c.
Ray, Dennis M. JPol 31(1969):583-585. 1064d. Shillinglaw, Geoffrey. IA 44(1968):601-603. 1064e. Woot-
en, Clyde C. JAS 27:620-622. 1064f. Yahuda, M.B.
PSt 16(1968):329-331.

1065. Kemp, Geoffrey. "Controlling Arms in the
Middle East: Some Preliminary Observations," WT 23:
285-291.

1066. Larson, Arthur. "Last Chance on Nuclear
Nonproliferation?" SatR 50,xl:21-24.

1067. Lepper, Mary K. "The Nuclear Test Ban
Treaty 1963: Demands and Supports." Florida State [PhD
diss] 1966. DA 27(1966):2576A

1068. McBride, James H. "The Nuclear Test Ban
Treaty and United States National Security," Georgetown [PhD diss] 1966. DA 27:521A.

1069. Peterson, Sophia. The Nuclear Test Ban
Treaty and Its Effect on International Tension. Los
Angeles: Security Studies Project, U of California
(64).

1070. Rosen, Steven. "Proliferation Treaty Controls and the IAEA," JCR 11:168-175.

1071. Schlesinger, James R. "Nuclear Spread," YR
57,i:66-84.

1072. Simmons, Norman L. "An Analysis of the Op-
position to the United States Arms Control Policy,"
American [PhD diss] 1967. DA 28:4241A.

1073. Stone, Jeremy J. "The Anti-Missile Folly,"
NL 50,i:13-15.

1074. Sugg, Howard A.I. "Soviet Disarmament
Theory Since 1959: An Analytical Study," American [PhD
diss] 1967. DA 28:1501A.

1075. Wu, Yuan-li. Arms Control Arrangements for
the Far East. Stanford: Hoover Institution (231).

1076. Zorga, Victor. "Arms and the Soviet Union,"
NRep 156,ii:13-15.

1077. U.S. Arms Control and Disarmament Agency.
Documents on Disarmament, 1966. Washington: Government Printing Office.

See also 850.

CULTURAL RELATIONS

1078. Barghoorn, F.C. "Cultural Exchanges
between Communist Countries and the United States,"
AAAPSS 372:113-123.

1079. Lawson, John H. "The Soviets and US Culture," NWR 35,ix:106-112.

1080. Trautmann, Fredrick W.E. "Louis Kossuth's
Audience Adaptation in his American Speaking Tour,
1851-1852," Purdue [PhD diss] 1966. DA 27:2646A.

THE MILITARY

1081.   Clavier, Philippe A. "Soviet Nuclear Defense Policy," MilR 47,i:72-77.

1082.   Collins, Edward M. "The Evolution of Soviet Strategy Under Khrushchev," Georgetown [PhD diss] 1966. DA 27:2584A.

1083.   Crane, Robert D. "The Structure of Soviet Military Thought," SST 7,i:28-34.

1084.   Erickson, John. "'The Fly in Outer Space': The Soviet Union and the Anti-Ballistic Missile," WT 23:106-114.

1085.   Galay, Nikolai. "The Problems of War and Peace," BISUSSR 14,ii:3-16.

1086.   Gallagher, Matthew. "Fifty Years of the Soviet Armed Forces," Survey 65:75-83.

1087.   Gately, Matthew J. "Soviet Airborne Operations in World War II," MilR 47,i:14-20.

1088.   Halperin, Morton H. Contemporary Military Strategy. Boston: Little, Brown (x,156).

1089.   Hashavia, Arie. "The Soviet Fleet in the Mediterranean," MilR 47,ii:79-81.

1090.   Kolkowicz, Roman. "The Impact of Modern Technology on the Soviet Officer Corps," Orbis 11:378-393.

1091.   Kolkowicz, Roman. The Soviet Military and the Communist Party. Princeton: Princeton U P (xvi, 429). Rev. 1091a. Coles, Harry L. AHR 73:864-865. 1091b. G.,R.R. EE 16,ix:55-56. 1091c. Garthoff,

Raymond L. RusR 27(1968):94. 1091d. Johnston, Robert
H. IJ 23:168-169. 1091e. Mackintosh, Malcolm. PoC
17,i(1968):36-37. 1091f. Miller, Wright. IA 44(1968):
562-563. 1091g. Rubinstein, Alvin Z. CH 53:246.
1091h. Schwartz, Harry. SatR 50,xxix:40. 1091i.
Tucker, Frank H. CSlSt 3(1969):154-155.

1092. Mackintosh, Malcolm. Juggernaut: A History
of the Soviet Armed Forces. New York: Macmillan
(320). Rev. 1092a. Duke, James B. AAAPSS 381(1969):
178. 1092b. Garthoff, Raymond L. RusR 27(1968):260.
1092c. Jacobs, Walter D. WAUS 130:186-187. 1092d.
Kolkowicz, Roman. APSR 62(1968):658-659. 1092e. Newman, William. LJ 92:2771. 1092f. Miller, Wright. IA
44(1968):562-563.

1093. McColl, Robert W. "The Oyüwan Soviet Area,
1927-1932," JAS 27:41-60.

1094. Murphy, F.M. "The Soviet Navy in the Mediterranean," USNIP 93:38-44.

1095. Odom, William E. "Soviet Training Economies," MilR 47,ix:81-85.

1096. Schwartz, Leonard E. "Manned Orbiting Lab-
oratory for War or Peace," IA 43:51-64. [Space Race
and Objectives and the Cold War.]

1097. Sterling, Claire. "The Soviet Fleet in the
Mediterranean," Reporter 37,x:14-18.

1098. Taylor, John W.R. "Soviet Airpower," MilR
47,xii:16-20.

1099. Wolfe, Thomas W. "Soviet Military Policy at
the Fifty Year Mark," CH 53:206-216,244-246.

1100. Wolfe, Thomas W. "Soviet Military Policy on
the Eve of the Fifty-Year Mark," SSU 6,iii:149-168.

1101.   Wolfe, Thomas W.   Soviet Military Policy at the Fifty-Year Mark.   Santa Monica: Rand Corp. (41).

1102.   Wolfe, Thomas W.   Soviet Military Policy Trends Under the Brezhnev-Kosygin Regime.   Santa Monica: Rand Corp. (29).

1103.   Anon.   The Changing Strategic Military Balance, USA vs. USSR. [By a Special Subcommittee of the National Strategy Committee, American Security Council] Chicago (103).   Rev. 1103a. Dobriansky, Lev. E. UQ 23:276-278.

1104.   Anon.   The Soviet Military Technological Challenge.   Washington: Center for Strategic Studies, Georgetown U (xvii,98).   Rev. 1104a. Stockwell, Richard W.   SlavR 27(1968):668-669.

See also 752, 1016, 1027, 1433, 1551.

VI. Ideology and Philosophy

IDEOLOGY

1105. Armstrong, John A. Ideology, Politics, and Government in the Soviet Union: An Introduction. [Rev. ed] New York: Praeger (xviii,173). Rev. 1105a. Frankel, Theodore. CSlSt 2(1968):427-429.

1106. Brzezinski, Zbigniew. "Communist State Relations: The Effect on Ideology," EE 16,iii:2-7.

1107. Chambre, Henri. "Soviet Ideology," SovS 18, iii:314-327.

1108. Harris, Nigel. "The Owl of Minerva," SovS 18:328-339.

1109. Schlesinger, Rudolf. "More Observations on Ideology," SovS 19:87-99.

1110. Smolansky, Oles M. "Moscow and the Problem of National Socialism: An Ideological Approach." CSlSt 1,ii:172-195.

See also 131, 1677.

MARXISM

1111. Acton, H.B. What Marx Really Said. New York: Schocken Books (vi,148). Rev. 1111a. Ritchie, A.M. P 43(1968):381-383.

1112. Avineri, Shlomo. The Social and Political Thought of Karl Marx. New York: Cambridge U P (viii, 269).

1113.   Baxandall, Lee.   "Marxism and Aesthetics: A
Critique of the Contribution of George Plekhanov,"
JAAC 25:267-279.

1114.   Blake, William N.   "Education in Karl Marx's
Concept of Labor," Alberta [PhD diss] 1967.

1115.   Blanchette, Oliva.   "The International Symposium on Marx and the Western World," IPQ 7,i:129-
137.

1116.   Carmichael, Joel.   Karl Marx, the Passionate
Logician.   New York: Scribners (viii,262).

1117.   Csikszentmihalyi, Mihalyi.   "Marx: A Socio-
Psychological Evaluation," ModA 11:272-282.

1118.   Daniel, Norman.   Marx and Soviet Reality.
Chester Springs: Dufour.

1119.   Dunayevskaya, Raya.   China, Russia, USA--
State-Capitalism and Marx's Humanism, or Philosophy
and Revolution.   Detroit: News and Letters (61).

1120.   Easton, Loyd D. and Guddat, Kurt H., eds.
Writings of the Young Marx on Philosophy and Society.
Garden City: Anchor (ix,506).

1121.   Engels, Friedrich and Marx, Karl.   The Communist Manifesto. [Intr. by A.J.P. Taylor, tr. by
Samuel Moore] Baltimore: Pelican (124).

1122.   Fetscher, Irving.   "New Tendencies in Marxist Philosophy," EE 16,v:9-14.

1123.   Eorsi, Istvan.   "One Hundred Years of Das
Kapital," EE 16,xi:24-26.

1124.   Garaudy, Roger.   Karl Marx: The Evolution of
His Thought.   New York: International (195).

1125. Goodman, Donald F. "Freedom, the Person and Community: Berdyaev and the Marxist Leaven," Fordham [PhD diss] 1967. DA 28(1968):4211A.

1126. Gregor, A. James. "Marxism and Ethics: A Methodological Inquiry," PPR 28:368-384.

1127. Hoffman, Robert. "Marx and Proudhon: A Reappraisal of Their Relationship," Historian 29:409-430.

1128. Hogan, Homer. "The Basic Perspective of Marxism-Leninism," SST 7:297-317. Rev. 1128a. Jordan, Z.A. SST 7:340-342.

1129. Irizarry, Carmen. "Spain's New Marxism," NL 50,i:10-12.

1130. Johnston, William M. "Karl Marx's Verse as a Foreshadowing of his Early Philosophy," JHI 28,ii: 259-268.

1131. Koren, Henry J. Marx and the Authentic Man. A First Introduction to the Philosophy of Karl Marx. Pittsburgh: Duquesne U P (150).

1132. Laski, Harold J. "The Communist Manifesto" An Introduction with the Original Text and Prefaces by Marx and Engels. New York: Pantheon (179).

1133. Lemberg, Eugen. "The Intellectual Shift in East-Central European Marxism-Leninism," ModA 11:131-143.

1134. Lichtheim, George. "On the Interpretation of Marx's Thought," Survey 62:3-14.

1135. Lobkowicz, Nicholas, ed. Marx and the Western World. Notre Dame and London: U of Notre Dame P (xix,444). Rev. 1135a. Bocheński, J.M. SST 7:253-255.

1136. MacIntyre, Alasdair. "Herbert Marcuse: From Marxism to Pessimism," Survey 62:38-44.

1137. Martel, Harry and Selsam, Howard, eds. Reader in Marxist Philosophy. New York: International (384). Rev. 1137a. Blakeley, T.J. WJ 11(1969):89-90.

1138. McInnes, Neil. "Havemann and the Dialectic," Survey 62:25-37.

1139. McInnes, Neil. "Marxist Philosophy," Encyclopedia of Philosophy 5:173-176.

1140. Melson, Robert F. "Marxists in the Nigerian Labour Movement: A Case Study in the Failure of Ideology," Massachusetts Institute of Technology [PhD diss] 1967.

1141. Mlikotin, Anthony M. "Yugoslav Revision of Marxist Aesthetics: A Review Article," SEEJ 11:322-338.

1142. Pachter, Henry M. "Marxism and America's New Left," Survey 62:104-113.

1143. Petrovic, Gajo. Marx in the Mid-Twentieth Century: A Yugoslav Philosopher Considers Karl Marx's Writings. New York: Doubleday-Anchor (iv,506). Rev. 1143a. Parsons, Howard. PPR 29(1968):137-139. 1143b. de Roover, Raymond. LJ 92:2763.

1144. Planty-Bonjour, Guy. The Categories of Dialectical Materialism: Contemporary Soviet Ontology [Tr. by T.J. Blakely] New York and Washington: Praeger (vi,182). Rev. 1144a. De George, Richard T. SlavR 28 (1969):166-167. 1144b. Kamenka, Eugene. RusR 27 (1968):474-476.

1145. Rusinow, Dennison I. "Marxism Belgrade Style," Antioch Review 27,iv:477-490.

1146. Schaffer, H.G., ed. The Communist World,
Marxist and Non-Marxist Views. New York: Appleton-
Century-Crofts (558).

1147. Somerville, John. The Philosophy of Marxism. An Exposition. New York: Random House (vi,214).

1148. Sowell, Thomas. "Marx's Capital after One
Hundred Years," CJEPS 33:50-74.

1149. Tucker, Robert C. "The Deradicalization of
Marxist Movements," APSR 61:343-358.

1150. Wolfe, Bertram D. Marxism. 100 Years in the
Life of a Doctrine. New York: Delta (404). Rev.
1150a. Blakeley, T.J. WJ 11(1970):498-499.

1151. Yanowitch, Murray. "Alienation and the
Young Marx in Soviet Thought," SlavR 26:29-53.

1152. Zeitlin, Irving. Marxism: A Re-Examination.
Princeton: Van Nostrand (v,170). Rev. 1152a. Blakeley, T.J. WJ 10(1969):371-377.

        See also 29, 34, 675, 1186, 1202, 1240, 1386.

LENINISM

1153. Abram, Irwin. "The Bolshevik Revolution:
Fifty Years After," Antioch Review 27:421-424.

1154. Bocheński, J.M. "Discussion: Thomism and
Marxism-Leninism," SST 7:154-168.

1155. Lieberstein, Samuel. "Leninism: A Study in
the Sociology of Political Alienation," California,
Berkeley [PhD diss] 1967. DA 28:4097A.

1156   Meyer, Alfred G. Leninism. New York, Washington and London: Praeger (324).

See also 1128, 1133, 1266.

"NATIONAL COMMUNISM"

See 906.

OTHER "ISMS"

1157. Blackmer, Donald L.M. "Italian Communism
and the International Communist Movement, 1956-1965,"
Harvard [PhD diss] 1967.

1158. Buick, A. and Jerome, W. "Soviet State Capitalism? The History of an Idea," Survey 62:58-71.

1159. Ebenstein, William. Today's Isms: Communism - Fascism - Capitalism - Socialism. Englewood
Cliffs: Prentice-Hall (xii,262). Rev. 1159a. Arnopoulos, P.J. CSlSt 1:496-500.

1160. Eisenberg, Rafael. The East-West Conflict:
Psychological Origin and Resolution. New York: Diplomatic (230). Rev. 1160a. Christ, John M. LJ 92:1163.

1161. Davis, Horace B. Nationalism and Socialism:
Marxist and Labor Theories of Nationalism to 1917. New
York and London: Monthly Review (xiv,248).

1162. Galbraith, John K. "Capitalism, Socialism,
and the Future of the Industrial State," AM 219,vi:61-
67.

1163. Hollander, Paul. "Observations on Bureaucracy, Totalitarianism, and the Comparative Study of
Communism," SlavR 26:302-307.

1164. Landreth, Harry. "Creeping Capitalism in
the Soviet Union?" HBR 45:133-140.

1165. Lichtheim, George. "Is Communism Dead?"
Com 44,iv:62-67.

1166. Preston, Nathaniel S. Politics, Economics,
and Power: Ideology and Practice Under Capitalism,
Socialism, Communism, and Fascism. New York: Macmillan (xiv,242).

1167. Riasanovsky, Nicholas V. "The Emergence of
Eurasianism," CalSlSt 4:39-72.

1168. Roberts, Paul C. "An Administrative Analysis of Oskar Lange's Theory of Socialist Planning,"
Virginia [PhD diss] 1967. DA 28(1968):2875A.

1169. Ward, Benjamin. "Marxism-Horvatism: 'A Yugoslav Theory of Socialism'," AER 57:509-523.

1170. Zekulin, Gleb. "Stalinism in Arts," CSlSt
1:117-118.

See also 343, 2091.

COMMUNIST THEORY

1171. Cattell, David T. "A Neo-Marxist Theory of
Comparative Analysis," SlavR 26:657-662.

1172. Kautsky, John H. "Communism and the Comparative Study of Development," SlavR 26:13-17.

1173. Meyer, Alfred G. Communism. New York: Random House (x,241).

1174. Rucker, Robert C. "On the Comparative Study
of Communism," WP 19:242-257.

1175. Shaffer, Harry G. "Premises of Communism,"
QQ 74:257-265.

See also 874.

PROPAGANDA AND COMMUNICATIONS

1176. Havighurst, Clark C., ed. _International Control of Propaganda_. Dobbs Ferry: Oceana.

1177. Horak, Stephan M. "The United States in Lenin's Image," _UQ_ 23:226-237.

1178. Kempers, F. "Freedom of Information and Criticism in Yugoslavia, Part I: The Political Ideological Background." _Gazette_ 13:3-21,317-336.

1179. Markham, James W. _Voices of the Red Giants: Communications in Russia and China_. Ames, Iowa State U P (513). Rev. 1179a. Gretton, George. _IA_ 44(1968): 305-306. 1179b. Grossman, Alfred. _EE_ 17,vi(1968): 56. 1179c. Hollander, Gayle D. _POQ_ 32(1968):326-327. 1179d. Mond, Georges H. _CS1P_ 10(1968):229-233.

1180. Powell, David. "The Effectiveness of Soviet Anti-Religious Propaganda," _POQ_ 31:366-380.

1181. Rogers, Rosemarie S. "The Soviet Audience: How it Uses the Mass Media," Massachusetts Institute of Technology [PhD diss] 1967.

See also 806.

ANTI-COMMUNISM IN THE WEST

1182. Anon. "Liberal Anti-Communism Revisited. A Symposium," _Com_ 44,iii:31-79.

See also 965, 1713.

PHILOSOPHY

1183. Avineri, Shlomo. "The Hegelian Origins of
Marx's Political Thought," RM 21,i:33-56.

1184. Bar-Hillel, Yehoshua. "Bolzano, Bernard
(1781-1848)," Encyclopedia of Philosophy 1:337-338.

1185. Beemans, Pierre J. "Scientific Atheism in
the Soviet-Union: 1917-1954," SST 7:234-242.

1186. Biddulph, Howard L. "Karl Marx's Early
Thought in Soviet Philosophy," Indiana [PhD diss]
1966. DA 27:4308A.

1187. Blakeley, Thomas J. "Current Soviet Views
on Existentialism," SST 7:333-339.

1188. Bocheński, J.M. "Survey: Relevant Recent
Books," SST 7:52-58.

1189. Bushurov, G.K. "Toward an Assessment of the
Historical-Philosophical Views of Vladimir Solovyov,"
Soviet Studies in Philosophy 6 (Winter,1967-1968):42-
51.

1190. Butenko, A.P. "Societal Laws and Forms In-
volved in the Evolution Toward Socialism," SST 6:23-
33.

1191. Čapek, Milič. "Czechoslovak Philosophy,"
Encyclopedia of Philosophy 2:287-288.

1192. Chisholm, Roderick M. "Marty, Anton (1847-
1914)," Encyclopedia of Philosophy 5:170-171.

1193. Christoff, Peter K. "Khomyakov, Aleksei
Stepanovich (1804-6o)," Encyclopedia of Philosophy 4:
335-336.

1194. Christoff, Peter K. "Kireevsky, Ivan Vasilievich (1805-56)," Encyclopedia of Philosophy 4:342-343.

1195. De George, Richard T. "Fedor Vasilevich Konstantinov," Soviet Leaders:236-241.

1196. De George, Richard T. "Philosophy," Science and Ideology in Soviet Society:47-81,150-155.

1197. Dye, James W. "Berdyaev, Nikolai (1874-1948)," Encyclopedia of Philosophy 1:285-287.

1198. Eliade, Mircea. "Ionescu, Nae (1890-1940)," Encyclopedia of Philosophy 4:212.

1199. Eliade, Mircea. "Radulescu-Motru, Constantin (1868-1954)," Encyclopedia of Philosophy 7:63-64.

1200. Eliade, Mircea. "Rumanian Philosophy," Encyclopedia of Philosophy 7:233-234.

1201. Gontarev, G.A. "The Treatment of Problems of Marxist Ethics in the Postrevolutionary Works of Lenin," Soviet Studies in Philosophy 6,iii:34-41.

1202. Elliott, Charles F. "Problems of Marxist Revisionism," JHI 28,i:71-86.

1203. Hanson, Norwood R. "Copernicus, Nicolas (1473-1543)," Encyclopedia of Philosophy 2:219-222.

1204. Hingley, Ronald. Nihilists. London: Weidenfeld and Nicolson (128).

1205. Hiz, H. "Chwistek, Leon (1884-1944)," Encyclopedia of Philosophy 2:112-113.

1206. Hodges, Donald C. "Yugoslav Philosophers in the Struggle Against Bureaucracy," FSUSP 1:77-94.

1207. Joravsky, David. "Deborin, Abram Moiseevich (1881-1963)," Encyclopedia of Philosophy 2:309-310.

1208. Jordan, Z.A. "Ajdukiewicz, Kazimierz (1890-1963)," Encyclopedia of Philosophy 1:62-63.

1209. Jordan, Z.A. "Kotarbiński, Tadeusz," Encyclopedia of Philosophy 4:361-363.

1210. Jordan, Z.A. The Evolution of Dialectical Materialism: A Philosophical and Sociological Analysis. New York: St. Martin's (xvi,490). Rev. 1210a. De George, Richard T. SlavR 28(1969):166-167. 1210b. MacIntyre, Alasdair. Survey 67(1968):139-142.

1211. Kamenka, Eugene. "Philosophers in Moscow," Survey 62:15-24.

1212. Kamenka, Eugene. "Philosophy Under Communism," Encyclopedia of Philosophy 2:163-168.

1213. Kamenka, Eugene. "Tolstoy, Count Lev Nikolaevich (1828-1910)," Encyclopedia of Philosophy 8: 146-149.

1214. Kemball, R.J. "Russian 19th Century Thought-Recent Source Material," SST 7:211-233 [about Herzen and Čaadaev].

1215. Kliger, George. "Radical Realism, Sense-Contents and Ontology: A Critical Examination of Some Aspects of Tadeusz Kotarbinski's Philosophy," Minnesota [PhD diss] 1967. DA 28(1968):4664A.

1216. Kline, George L. "Bazarov, Vladimir Alexandrovich (1874-1939)," Encyclopedia of Philosophy 1:262.

1217. Kline, George L. "Bogdanov, Alexander Aleksandrovich (1873-1928)," Encyclopedia of Philosophy 1: 331.

1218. Kline, George L. "Chicherin, Boris Nikolaye-vich (1828-1904)," Encyclopedia of Philosophy 2:86-87.

1219. Kline, George L. "Frank, Simon Lyudvigovich (1877-1950)," Encyclopedia of Philosophy 3:219-220.

1220. Kline, George L. "Herzen, Alexander Ivano-vich (1812-70)," Encyclopedia of Philosophy 3:494-495.

1221. Kline, George L. "Kavelin, Konstantin Dmi-trievich (1818-85)," Encyclopedia of Philosophy 4:327-328.

1222. Kline, George L. "Leontyev, Konstantin Nikolayevich (1831-91)," Encyclopedia of Philosophy 4:436-437.

1223. Kline, George L. "Lunacharski, Anatoli Vasilyevich (1875-1933)," Encyclopedia of Philosophy 5:109.

1224. Kline, George L. "Philosophy Holdings in Soviet and East-European Libraries," SST 7:169-172.

1225. Kline, George L. "Pisarev, Dmitri Ivanovich (1840-68)," Encyclopedia of Philosophy 6:312.

1226. Kline, George L. "Russian Philosophy," Encyclopedia of Philosophy 7:258-268.

1227. Kline, George L. "Shestov, Leon (1866-1938)," Encyclopedia of Philosophy 7:433-434.

1228. Kline, George L. "Skovoroda, Gregory Sav-vich (1722-94)," Encyclopedia of Philosophy 7:461.

1229. Kline, George L. "Solovyov, Vladimir Serge-yevich (1853-1900)," Encyclopedia of Philosophy 7:491-493.

1230. Kline, George L. "Volski, Stanislav (1880-1936 [?])," Encyclopedia of Philosophy 8:261-262.

1231. Kovesi, Julius. "Hungarian Philosophy," Encyclopedia of Philosophy 4:93-95.

1232. Kovesi, Julius. "Palagyi, Menyhert (1859-1924)," Encyclopedia of Philosophy 6:18-19.

1233. Kovesi, Julius. "Pauler, Akos (1876-1933)," Encyclopedia of Philosophy 6:59-60.

1234. Krzywicki-Herburt, George. "Polish Philosophy," Encyclopedia of Philosophy 6:363-370.

1235. Krzywicki-Herburt, George. "Twardowski, Kazimierz (1866-1938)," Encyclopedia of Philosophy 8: 166-167.

1236. Laszlo, Ervin, ed. Philosophy in the Soviet Union: A Survey of the Mid-Sixties. New York: Praeger (208). Rev. 1236a. Kamenka, Eugene. RusR 27(1968): 474-476.

1237. Laszlo, Ervin. "Trends in East-European Philosophy. A Case Study on Hungary," SST 7,ii:130-141.

1238. Lejewski, Czesław. "Leśniewski, Stanisław (1886-1939)," Encyclopedia of Philosophy 4:441-443.

1239. Lejewski, Czesław. "Łukasiewicz, Jan (1878-1956)," Encyclopedia of Philosophy 5:104-107.

1240. Lessing, Arthur. "Marxist Existentialism," RM 20,iii:461-482.

1241. Levickij, Sergej. "O metafizičeskom legkomyslii," NŽ 89:228-243.

1242. Lobkowicz, Nicholas. Theory and Practice.
Notre Dame: U of Notre Dame P (442).

1243. MacMaster, Robert E. Danilevsky: A Russian
Totalitarian Philosopher. Cambridge: Harvard U P
(xiii,368). Rev. 1243a. Benson, Sumner. JMH 41(1969):
280-283. 1243b. Clarkson, Jesse D. AHR 73(1968):861-
862. 1243c. Kristof, Ladis K. RusR 27(1968):241-243.
1243d. Schwarz, R.W. LJ 92:1167. 1243e. Seton-Watson, Hugh. SEER 46,cvi(1968):267-269. 1243f. Sker-
pan, Alfred A. Historian 30(1968):267-269.

1244. Marković, Mihailo. "Yugoslav Philosophy,"
Encyclopedia of Philosophy 8:359-364.

1245. McCall, Storrs, comp. Polish Logic 1920-
1939. [Intr. by Tadeusz Kotarbiński] London: Oxford U
P (viii,406).

1246. McInnes, Neil. "Lukács, Georg," Encyclopedia of Philosophy 5:102-104.

1247. Meyer, Alfred G. "Lev Davidovich Trotsky,"
PoC 16,vi:30-40.

1248. Mostowski, Andrzej. "Tarski, Alfred," Encyclopedia of Philosophy 8:77-81.

1249. O'Rourke, James J. "Notes and Comments:
Value Theory," SST 7,111:243-246.

1250. Parsons, Howard L. Soviet Philosophers
Speak: Some Contemporary Views. New York: American
Institute of Marxist Studies (46).

1251. Parsons, Howard L. "Soviet Philosophers
Speak," NWR 35,vi:31-34.

1252. Pavićević, Buko. "Petronievic, Branislav
(1875-1954)," Encyclopedia of Philosophy 6:128-129.

1253. Pethybridge, Roger. "The Assessment of
Ideological Influence on East Europeans," POQ 31:38-
50.

1254. Petrović, Gajo. "Plekhanov, Georgii Valen-
tinovich (1856-1918)," Encyclopedia of Philosophy 6:
347-350.

1255. Plekhanov, G.V. Essays in the History of
Materialism New York: Fertig (287).

1256. Randall, Francis B. N.G. Chernyshevskii.
New York: Twayne (178). Rev. 1256a. Moser, Charles A.
SlavR 27(1968):680-681.

1257. Révész, László. "Political Science in Eastern Europe: Discussion and Initial Steps," SST 7,iii:
185-210.

1258. Rosenthal, M. and Yudin, P., eds. A Dictionary of Philosophy. Moscow: Progress Publishers
(494).

1259. Scanlan, James P. "Belinski, Vissarion
Grigoryevich (1811-48)," Encyclopedia of Philosophy 1:
277.

1260. Scanlan, James P. "Bulgakov, Sergey Nikolayevich (1871-1944)," Encyclopedia of Philosophy 1:
421-423.

1261. Scanlan, James P. "Florensky, Paul Alexandrovich (1882-1940[?])," Encyclopedia of Philosophy 3:
205-206.

1262. Scanlan, James P. "Chernyshevski, Nikolai
Gavrilovich (1828-89)," Encyclopedia of Philosophy 2:
86.

1263. Scanlan, James P. "Koslov, Alexey Alexandrovich (1831-1901)," Encyclopedia of Philosophy 4:363.

1264. Scanlan, James P. "Lapshin, Ivan Ivanovich (1870-1952)," Encyclopedia of Philosophy 4:363.

1265. Scanlan, James P. "Lavrov, Peter Lavrovich (1823-1900)," Encyclopedia of Philosophy 4:402-404.

1266. Scanlan, James P. "Lenin, V.I.(1870-1924)," Encyclopedia of Philosophy 4:434-435.

1267. Scanlan, James P. "Lopatin, Leon Mikhailo-vich (1855-192o)," Encyclopedia of Philosophy 5:85-86.

1268. Scanlan, James P. "Mikhailovsky, Nicholas Konstantinovich (1842-1904)," Encyclopedia of Philoso-phy 5:310-311.

1269. Scanlan, James P. "Nikolaj Černyševskij and Soviet Philosophy," SST 7,i:1-27.

1270. Scanlan, James P. "Radishchev, Alexander Nikolayevich (1749-1802)," Encyclopedia of Philosophy 7:63.

1271. Scanlan, James P. "Rozanov, Vasily Vasilye-vich (1856-1919)," Encyclopedia of Philosophy 7:229-230.

1272. Scanlan, James P. "Vysheslavtsev, Boris Petrovich (1877-1954)," Encyclopedia of Philosophy 8:272-273.

1273. Scanlan, James P. "Shpet, Gustav Gustavo-vich (1879-1937)," Encyclopedia of Philosophy 7:433-434.

1274. Schiebel, Joseph. "Changing the Unchange-able. Historical Materialism and Six Versions of Eter-nal Laws of Historical Development," SST 7,iv:318-332.

1275. Šešić, Bogdan. "Petrović-Njegoš, Petar

(1813-1851)," Encyclopedia of Philosophy 6:129.

1276. Shein, Louis J. "Lev Shestov: A Russian
Existentialist," RusR 26:278-285.

1277. Shein, Louis J. "Lossky, Nicholas Onufriye-
vich (1870-1965)," Encyclopedia of Philosophy 5:86-87.

1278. Shein, Louis J. "N.O. Lossky's Intuitive
Epistemology," CS1St 1:365-378.

1279. Skolimowski, Henryk. Polish Analytical Philosophy. A Survey and A Comparison with British Analytical Philosophy. London: Routledge and Kegan Paul
(ix,275). Rev. 1279a. Jordan, Z.A. Journal of the
Royal Institute of Philosophy 43(1968):399-402.

1280. Skolimowski, Henryk. "Ingarden, Roman,"
Encyclopedia of Philosophy 4:193-195.

1281. Somerville, John. "Marxist Ethics, Deter-
minism, and Freedom," PPR 28:17-23.

1282. Stojković, Andrija. "Marković, Svetozar
(1846-1875)," Encyclopedia of Philosophy 5:164-166.

1283. Thomson, S. Harrison. "Hus, John (1369-
1415)," Encyclopedia of Philosophy 4:95-96.

1284. Tsanoff, Radoslav A. "Bulgarian Philosophy," Encyclopedia of Philosophy 1:423-424.

1285. Ulich, Robert. "Comenius, John Amos (1592-
1670)," Encyclopedia of Philosophy 2:146-147.

1286. Uytman, John D. "Pavlov, Ivan Ivanovich
(1840-1936)," Encyclopedia of Philosophy 6:61-63.

1287. Wasiolek, Edward. "Dostoyevsky, Fyodor Mi-
khailovich (1821-81)," Encyclopedia of Philosophy 2:
411-412.

1288. Wellek, René. "Masaryk, Tomáš Garrigue
(1850-1937)," Encyclopedia of Philosophy 5:176-177.

1289. Whyte, Lancelot L. "Boscovich, Roger Joseph
(1711-1787)," Encyclopedia of Philosophy 1:350-352.

1290. Woodcock, George. "Bakunin, Michael (1814-
76)," Encyclopedia of Philosophy 1:244-246.

1291. Woodcock, George. "Kropotkin, Peter (1842-
1921)," Encyclopedia of Philosophy 4:365-366.

1292. Zeldin, Mary-Barbara. "Chaadaev, Pyotr
Yakovlevich (1794-1856)," Encyclopedia of Philosophy :
2:71-72.

1293. Zeldin, Mary-Barbara. "Spir, Afrikan Alexandrovich (1837-90)," Encyclopedia of Philosophy 7:
544.

        See also 9, 18, 395, 669, 694, 695, 1083,
1120, 1122, 1128, 1137, 1139, 1143, 1147, 1154, 1656,
1997, 2185.

                        RELIGION

GENERAL

1294. Armstrong, Benjamin L. "The Attitude of the
Soviet State to Religion 1959-1965, as Expressed in
Official Russian Periodicals," New York [PhD diss]
1967. DA 28(1968):4502A.

1295. Birnbaum, Norman. "Eastern Europe and the
Death of God," Com 44,i:69-73.

1296. Dunn, Ethel. "Russian Sectarianism in New
Soviet Marxist Scholarship," SlavR 26:128-140.

1297. Garsoïan, Nina G. The Paulician Heresy:
A Study of the Origin and Development of Paulicianism
in Armenia and the Eastern Provinces of the Byzantine
Empire. The Hague and Paris: Mouton (293). Rev.1297a.
Toumanoff, Cyril. AHR 74(1969):961-962.

1298. Gimbutas, Marija. "Ancient Slavic Religion:
A Synopsis," THRJ [F7]:738-759.

1299. Konstantinov, Prot. D. Religioznoe dviženie
soprotivlenija v SSR. Canada: SBONR (71).

1300. Loeschcke, Walter. Apostles and Evange-
lists. Recklinghausen: Aurel Bongers (Dist. in U.S.
by Taplinger (80)

1301. Manning, Clarence A. "Religion in the USSR
and East Europe: A footnote to the New Catholic Encyclopedia," UQ 23:344-353.

1302. Powell, David E. "Anti-Religious Propaganda
in the Soviet Union, 1959-1963," Yale [PhD diss] 1967.
DA 28:272A.

1303. Rothenberg, Joshua. "The Status of Cults,"
PoC 16,v:119-124.

1304. Anon. "Is God Alive?" [Pest Megyei Hirlap
4 July], EE 16,xii:28-31.

        See also 184, 196, 197, 297, 362, 1180, 1185.

CHRISTIANITY

1305. Alexeev, Wassilij. "The Russian Orthodox
Church Under German Occupation, 1941-1945," Minnesota
[PhD diss] 1967. DA 28(1968):2761A.

1306. Bogolepov, A.A. "Pravoslavnaja cerkov' v

Sovetskom Sojuze," Zapiski [Fl]:87-133. [Synopsis in English: "The Orthodox Church in the Soviet Union."]

1307. Bourdeaux, Michael. "Reform and Schism," PoC 16,v:108-118.

1308. Constantelos, Demetrios J. The Greek Orthodox Church: Faith, History, and Practice. [Foreword by Archbishop Iakovos] New York: Seabury (127).

1309. Edwards, David W. "Orthodoxy During the Reign of Tsar Nicholas I: A Study in Church-State Relations," Kansas State [PhD diss] 1967. DA 28:1758A.

1310. Hutten, Kurt. Iron Curtain Christians: The Church in Communist Countries Today. [Tr. by Walter G. Tillmanns] Minneapolis: Augsburg (495). Rev. 1310a. Ruoss, G. Martin. LJ 92:2579.

1311. Stroyen, W.B. Communist Russia and the Russian Orthodox Church. Washington: Catholic U of America P (161).

1312. Struve, Nikita. Christians in Contemporary Russia. [Tr. by Lancelot Sheppard and A. Manson] New York: Scribner (464). Rev. 1312a. Bociurkiw, Bohdan R. IJ 23:313-314. 1312b. Klimenko, Michael. CSlSt 2 (1968):136-137.

See also 76, 256, 285, 381, 388, 634.

JUDAISM

1313. Ami, Ben. Between Hammer and Sickle. Philadelphia: Jewish Publication Society (x,307). Rev. 1313a. Aynot, Rosalind V. PoC 16,v:136-137. 1313b. Rubin, Ronald I. SatR 50,xxxv:35.

1314. Bettelheim, B. "Survival of the Jews," NRep 157:23-30.

1315. Friedberg, Maurice. "On Reading Recent Soviet Judaica," Survey 62:167-177.

1316. Gitelman, Zvi. The Jews," PoC 16,v:92-101.

1317. Hoffseyer, Benjamin. "Rabbi Chaim Tchernowitz, 'Rav Tzair' and the Yeshiva of Odessa," Yeshiva [PhD diss] 1967. DA 28:1987A.

1318. Holotik, Ludovit. "The 'Jewish Problem' in Slovakia," EEQ 1:31-37.

1319. Kissman, Joseph. "Rumania," AJY 68:403-406.
[Summary of Judaism and Jewish affairs in Rumania during 1967.]

1320. Rothenberg, Joshua. "How Many Jews Are There in the Soviet Union?" JSS 29,iv:234-240.

1321. Rubin, Ronald I. "Soviet Jewry and the United Nations: The Politics of Non-Governmental Organizations," JSS 29,iii:139-154.

1322. Shapiro, Leon. "Bulgaria," AJY 68:411-413.
[Summary of state of Judaism and Jewish affairs in Bulgaria in 1967.]

1323. Shapiro, Leon. "Hungary," AJY 68:399-402.
[Summary of state of Judaism and Jewish affairs in Hungary during 1967.]

1324. Shapiro, Leon. "Poland," AJY 68:389-394.
[Summary of Judaism and Jewish affairs in Poland during 1967.]

1325. Shapiro, Leon. "Soviet Union," AJY 68:377-388. [Summary of Judaism and Jewish affairs in the Soviet Union during 1967.]

1326. Shapiro, Leon. "Yugoslavia," AJY 68:407-

410. [Summary of Judaism and Jewish affairs in Yugoslavia during 1967.]

1327. Szajkowski, Zosa. "Paul Nathan, Lucien Wolf, Jacob H. Schiff and the Jewish Revolutionary Movements in East Europe (1903-1917)," Pt. I. JSS 29, i:3-26; Pt. II. JSS 29,ii:75-91.

1328. Wiesel, Elie. "Will Soviet Jewry Survive?" Com 43,ii:47-52.

1329. Anon. "Czechoslovakia," AJY 68:395-398. [Summary of Judaism and Jewish affairs in Czechoslovakia during 1967.]

See also 268, 328, 1340.

ISLAM

1330. Bennigsen, Alexandre and Lemercier-Quelquejay, Chantal. Islam in the Soviet Union. [Intr. by Geoffrey E. Wheeler] New York and Washington: Praeger (xxii,272). Rev. 1330a. Ahmad, Aziz. IJ 23:315-316. 1330b. Allworth, Edward. SlavR 28(1969):143-145. 1330c. Carlisle, Donald S. PoC 16,v:132-134. 1330d. Imam, Zafar. IA 43:762-763. 1330e. LeCompte, Garé. CSlSt 2(1968):410-412. 1330f. Pierce, Richard A. AAAPSS 378(1968):153-154. 1330g. Rubinstein, Alvin Z. CH 55(1968):299. 1330h. Rupen, Robert A. APSR 62 (1968):1002-1003. 1330i. Shipman, Joseph C. LJ 92: 1834. 1330j. Wileman, D. GJ 134(1968):94-95. 1330k. Zenkovsky, Serge A. RusR 27:344-350; AHR 73(1968): 1201-1202.

VII. Public Affairs, Law, and Government

GENERAL

1331. Grote, Manfred W.H. "A New West German Policy toward Eastern Europe," Maryland [PhD diss] 1967. DA 28:3245A.

1332. Hauptmann, Jerzy. "Changes in Eastern Europe," CEJ/SB 15,iv:111-114.

1333. Hazard, John N. "Mali's Socialism and the Soviet Legal Model," YLJ 77:28-69.

1334. Kos-Rabcewicz-Zubkowski, L. "Droit international commercial dans les rapports Est-Ouest," CYIL 5:159-192.

1335. Ramundo, Bernard A. Peaceful Coexistence: International Law in the Building of Communism. Baltimore: Johns Hopkins P (272). Rev. 1335a. Leinbach, Philip E. LJ 92:1941.

1336. Rubinstein, Alvin Z. "Balkan Kaleidoscope," CH 52:220-226,244-245.

1337. Sidzikauskas, Vaclovas. "The Problem of the Baltic States in Today's World," BR 34:3-7.

1338. Wolff, R.L. The Balkans in Our Time. New York: Norton (618).

See also 279, 742.

JOURNALISM

1339. Clarkson, Stephen H. "Yankee Imperialism

and Indian Independence: Two Soviet Publications on India," CJEPS 33:298-303.

1340. Decter, Moshe, ed. Israel and the Jews in the Soviet Mirror: Soviet Cartoons on the Middle East Crisis. New York: Conference on the Status of Soviet Jews (49).

1341. Dobriansky, Lev E. "From Moscow's Izvestia to Washington's Post," UQ 23:332-343.

1342. Gruliow, Leo. "Notes from a Pravda-Watcher," Antioch Review 27:440-457.

1343. Hollander, Gayle D. "Recent Developments in Soviet Radio and Television News Reporting," POQ 31 (Fall):359-362.

1344. Hollander, Gayle D. Soviet Newspapers and Magazines. Cambridge: Center for International Studies, Massachusetts Institute of Technology (137).

1345. Kerr, Walter B. "The House of Pravda," SatR 50,xlix:60-61.

1346. Whelan, Joseph G. "The Press and Krushchev's Withdrawal from the Moon Race," POQ 32,i:65-73.

See also 187, 1294, 1452.

ALBANIA

1347. Logoreci, Anton. "Albania and China: Incongruous Alliance," CH 52:227-231.

1348. Logoreci, Anton. "Albania: The Anabaptists of European Communism," PoC 16,iii:22-28.

1349. Anon. "Albania's Cultural Revolution," EE 16,iv:27-29.

BULGARIA

1350. Anon. "What's Under the Beatle Haircuts?"
[Pogled 25 Sept 1967], EE 16,xii:33-34.

See also 15, 717.

CZECHOSLOVAKIA

1351. Barcata, Louis. "Šik versus Schweik in
Czechoslovakia," EE 16,ii:21-22.

1352. Davis, Robert G. "Letter from Czechoslovakia," NL 50,xix:10-12.

1353. Jicinska, B. "Czechoslovakia's Oldest Pro-
fession," EE 16,vii:23-24.

1354. Schwartz, Morton. "Czechoslovakia: Toward
One-Party Pluralism?" PoC 16,i:21-27.

1355. Sterling, Claire. "The Rickety Czech 'New
Model'," Reporter 36,xi:22-24.

1356. Vaculik, Ludvik. "Culture and Party in
Czechoslovakia," EE 16,ix:18-20.

1357. Yglesias, Jose. "Letter from Prague,"
Nation (U.S.) 204,ii:59-61.

1358. Anon. "Little-Known Czechoslovakia,"
[Excerpts from MY 1967], EE 16,x:27-29.

1359. Anon. "The Slansky Trial Revisited," EE 16,
viii:18-20.

See also 180, 705, 747.

FINLAND

1360. Crosby, William D. "Consular Power--Most
Favored Nation Clause--Construction of 1934 Treaty of
Friendship, Commerce and Consular Rights with Finland:
Mentula v. State Land Board (Oregon 1966),"
ColumJTransnatL 6:154-159.

See also 335.

EAST GERMANY

1361. Hornsby, Lex, ed. Profile of East Germany
Toronto: International Publications Service (120).

1362. Muray, Leo. "Profile of East Germany," NRep
156,xiii:6-8.

1363. Planck, Charles R. The Changing Status of
German Reunification in Western Diplomacy, 1955-1966.
Baltimore: Johns Hopkins P (vii,65). Rev. 1363a.
Adams, John C. SlavR 27(1968):664-665.

1364. Schmitt, Hans A. "Men and Politics in East
Germany," CH 52:232-237.

1365. Sylvester, Anthony. "The Other Side of the
Wall," EE 16,vi:3-7.

1366. Váli, Ferenc A. The Quest for a United Germany. Baltimore: Johns Hopkins U P (xii,318). Rev.
1366a. Adams, John C. SlavR 27(1968):664-665. 1366b.
Plischke, Elmer. WAUS 130:214-216.

1367. Van Altena, John,Jr. "The Flight that
Failed," EE 16,vii:2-11.

GREECE

1368. Doumas, C.L. "Political Climate and Political Methods in Contemporary Greece," SoQ 5,ii:151-168.

1369. Rousseas, Stephen. "The Deadlock in Greece," Nation (U.S.) 204,xiii:390-395.

1370. Rousseas, Stephen, Starobin, Herman and Lenzer, Gertrud. The Death of a Democracy: Greece and the American Conscience. New York: Grove (xii,268). Rev. 1370a. McNeill, William H. SlavR 27(1968):665-666.

1371. Walzer, Michael. "The Condition of Greece," Dissent (Jul-Aug):421-431.

HUNGARY

1372. Csabafi, Imre. "Hungarian Air Code," JAirL 33:457-464.

1373. Held, Joseph. "An Apologia for Kadar," EE 16,v:22-23.

1374. Laszlo, E. The Communist Ideology in Hungary: Handbook for Basic Research. New York: Humanities.

1375. Lendvai, Paul. "Hungary: Change vs. Immobilism," PoC 16,ii:11-17.

1376. Neuburg, Paul. "All Quiet on the Eastern Front," PR 34,iii:447-457.

1377. Sterling, Claire. "Hungary: The Mechanism and the Marionettes," Reporter 36,ix:25-27.

See also 703.

POLAND

1378. Finestone, Harold. "Reformation and Recidivism Among Italian and Polish Criminal Offenders," AJS 72:575-588.

1379. Gamarnikow, Michael. "Poland: Political Pluralism in a One-Party State," PoC 16,iv:1-14.

1380. Johnson, A. Ross. "Warsaw: Politics and the Intellectual," EE 16,vii:12-16.

1381. Koziebrodski, Leopold B. "Administrative and Civil Law in the Regulation of Property Rights in Present-Day Poland," AJCL 15:772-781.

1382. Lasok, D. "Matrimonial Property - Polish Style," ICLQ,i:230-242.

1383. Lasok, Dominik. "Polish System of Private International Law," AJCL 15:330-351.

1384. Nitzburg, Arthur R. "Polish Systems of Inheritance," PolR 12,i:12-38.

1385. Ptakowski, Jerzy. "Gomulka and His Party," EE 16,v:2-7.

1386. Seidler, Grzegorz L. "Marxist Legal Thought in Poland," SlavR 26,iii:382-394.

1387. Shanor, Donald R. "Poland," AM 220,vi:36-44.

1388. Szpunar, Adam. "The Law of Tort in the Polish Civil Code," ICLQ 16,i:86-102.

1389. Terrill, Ross. "The Polish Concensus," NRep 156,xxi:17-22.

See also 355, 357, 377, 378, 384, 673, 681, 682, 685.

RUMANIA

1390. Ceausescu, Nicolae. "The Rumanian Course," [Excerpts from 7 May 1967. Scinteia] EE 16,vi:13-16.

1391. Cismarescu, Michael. "Rumania's Changing Legal Code," EE 16,viii:16-17.

1392. Sporea, Constantin. "Reshaping the Rumanian Party," EE 16,x:8-12.

See also 387.

THE SOVIET UNION

GENERAL

1393. Adams, Jan S. "'People's Control' in the Soviet Union," WPQ 20:919-929.

1394. Bandyopadhyaya, Jayantanuja. "Whither Russia? The Changes Ahead," PoC 16,i:41-44.

1395. Barry, Donald D. "Motor-Car in Soviet Criminal and Civil Law," ICLQ 16:56-85.

1396. Beerman, R. "The Grain Problem and Anti-Speculation Laws," SovS 19,i:127-129.

1397. Brezhnev, Leonid. "Thus Spake Leonid Brezhnev," Reporter 37,x:19.

1398. Bush, Keith. "The Reforms: A Balance Sheet," PoC 16,iv:30-41.

1399. Butler, William E. The Law of Soviet Territorial Waters: A Case Study of Maritime Legislation
and Practice. New York, Washington, London: Praeger
(xvii,192). Rev. 1399a. Fenwick, Charles G. WAUS
130:143-144. 1399b. Fisher, Joel M. SlavR 28(1969):
169. 1399c. Johnson, D.H.N. ICLQ 17(1968):794-795.
1399d. Taylor, Pauline B. RusR 27(1968):487.

1400. Butler, William E. "Self Determination in
Soviet International Law," SAIS Review 12,i:32-39.

1401. Butler, William E., comp. "Soviet International Law: Diplomatic and Consular Law," SStD 3,ii-
iii:1-148.

1402. Butler, William E. "Soviet Law: An 'Enigma'
Unravelled," PennBAQ 38:275-280. [Comment on No. 1414]

1403. Butler, William E., Berman, Harold J.,comp.
and trans. "Soviet Public International Law," SStD 3,
iv:1-95.

1404. Butler, William E. "Soviet Territorial
Waters," WAUS 130:17-25.

1405. Buxarin, N.I. Put' k socializmu v Rossii:
Izbrannye proizvedenija. [Ed., with intr. by Sidney
Heitman, tr. of intr. and notes by Eugenia Zhiglevich]
New York: Omicron (416). Rev. 1405a. Walker, Franklin
A. AHR 73(1968):1205.

1406. Cattell, David T. "The Fiftieth Anniversary: A Soviet Watershed?" CH 53:224-229.

1407. Clarke, Roger A. "The Composition of the
USSR Supreme Soviet, 1958-1966," SovS 19:53-65.

1408. Clarkson, Jesse D. "Russia and the Future,"
RusR 26:361-375.

1409.   Davis, Jerome. "After Fifty Years," NWR 35, ix:73-75.

1410.   Edgerton, William H. "Patent Protection for Pharmaceutical Products in the U.S.S.R.," JPOS 49:835-840.

1411.   Gibian, George. "From an Observer's Note-book," PoC 16,ii:57-64.

1412.   Gilison, Jerome M. "New Factors of Stability in Soviet Collective Leadership," WP 19,iv:563-581.

1413.   Hammer, Darrell P. "Bureaucracy and the 'Rule of Law' in Soviet Society," SWIF [F6]:87-110.

1414.   Hanson, Robert D. "The Evolving Enigma of the Soviet Legal System," PennBAQ 38:74-80. [Cf. No. 1402.]

1415.   Hanson, Robert D. "Soviet Law--A Reply to an Attack," PennBAQ 38:463-465. [Reply to No. 1402.]

1416.   Hendel, Samuel. "The U.S.S.R. after Fifty Years: An Overview," USSR after 50 Yrs [F2]:3-38.

1417.   Hough, Jerry. "The Soviet Elite: I. Groups and Individuals," PoC 16,i:28-35.

1418.   Hough, Jerry. "The Soviet Elite: II. In Whose Hands the Future?" PoC 16,ii:18-25.

1419.   Johnson, E.L. "Matrimonial Property in Soviet Law," ICLQ 16:1106-1134.

1420.   Kulski, Wladyslaw W. "Politics and the Party: Continuing Revolution or New Conservatism?" SWIF [F6]:41-62.

1421. Levine, Isaac D. "The Crises Ahead," PoC 16,i:44-46.

1422. Lewytzkyj, Borys. "Generations in Conflict," PoC 16,i:36-40.

1423. McClure, Timothy. "The Politics of Soviet Culture, 1964-1967," PoC 16,ii:26-43.

1424. Meyer, Alfred G. "The Soviet Political System," USSR after 50 Yrs [F2]:39-60.

1425. Micklin, Philip P. "The Baykal Controversy: A Resource Use Conflict in the U.S.S.R.," NRJ 7:485-498.

1426. Mieczkowski, Z. "The Soviet Post-Stalin Approach to the Unity of Economic and Administrative Divisions," ESEE 12:84-98.

1427. Miller, Wright. "The Social and Cultural Record," USSR after 50 Yrs [F2]:101-123.

1428. Morgan, Patrick M. "The System of Formal Honorary Awards in the Soviet Union," Yale [PhD diss] 1967. DA 29:942A.

1429. Pomeroy, William J. Half a Century of Socialism: Soviet Life in the Sixties. New York: International Publishers (125).

1430. Pomeroy, William J. "Soviet Democracy Expands," NWR 35,ix:95-103.

1431. Remington, Robin A. "The Growth of Communist Regional Organization, 1949-1962," Indiana [PhD diss] 1966. DA 27(1966):2587A.

1432. Rudden, Bernard. "Soviet Tort Law," NYULRev 42:583-630.

1433. Scott, Harriet F. "New Soviet Defense Minister," <u>MilR</u> 27,vii:33-36.

1434. Schapiro, Leonard. <u>The Government and Politics of the Soviet Union</u>. London: Hutchinson U Library (176).

1435. Shapiro, Jane P. "Rehabilitation Policy and Political Conflict in the Soviet Union, 1953-64," Columbia [PhD diss] 1967. <u>DA</u> 31(1971):4869A.

1436. Smith, Jessica. "Soviet Democracy and How it Works," <u>NWR</u> 35,i:33-43;ii:46-54;iii:39-48;iv:40-49; v:39-47;vi:46-51;vii:51-57.

1437. Sorokin, Pitirim A. "The Essential Characteristics of the Russian Nation in the Twentieth Century," <u>AAAPSS</u> 370:99-115.

1438. Strong, Augusta. "Soviet Women Greet Their Sisters from Many Nations," <u>NWR</u> 35,ix:124-127.

1439. Thomas, John R. "Technology and Nationalism," <u>Survey</u> 65:96-107.

1440. Wolfe, Bertram D. "Reflections on the Future of the Soviet System," <u>RusR</u> 26:107-128.

1441. Wolfe, Bertram D. "Reflections on the Soviet System: The Durable Core of Totalitarianism," <u>USSR</u> after 50 Yrs. [F2]:125-157.

1442. Anon. <u>Report of Court Proceedings in the Case of the Anti-Soviet Trotskyite Centre Heard before the Military Collegium of the Supreme Court of the U.S.S.R., Moscow, January 23-30, 1937: Verbatim Report</u>. New York: Howard Fertig (vi,580).

See also 547, 619, 765, 790, 927, 1055,1105.

COMMUNIST PARTY

1443. Fainsod, Merle. "Roads to the Future," PoC 16,iv:21-23.

1444. Field, Mark G. "Soviet Society and Communist Party Controls: A Case of 'Constricted' Development," Donald W. Treadgold, ed., Soviet and Chinese Communism: Similarities and Differences, 185-211. Seattle: U of Washington P.

1445. Heldman, Dan C. "Ideology, Science, and the Party: The Need for Controls," PoC 16,i:67-71.

1446. Hodnett, Grey. "What's in a Nation?" PoC 16,v:2-15.

1447. Hoffmann, Erik P. "Ideological Administration in the Soviet Union, 1959-1963: A Study of the Communications Behavior of the Communist Party," Indiana [PhD diss] 1967. DA 28:3745A.

1448. Joravsky, David. "Bosses and Scientists," PoC 16,i:72-75.

1449. Levi, Arrigo. "The Evolution of the Soviet System," PoC 16,iv:24-29.

1450. Lyons, Eugene. Workers Paradise Lost: Fifty Years of Soviet Communism: A Balance Sheet. New York: Funk and Wagnall (387). Rev. 1450a. Chamberlin, William H. ModA 12,iii(1968):202-203. 1450b. Chamberlin, William H. RusR 27(1968):231-236. 1450c. Fedenko, P. BISUSSR 15,v(1968):29-34. 1450d. Ivsky, Oleg. LJ 92:3047. 1450e. Jacobs, Walter D. WAUS 130(1968): 262-264. 1450f. Zemel's, L. NŽ 90(1968):301-303.

1451. Meissner, Boris. "The Soviet Union Under Brezhnev and Kosygin," ModA 11,ii:7-23.

See also 1672.

REPUBLICS

1452. Critchlow, James. "Broadcasting in the
Uzbek SSR," CAR 15,iii:260-262.

1453. Lelis, Jāzeps. "Latviešu trimdas sabriedrī-
bas izvērtējums," JGai 63:40-48.

1454. Sabaliúnas, Leonas. "Litauische Exilorgani-
sationen und ihre Tätigkeit," AB 6:207-219.

1455. Starcs, Pēteris. "Latviešu nacionālās
eksistences problēmu pētīšana," Archīvs 8:11-22.

NATIONAL MINORITIES

1456. Conquest, Robert, ed. Soviet Nationalities:
Policy in Practice. New York: Praeger (160). Rev.
1456a. Armstrong, John A. AAAPSS 377(1968):173-174.
1456b. Jacobs, Walter D. WAUS 130(1968):262-264.
1456c. Leinbach, Philip E. LJ 92:3046.

1457. Gidney, J.B. A Mandate for Armenia. Kent:
Kent State U P (270).

1458. Heiman, Leo. "Ukraine: 1966," UQ 23:43-64.

1459. Pipes, Richard. "'Solving' the Nationality
Problem," PoC 16,v:125-131.

1460. Remeikis, Thomas. "The Evolving Status of
Nationalities in the Soviet Union," CSlSt 1:404-423.

1461. Sabaliúnas, Leonas. "Elections in Lithuania," EE 16,vii:24-26.

See also 1676, 1920.

TURKEY

1462. Cihan, Ali F. <u>Treatise on Socialist Turkey</u>.
Washington: Joint Publications Research Bureau (ii,
146).

1463. Golbert, Albert. "Legal Incentives and
Realities of Private Foreign Investment in Turkey,"
<u>AJCL</u> 15,2:351-360.

1464. Kuchenberg, Thomas C. "The OECD Consortium
to Aid Turkey," <u>StudLEconDev</u> 2,Study 1:91-106.

1465. Lawson, Ruth C. "New Regime in Turkey," <u>CH</u>
52:105-110.

See also 938.

YUGOSLAVIA

1466. Ames, Kenneth. "Yugoslavia's Crumbling Federation," <u>NL</u> 50,xii:10-12.

1467. Clesner, Herschel F. "Foreign Investment
and Technical Agreements in Yugoslavia--1967," <u>Idea</u>
11:21-36.

1468. Johnson, A.R. "The Dynamics of Communist
Ideological Change in Yugoslavia, 1945-53," Columbia
[PhD diss] 1967. <u>DA</u> 28(1968):4225A.

1469. Jukić, Ilija. "Tito's Last Battle," <u>EE</u> 16,
iv:2-11.

1470. Magner, Thomas F. "Language and Nationalism
in Yugoslavia," <u>CSlSt</u> 1:333-347.

1471. Mihajlov, Mihajlo. "The Unspoken Defense
of Mihajlo Mihajlov," <u>NL</u> 50,x:3-16.

1472. Pawel, Ernst. "Yugoslav Report: Three Generations," <u>PR</u> 34,iv:606-613.

1473. Prpic, George J. "New Era in Yugoslavia,"
<u>America</u> 116,xiv(8 April):528-530.

1474. Stankovic, Slobodan. "Yugoslavia's Critical
Year," <u>EE</u> 16,iv:12-17.

1475. Sylvester, Anthony. "Intellectual Ferment
in Yugoslavia," <u>Survey</u> 62:121-128.

See also 705.

VIII. Economics

GENERAL

1476. Berman, Harold J. and Garson, John R. "Possible Effects of the Proposed East-West Trade Relations Act upon U.S. Import, Export, and Credit Controls," VandLRev 20(Mar):297-302.

1477. Berman, Harold J. and Garson, John R. "U.S. Export Controls--Past, Present and Future," CLRev 5 (May):791-890.

1478. Brenman, Andrew H. "Economic Reform in Austria, 1852-1859," Princeton [PhD diss] 1966. DA 27 (1966):2473A.

1479. Brzeski, Andrzej. "Finance and Inflation under Central Planning," Oe-W 12:177-190;278-297.

1480. Brzeski, Andrzej. "Price System in Eastern Europe: CESES International Seminar in Florence, September 1966," Oe-W 12:99-101.

1481. Burck, Gilbert. "East Europe's Struggle for Economic Freedom," Fortune 75,v:124-127,234,236,241-242.

1482. Burck, Gilbert. "The Challenging East European Market," Fortune 76,i:122-124,172,177-178,180.

1483. Dārziņš, Ansis L. "Pārdomas par dažām Latvijas sociāli saimnieciskām problēmām," JGai 66:40-45.

1484. Erlich, Alexander. "Economic Reforms in Communist Countries," Dissent (May-Jun):311-319.

1485. Fallenbuchl, Z.M. "Collectivization and Economic Development," CJEPS 33:1-15.

1486. Fox, Alan and Galenson, Walter. "Earnings and Employment in Eastern Europe, 1957 to 1963," QJE 81,ii:220-240.

1487. Frankel, Theodore. "Economic Reform: A Tentative Appraisal," PoC 16,iii:29-41.

1488. Gamarnikow, Michael. "New Tasks for the Trade Unions," EE 16,iv:18-26.

1489. Gamarnikow, Michael. "The New Role of Private Enterprise," EE 16,viii:2-9.

1490. Hunter, Louis C. "The Living Past in the Appalachias of Europe: Water Mills in Southern Europe," T&C viii:446-466.

1491. Ischboldin, B.S. Genetic Economics. St. Louis. Rev. 1491a. Timašev, N.S. NŽ 89:295-296.

1492. Lukin, L. and Zavolzhsky, S. "Bourgeois Criticism of Socialist Economic Co-operation," IA 43, i:8-13.

1493. McWilliams, Carey. "The Outmoded Wall," Nation(U.S.) 205,v:138-140.

1494. Mieczkowski, Bogdan. "The Unstable Soviet Bloc Economies," EE 16,x:2-7.

1495. Miroshnichenko, B. "The International Significance of Soviet Planning Experience," IA 43,i:10-16.

1496. Pervushin, S.P., et al. Production, Accumulation and Consumption. [A.I. Notkin, Ia. B. Kvasha, S.A. Kheinman, V.G. Venzher from Voprosy èkonomii,9, xi,x,ix, Jan.-Feb.-Mar. 1967] White Plains, Interna-

tional Arts and Sciences P (IV-V,174). Rev. 1496a.
Labsvirs, Janis. CSlSt 1:302-304.

1497. Pryor, Frederic L. "Evaluation of Economic
Systems: A Review Article," SovS 18:356-361.

1498. Roucek, Joseph S. "Changing Aspects of the
COMECON," CEJ/SB 15,viii-ix:223-237.

1499. Shaffer, Harry G. "Beruházás as emberi
tökébe: egy megjegyzés," ["Investment in Human Capital: Comment"] György Szakolczai, ed. A gazdasági
növekedés feltételei, 354-363. Budapest: Közgazdasági
és Jogi Könyvkiadó.

1500. Šik, Ota. Plan and Market under Socialism.
[Tr. by Eleanor Wheeler] White Plains: International
Arts and Sciences P (382).

1501. Sirc, Ljubo. "Economics of Collectivization," SovS 18:362-370.

1502. Taylor, Norman W. "Adam Smith's First Russian Disciple," SEER 45,cv:425-438.

1503. Triska, Jan F. "The Party Apparatchiks at
Bay," EE 16,xii:2-8.

1504. Turgeon, Lynn. "How Important Are the
Reforms?" Monthly Review (Jan):27-33.

1505. Zentner, Peter. East-West Trade: A Practi-
cal Guide to Selling in Eastern Europe. London: Par-
rish (300).

1506. Anon. "The Cost of Communism [ECE report on
Europe's Economic Growth]," Economist 223:702-704.

1507. Anon. "A New Role for Bankers," [Excerpts
from Nepszabadsag 12 May 1967] EE 16,ix:26-28.

1508. Anon. "Recent Developments in Trade Between Eastern and Western European Countries," Economic Bulletin for Europe 19,i:38-55.

1509. Anon. "Toward the Computer Age," EE 16,vi: 9-12.

See also 5, 165, 284, 723, 724, 744, 749, 796, 914, 917, 966, 991, 1000.

ALBANIA

1510. Prybyla, Jan S. "Albania's Economic Vassalage," EE 16,i:9-14.

BULGARIA

1511. Coussens, S.H. "Changes in Bulgarian Agriculture," Geography 52(Jan):12-22.

1512. Anon. "Bulgaria's Bureaucratic Miasma," [Pogled 30 Jan 1967]. EE 16,v:24-26.

1513. Anon. "The Slowdown in Shipping," [Excerpts from Otechesten Front 2 Jun 1967]. EE 16,x:25-26.

See also 13.

CZECHOSLOVAKIA

1514. Frejka, Tomas. "The Development of the Industrial Distribution of the Labor Force in Czechoslovakia," ILRR 21,i:3-17.

1515. Holesovsky, Vaclav. "Prague's Economic Model," EE 16,ii:13-16.

1516. Kanturek, Jiri. "Reform 1967: Full Victory or Hesitant Steps?" EE 16,ii:29-31.

1517. Lazarcik, Gregor. "The Performance of

Czechoslovak Agriculture Since World War II," SEEA
[F5]:385-406. Rev. 1517a. Ernst, Maurice. SEEA [F5]:
407-410.

1518. Mares, Vaclav E. "Czechoslovakia's Half
Century," CH 52:200-207.

1519. Prasad, S. Benjamin. "Prague Goes Pragmat-
ic," CJWB 2,ii:73-78.

1520. Selucky, Radoslav. "The Specter of Unem-
ployment," [Excerpts from Priroda a Společnost 11:
1967] EE 16,ix:23-25.

1521. Steiner, Bruno. "Autos: The Coming Struggle," EE 16,ii:32-33.

See also 224, 1479.

EAST GERMANY

1522. Homze, Edward L. Foreign Labor in Nazi Germany. Princeton: Princeton U P (xviii,350).

1523. Seotis, Jean. "East Germany and ECE," IC
561:49-53.

1524. Villmow, Jack R. "A Regional Analysis of
East German Industrialization in the 1950's," CSlSt 1:
424-460.

See also 1479.

GREECE

1525. Nugent, Jeffrey B. "Economic Thought, Investment Criteria, and Development Strategies in
Greece--A Postwar Survey," EDCC 15,iii:331-335.

HUNGARY

1526.   Brown, Alan A.   "The Economies of Centrally
Planned Foreign Trade: The Hungarian Experience," Harvard [PhD diss] 1967.

1527.   Anon.   "A Future for Private Plots,"
[Fizyelo 7 Dec 1966] EE 16,iv:32-34.

See also 340, 341, 1479.

POLAND

1528.   Flemming, George J.   "Making a Living in
Poland," EE 16,ix:3-8.

1529.   Flemming, J.   "The Polish Eagle Looks West,"
EE 16,x:16-20.

1530.   Gamarnikow, M.   "Poland's Foreign Trade with
East and West," P&G 11,iii/iv:36-53.

1531.   Anon.   "Concessionaires, Cooperatives and
Commissions," [Excerpts from Życie Warszawy] EE 16,
viii:26-27.

1532.   Anon.   "The Cult of the Dollar," [Kultura
26 Mar 1967] EE 16,vii:29-31.

1533.   Anon.   "Industrial Cooperation with the
West," [Rynki Zagraniczne 28 Jan 1967] EE 16,v:26-28.

See also 228, 368, 1479.

RUMANIA

1534.   Cioranescu, George.   "How Efficient is Rumanian Agriculture?" EE 16,ix:9-13.

1535. Montias, John M. <u>Economic Development in</u>
<u>Communist Rumania</u>. Cambridge and London: M.I.T. Press
(xiv,327). Rev. 1535a.Dallin, L.A.D. <u>AAAPSS</u> 377:219-
220. 1535b. Hoffman, George W. <u>GR</u> 59(1969):303-305.

1536. Anon. "A Critical Look at Rumania's Econ-
omy," [Excerpts from <u>Scinteia</u> 25 Dec 1967] <u>EE</u> 16,ii:
23-28.

THE SOVIET UNION

GENERAL

1537. Best, Paul J. "Some Notes on the Soviet
Foreign Insurance System," <u>Journal of Risk and Insur-</u>
<u>ance</u> 24:445-450.

1538. Hellie, Richard. "The Foundations of Russian Capitalism," <u>SlavR</u> 26:148-154.

1539. Hutchings, Raymond. "The Ending of Unem-
ployment in the USSR," <u>SovS</u> 9,i:29-52.

1540. Jackson, Marvin R.,Jr. "Soviet Project and
Design Organizations: Technological Decision Making
in a Command Economy," California, Berkeley [PhD diss]
1967. <u>DA</u> 28:4326A.

1541. Levine, Herbert S. "The Economy, Hard Spots
and Soft," <u>SWIF</u> [F6]:63-86.

1542. Matko, D.J.I. and Ticktin, H.H. "Some Notes
on the 1965 Yearbook," <u>SovS</u> 19,i:122-126.

1543. Meisak, Nikolai. "Novobirsk," <u>EW</u> 21,vii-
viii:25.

1544. Pickersgill, Joyce E. "Soviet Monetary
Policy and the Demand for Money, 1914 to 1937,"

Washington, Seattle [PhD diss] 1966. DA 27(1966): 4030A.

1545. Rostow, W.W. The Dynamics of Soviet Society. New York: Norton (320). Rev. 1545a. Gekker, Paul. MLabR 90,xi:68.

1546. Schwartz, Harry. The Soviet Union: Communist Economic Power. Chicago: Scott, Foresman (72).

1547. Shaffer, Harry G. "Do the U.S. and Soviet Economies Show Signs of Convergence?" Jan S. Prybyla, ed., The Triangle of Power, Conflict and Accommodation: The United States, the Soviet Union and Communist China, 39-51. University Park: Pennsylvania State U.

1548. Spulber, Nicolas. "Economic Modernization," US and EEur [F3]:57-80.

1549. Zauberman, Alfred. Aspects of Planometrics. [With contributions by A. Bergstrom, T. Kronsjö, and E.J. Mishan with M.J. Ellman] New Haven: Yale U P (xii,318). Rev. 1549a. Lamed, Stefan. CSlSt 3(1969): 577-579. 1549b. Montias, John M. SlavR 28(1969):158-160.

See also 197, 393, 459, 723, 724, 781, 829, 834, 838, 1095, 1158, 1426, 1479, 1593, 1680.

AGRICULTURE

1550. Bernstein, Thomas P. "Leadership and Mass Mobilisation in the Soviet and Chinese Collectivisation Campaigns of 1929-30 and 1955-56: A Comparison," ChQ 31:1-47.

1551. Conklin, David W. "Essays on Soviet Agriculture and Decentralization Reforms," Massachusetts Institute of Technology [PhD diss] 1967.

1552. Gagarin, Grigori. "Development of Soviet Agronomy," SSU 8,iii:36-53.

1553. Harris, Lement. "New Stage in Agriculture," NWR 35,ix:90-94.

1554. Jasny, Naum M. "Production Costs and Prices in Soviet Agriculture," SEEA [F5]:212-257. Rev. 1554a. Raup, Philip M. SEEA [F5]:258-264.

1555. Joravsky, David. "Ideology and Progress in Crop Rotation," SEEA [F5]:156-172. Rev. 1555a. Arnheim, Norman,Jr. SEEA [F5]:173-184.

1556. Judy, Richard W. and Walters, Harry E. "Soviet Agricultural Output by 1970," SEEA [F5]:306-344. Rev. 1556a. Chapman, Janet G. SEEA [F5]:345-355.

1557. Klatt, Werner. "Fifty Years of Soviet Agriculture," Survey 65:84-95.

1558. Laird, Roy D. "Khrushchev's Administrative Reforms in Agriculture: An Appraisal," SEEA [F5]:29-50. Rev. 1558a. Swearer, Howard R. SEEA [F5]:51-56.

1559. Mensheha, Mark P. "Soviet Agriculture Potentialities and Reality," AAAG 57:184.

1560. Nimitz, Nancy. "Farm Employment in the Soviet Union, 1928-1963," SEEA [F5]:175-205. Rev. 1560a. Durgin, Frank A.,Jr. SEEA [F5]:206-211.

1561. Schwartz, Janet S. "The Meaning of Work in the Soviet System," Cornell [PhD diss] 1967. DA 28: 4301A.

1562. Volin, Lazar. "Khrushchev and the Soviet Agricultural Scene," SEEA [F5]:1-21. Rev. 1562a. Popluiko, Anatole I. SEEA [F5]:22-28.

See also 189, 205, 213, 232, 240, 241, 248, 318, 1636, 1657.

INDUSTRY AND MANAGEMENT

1563. Abouchar, Alan J. "The Spatial Efficiency
of the Soviet Cement Industry before World War II,"
California, Berkeley [PhD diss] 1966. DA 27(1966):
857A.

1564. Abouchar, Alan J. "Rationality in the Pre-
war Soviet Cement Industry," SovS 19,ii:211-231.

1565. Allen, Charles R.,Jr. "The Soviet Trade
Unions and the Economic Reform," NWR 35,ix:86-89,105.

1566. Allen,Charles R.,Jr. "Trade Unions in the
USSR: A Revealing New Study," NWR 35,viii:50-54.

1567. Bone, Robert M. "Regional Planning and
Economic Regionalization in the Soviet Union," LE
xliii:347-354.

1568. Conquest, Robert, ed. Industrial Workers in
the U.S.S.R. New York: Praeger (144). Rev. 1568a.
Hamilton, F.E.I. IA 44,ii:348. 1568b. Leinbach,
Philip E. LJ 92,xvi:3046.

1569. DeFelice, Frank. "Soviet Physical Distribution: The Case of Processed Foods," North Carolina,
Chapel Hill [PhD diss] 1967. DA 28(1968):4325A.

1570. Dolan, Edwin G. "Structural Interdependence
of the Soviet Economy Before the Industrialization
Drive," SovS 19,i:66-73.

1571. Goldman, Marshall I. "Economic Revolution
in the Soviet Union," FA 45:319-331.

1572. Guest, B. Ross. "Soviet Gas Pipeline Development During the Seven-Year Plan," PG xix:189-192.

1573. Kahan, Arcadius. "Government Policies and
the Industrialization of Russia," JEH 27:460-477.

1574. Koropeckyj, Iwan S. "The Development of Soviet Location Theory before the Second World War-I," SovS 19:1-28;232-244.

1575. Nash, Edmund. "The New Five-Day Workweek in the Soviet Union," MLabR 90,viii:18-19.

1576. Nash, Edmund. "Western Influences on the U.S.S.R.'s New Incentives System," MLabR 90,iv:37-40.

1577. Prociuk, S.G. "The Manpower Problem in Siberia," SovS 19,ii:190-210.

1578. Richman, Barry M. Management Development and Education in the Soviet Union. East Lansing: Michigan State U P (xviii,308). Rev. 1578a. Earle, A. F. SEER 46,cvii(1968):554-555. 1578b. Ryavec, Karl W. SlavR 28(1969):164-166.

1579. Roosa, Ruth A. "The Association of Industry and Trade, 1906-1914: An Examination of the Economic Views of Organized Industrialists in Prerevolutionary Russia," Columbia [PhD diss] 1967.

1580. Rushing, Francis W. "An Analysis of the Chemical Industry in the Soviet Union during the Seven Year Plan, 1959-1965," North Carolina, Chapel Hill [PhD diss] 1967. DA 28:2848A.

1581. Smith, Howard R. "Robber Baron and Russian Manager," CJWB 2,vi:73-79.

1582. Stanley, Emilio J. "Regional Distribution of Soviet Industrial Manpower 1940-1955," Michigan [PhD diss] 1967. DA 28:2474B.

1583. Treml, Vladimir G. "New Soviet Capital Data," SovS 18:290-295.

1584. Von Laue, Theodore H. "Russian Peasants in the Factory," Val R. Lorwin, ed. Labor and Working

Conditions in Modern Europe, 73-85. New York: The
Macmillan Co.; London: Collier-Macmillan Limited.

1585. Zile, Zigurds L. "Private Rights in a Collective Society: A Study of the Non-Socialist Effort
in Soviet Urban Housing Construction," Harvard [PhD
diss] 1967.

          See also 444, 488, 605, 1599, 1620, 1666,
1680, 1681.

ECONOMIC GROWTH AND DEVELOPMENT

1586. Balinsky, Alexander, and Bergson, Abram.
Planning and the Market in the USSR. New Brunswick:
Rutgers U P (132). Rev. 1586a. Novak, Victor. LJ 92:
2560. 1586b. Anon. EE 16,vii:58-59.

1587. Bilbija, Žarko G. "Economic Values and the
Value of Economics: A Review of Agrarianism and its
Economic Theories," FSUSP 1:54-76.

1588. Blok, G. "Changing the Nature of Siberia,"
EW 21,i/ii:22-23.

1589. Bor, Mikhail. *Aims and Methods of Soviet
Planning*. London: Lawrence and Wishart (255). Rev.
1589a. Hunter, Holland. AAAPSS 378(1968):204. 1589b.
Spulber, Nicolas. AER 58(1968):1000-1002. 1589c.
Zauberman, Alfred. IA 44(1968):844.

1590. Chandra, N.K. "Long-Term Economic Plans and
Their Methodology," SovS 18,iii:296-313.

1591. Chirovsky, Nicholas L. "First Stage of the
New Soviet Plan, 1966-1970," UQ 23:299-313.

1592. Conolly, Violet. *Beyond the Urals: Economic
Developments in Soviet Asia*. London, New York and
Toronto: Oxford U P (xx,420). Rev. 1592a. Gibson,
James R. IJ 23,iv:645-646.

1593. Dobb, Maurice. "Fifty Years' Achievement:
The First Socialist Economy," NWR 35,ix:76-85.

1594. Dobb, Maurice. Soviet Economic Development
Since 1917. [rev. and enl. ed.] International Publications (515). Rev. 1594a. Bernt, H.H. LJ 92:1152.

1595. Fallenbuchl, Z.M. "Economic Policy of the
Period of Transition from Capitalism to Socialism,"
CS1P 9:245-269.

1596. Feiwel, George R. The Soviet Quest for Eco-
nomic Efficiency: Issues, Controversies, and Reforms.
New York: Praeger (xxii,420). Rev. 1596a. Bunyan,
James. RusR 27(1968):257. 1596b. Pryor, Frederic L.
SlavR 28(1969):160-161.

1597. Gekker, Paul. "The Soviet Bank for Foreign
Trade and Soviet Banks Abroad: A Note," EP 7:183-197.

1598. Goldman, Marshall I. "Soviet Economic
Growth Since the Revolution," CH 53:230-235.

1599. Granick, David. Soviet Metal-Fabricating
and Economic Development: Practice versus Policy.
Madison, Milwaukee, and London: U of Wisconsin P (xiv,
367). Rev. 1599a. Baranson, Jack. AER 58,iv(1968):
1028-1029. 1599b. Clark, M. Gardner. AAAPSS 376
(1968):194-195. 1599c. Yanowitch, Murray. SlavR 26:
691-693.

1600. Halperin, Ernst. "Beyond Libermanism," PoC
16,i:47-49.

1601. Hardt, John P., et al. Mathematics and Com-
puters in Soviet Economic Planning. New Haven: Yale
U P (xxii,298). Rev. 1601a. Lal, K. CS1St 2(1968):
604-605. 1601b. Spulber, Nicolas. AER 58(1968):998-
1000.

European Economics East and West. Cleveland: World
(114). Rev. 1602a. Mieczkowski, Bogdan. CSlSt 3
(1969):131-133.

1603. Kaplan, Norman M. "The Growth of Output and
Inputs in Soviet Transport and Communications," AER
57:1154-1167.

1604. Kholov, Makhmadullo. "Half a Century of an
Asian Republic of the USSR," EW 21,ix-x:24.

1605. Klages, Walter J.,Jr. "The Economic Development of Russia: From Thesis to Anti-Thesis--The
Roots and Antecedents of Modern Soviet Strategy for
Economic Growth," Alabama [PhD diss] 1967. DA 28:
2871A.

1606. Laibman, David. "Profits and Planning: The
Discussions Among Soviet Economists," NWR 35,vi:59-63.

1607. Lee, Robert E. "The Growth and Development
of the Economy of Soviet Georgia," California, Los
Angeles [PhD diss] 1966. DA 27(1966):1976B.

1608. Liberman, Yevsei. "The Soviet Economic Reform," FA 46:53-63.

1609. Mazour, Anatole G. Soviet Economic Development: Operation Outstrip, 1921-1965. Princeton: Van
Nostrand (191). Rev. 1609a. Hamilton, F.E.I. IA 44
(1968):348. 1609b. Pospielovsky, Dimitry. RusR 27
(1968):259.

1610. McAuley, Alastair N.D. "Rationality and
Central Planning," SovS 18,iii:340-355.

1611. Miller, Margaret. The Economic Development
of Russia, 1905-1914: With Special Reference to Trade,
Industry and Finance. London: Frank Cass (vii,321).

1612. Miller, Margaret. "Management Reforms in Industry," CAR 15,ii:99-113.

1613. Miller, Margaret. "Notes on Industrial Development," CAR 15,iv:300-315.

1614. Mišalov, Jurij. "Xozjajstvennyj eksperiment," NŽ 89:183-197.

1615. Mote, Max E. "The Budget of Greater Leningrad, 1956-1960," SovS 19,ii:245-254.

1616. di Pierro, Alberto P. "Western Estimates of Soviet Industrial Growth: A Critical Appraisal," Virginia [PhD diss] 1967. DA 28:3314A.

1617. Rausch, Howard. "Russia's Economic Reformation," Reporter 37,viii:33-35.

1618. Shaffer, Harry G. "Economic Growth and Economic Rationality," in Samuel Hendel, The Soviet System in Theory and Practice, 3rd ed., 333-339. Princeton: Van Nostrand.

1619. Sharlet, Robert. "Soviet Union as a Developing Country: A Review Essay," JDA 2:270-276.

1620. Sharpe, Myron E., ed. Planning, Profit and Incentives in the USSR. White Plains: International Arts and Sciences P. (viii,337). Rev. 1620a. Campbell, Robert. SlavR 27(1968):669-671.

1621. Smolinski, Leon. "Planning Without Theory 1917-1967," Survey 64:108-128.

1622. Solecki, J.J. Russia-China-Japan, Economic Growth, Resources, Forest Industries: Ten Lectures. Vancouver: U of British Columbia (vi,289).

1623. Sonin, M. and Zhiltsov, E. "Economic Development and Employment in the Soviet Union," ILabR 96,
i:67-91.

1624. Wiles, Peter. The Pursuit of Affluence: The
Economic Record," USSR after 50 Yrs [F2]:61-99.

1625. Zaleski, Eugene. Planning Reforms in the
Soviet Union 1962-1966. [Tr. by Marie C. MacAndrew and
G. Warren Nutter] Chapel Hill: U of North Carolina P
(viii,203). Rev. 1625a. Bernt, H.H. LJ 92:2398.
1625b. Campbell, Robert. APSR 62(1968):656-657.
1625c. Frankel, Theodore. PoC 17,ii(1968):67. 1625d.
McAuley, Alastair. PSQ 84(1968):712-713. 1625e.
Pryor, Frederic L. SlavR 28(1969):160-161. 1625f.
Wiles, Peter. AER 58(1968):995-997.

See also 655, 838, 921, 1011, 1450.

WAGES AND PRICES

1626. Bradley, Michael E. "Wage Determination and
Incentive Problems in Soviet Agriculture," Cornell
[PhD diss] 1967. DA 28:10A.

1627. Cerniglia, Joseph S. Wages in the U.S.S.R.
1950-1966: Construction. Washington: U.S. Department
of Commerce, Bureau of the Census. [International Population Reports, Series P-95, No. 63] (36).

1628. Goldman, Marshall I. "Trade and the Consum-
er," Survey 64:129-142.

1629. Kirsch, Leonard J. "A Study of Soviet Economies: Wage Administration and Structure in the USSR
since 1956," Harvard [PhD diss] 1967.

TURKEY

1630. Korniyenko, Radmir P. Labor Movement in

Turkey (1918-63). Washington: Joint Publications Research Service (ii,157).

1631. Robinson, Richard D. High-Level Manpower in
Economic Development: The Turkish Case. Cambridge:
Harvard U P (121). Rev. 1631a. Webster, Donald E.
MEJ 22,ii(1968):225.

1632. Seidler, Lee. The Function of Accounting in
Economic Development: Turkey as a Case Study. New
York: Praeger (369).

See also 1463.

YUGOSLAVIA

1633. Anderson, Stephen S. "Economic 'Reform' in
Yugoslavia," CH 52:214-219.

1634. Burck, Gilbert. "Adam Smitović on the Sava,"
Fortune 75,v:128-133,242,244,246.

1635. Grossman, Gregory. Economic Systems. Englewood Cliffs: Prentice-Hall (120). Rev. 1635a. Laird,
William E. FSUSP,I:95-99.

1636. Halpern, Joel M. "Farming as a Way of Life:
Yugoslav Peasant Attitudes," SEEA [F5]:356-381. Rev.
1636a. Bicanić, Rudolf. SEEA [F5]:382-384.

1637. Karcic, Berislav. "The Role of Money,
Credit and Related Institutions in Postwar Yugoslavia
till 1960," Columbia [PhD diss] 1966. DA 28:1593A.

1638. Margold, Stella. "Yugoslavia's New Economic
Reforms," AJES 26,i:65-77.

1639. Trees, Robert. "The Organization, Operation, and Management of a Yugoslavian Economic Enterprise: The Case of New Combine, a Publicly Owned Firm

for the Wholesale Distribution of Agricultural Equipment and Supplies," Chicago [PhD diss] 1966.

1640. Ward, Benjamin N. The Socialist Economy: A Study of Organizational Alternatives. New York: Random House (ix,272). Rev. 1640a. Colberg, Marshall R. FSUSP 2(1968):50-53.

See also 730.

IX. Education and Psychology

EAST EUROPE

PSYCHOLOGY

1641. Brožek, Josef, comp. "Recent Slavic Books in Psychology," ConP 12:306-308.

1642. Kaczkowski, Henry. "Psychology in Poland," AP 22:79-80.

1643. Moss, C. Scott. "Visitation to Mental Health Programs in Eastern Europe," AP 22:452-456.

See also 177.

EDUCATION

1644. Bencédy, József. "Tendances et developpements recents dans l'éducation primaire et secondaire en Hongrie," IRE 13:332-344.

1645. Dixon, R.T. "Differentiated Education in Czechoslovakia," CER 4,i:3-8.

1646. Georgeoff, John. "Higher Education in Bulgaria," EdF 31:455-464.

1647. Georgeoff, John. "Patterns of Educational Administration and Supervision in Yugoslavia," PSc 3, ii:97-104.

1648. Grace, Sister Mary. "Poland's Contribution to Mathematics," MTe 60:383-386.

1649. Kazamias, Andreas M. Education and the Quest for Modernity in Turkey. Chicago: U of Chicago P (304).

1650. Kulich, Jindra. "The Communist Party and Adult Education in Czechoslovakia, 1945-1965," CER 11, 231-243.

1651. Kulich, Jindra. The Role and Training of Adult Educators in Czechoslovakia. Vancouver: Faculty of Education and Department of University Extension, U of British Columbia (131).

1652. Roucek, Joseph S. The Teaching of History. New York: Philosophical Library (vi,282).

1653. Thomas, John I. "The Evolvement of Communist Education in Albania," Connecticut [PhD diss] 1967. DA 28(1968):3576A.

1654. Organization for Economic Cooperation and Development (U.N.). The Education, Training, and Functions of Technicians: Yugoslavia. Paris: OECD Directorate for Scientific Affairs (89).

1655. Anon. "Exchange Program with Eastern Europe," SS 95,2294(14 Oct):345-346.

See also 65, 217, 1672, 1729.

THE SOVIET UNION

PSYCHOLOGY

1656. Payne, T.R. "The 'Brain-Psyche' Problem in Soviet Psychology," SST 7,ii:83-100.

EDUCATION

General

1657. Adams, Arthur E. "Informal Education in Soviet Agriculture," CER 11,ii:217-230.

1658. Alexandrov, P.S. "'The Eternal Spring Whose Name is Twenty Years'," NWR 35,ix:128-134.

1659. Anderson, Randall C. "An Inquiry-Oriented Approach for Studying the Soviet Human Condition," SocE 31:715-719.

1660. Azrael, Jeremy R. "Fifty Years of Soviet Education," Survey 64:45-60.

1661. Brickman, William W. "Khrushchev's Vision of the Future Soviet School," SS 95,2297(25 Nov):461-474.

1662. Brickman, William W., ed. "Soviet Education: Revolution to Evolution," SS 95,2297(25 Nov): 437-474.

1663. Chabe, Alexander. "Assessing Soviet Education," Education 88:172-180.

1664. Chabe, Alexander M. "Evaluating Soviet Education," SS 95,2297(25 Nov):458-461.

1665. Counts, George S. "The Creation of the New Soviet Man," SS 95,2297(25 Nov):438-444.

1666. DeWitt, Nicholas. "Educational and Manpower Planning in the Soviet Union," World Yearbook of Education, 1967: Educational Planning, 219-239.

1667. Dorotich, Daniel. "A Turning Point in the Soviet School. The 17th Party Congress and the Teaching of History," HEQ 7:295-311.

1668. Ernst, Karl D. "Moscow Conservatory: One Hundred Years Old," MEJrn 53,viii:107-109

1669. Fraser, Stewart. "Shattered Sino-Soviet Educational Relations," PDK 48:288-293.

1670. Froese, Leonhard. "Soviet Higher Education: Ideal and Reality," SS 95,2297(25 Nov):455-458.

1671. Goodman, Ann S. and Feshbach, Murray. Estimates and Projections of Educational Attainment in the U.S.S.R.: 1950-1985. [International Population Reports, Series P-91, No. 16] Washington, D.C.: U.S. Department of Commerce, Bureau of the Census: (23).

1672. Graham, Loren R. The Soviet Academy of Sciences and the Communist Party, 1927-1932. Princeton: Princeton U P (xvi,255). Rev. 1672a. Walsh, Warren B. RusR 27(1968):476-477.

1673. Grant, Nigel. "Problems and Developments in Teacher Education in the USSR," SS 95,2297(25 Nov): 451-455.

1674. King, Edmund J. "The Soviet Union: The Claims of Communism," Other Schools and Ours: A Comparative Study for Today, 217-255. New York: Holt, Rinehart and Winston.

1675. Law, David A. "A Comparative Study of the Concepts of Truth, Freedom, and Democracy in the American and Soviet Education Systems," Utah [PhD diss] 1966. DA 27:2326A.

1676. Lipset, Harry. "National Minority Languages in Soviet Education," SovS 19:181-189.

1677. Mickiewicz, Ellen P. Soviet Political Schools: The Communist Party Adult Instruction System. New Haven and London: Yale U P (ix,190). Rev. 1677a.

Bernt, H.H. LJ 92:2562-2563. 1677b. Grant, Nigel.
CER 12(1968):361-363. 1677c. Lane, D.S. PSt 16
(1968):129. 1677d. Pennar, Jaan. SlavR 29(1970):135-
136. 1677e. Schwartz, Joel J. APSR 62(1968):276-277.

1678. Mlikotin, Anthony M. "Soviet Methods of
Teaching Foreign Languages," MLJ 51:337-343.

1679. Moos, Elizabeth. "Soviet Education Today,"
NWR 35,ix:135-137.

1680. Noah, Harold J. Financing Soviet Schools.
New York: Columbia U P (xxiv,294). Rev. 1680a. Bernt,
H.H. LJ 92:2562-2563. 1680b. Lilge, Frederic. SlavR
27(1968):504-505.

1681. Noah, Harold J. "The Economics of Education," PoC 16,iv:42-52.

1682. Roucek, Joseph S. "The Training of Foreign
Students by Communist Countries," UQ 23:314-331.

1683. Rudman, Herbert C. "Problems of Higher Education in the Soviet Union," SS 95,2289(4 Mar):153-
154,156.

1684. Rudman, Herbert C. The School and the State
in the U.S.S.R. New York: Macmillan; London: Collier-
Macmillan (xviii,286). Rev. 1684a. Bernt, H.H. LJ
92:2562-2563. 1684b. Johnson, William H.E. CER 12
(1968):360. 1684c. Parker, Franklin. IRE 15(1969):
111.

1685. Schlesinger, Ina. "Soviet Education in
1966," SS 95,2297(25 Nov):448-450.

1686. Schlesinger, Ina. "Soviet Education, 1957-
67," SS 95,2297(25 Nov):444-448.

1687. Schwadron, Abraham A. "Music in Soviet Education," MEJrn 53,viii(Apr):87-93.

1688. Smith, Ronald E. "Guidance in Soviet Schools," Ohio State [PhD diss] 1966. DA 27(1966): 3699A.

1689. Taubman, William. The View from Lenin Hills: An American Student's Report on Soviet Youth in Ferment. New York: Coward-McCann (249).

1690. Anon. "The Aging Elite," SS 95,2286(21 Jan):39-40.

See also 207, 458, 1578, 1811, 2238, 2251.

Primary and Secondary

1691. Lebedyev, Pantyeleymon D. "Educational Techniques and Problems of Programmed Instruction in the USSR," IRE 13,i:26-39.

1692. Moser, James M. "Mathematics Education in the Secondary Schools of the Soviet Union," MTe 60, viii:885-892.

1693. Mueller, Francis J. "The Revolution at Sputnik-Plus-Ten," MTe 60,vii:696-706.

1694. Siemienkow, G. [Semencov] "Prepodavanie ximii v srednix školax Sovetskogs Sojuza v tridcatyx i sorokovyx godax," Zapiski [Fl]:57-65. [Synopsis in English: "The Teaching of Chemistry in the Secondary Schools of the U.S.S.R. in the Thirties and Forties."]

1695. Smith, Ronald E. "The Class Adviser in the Soviet School," The School Counselor (Nov):103-106.

1696. Zacek, Judith C. "The Lancastrian School Movement in Russia," SEER 45,cv:343-367.

1697. Ifft, Edward M. "Science Students at Moscow University," BAS (Apr):40-44.

See also 450.

Higher Education

1698. Odintsoff, B.N. "Pervye mecjacy avtonomii v Moskovskom universitete," Zapiski [F1]:47-56. [Synopsis in English: "The First Months of Moscow University's Autonomy."]

1699. Procuta, Ginutis. "The Transformation of Higher Education in Lithuania during the First Decade of Soviet Rule," Lituanus 13,i:71-92.

SLAVIC AND EAST EUROPEAN STUDIES IN AMERICA

1700. Birkenmayer, Sigmund S. "Syntax, Word Division, Punctuation: Their Place in the Teaching of Russian in College," MLJ 51,v:204-209.

1701. Buyniak, Victor O. "Slavic Studies in Canada: An Historical Review," CS1P 9:3-23. Rev. 1701a. Fallenbuchl, Z.M. CS1P 9:42-44. 1701b. Field, N.C. CS1P 9:34-37. 1701c. Ignatieff, L. CS1P 9:27-30. 1701d. Kos-Rabcewicz-Zubkowski, L. CS1P 9:40-42. 1701e. Pech, S.Z. CS1P 9:24-27. 1701f. Shein, L.J. CS1P 9:37-40. 1701g. Strong, J.W. CS1P 9:30-34. [Buyniak's response CS1P 9:45-49.]

1702. Fischer, George. American Research on Soviet Society: Guide to Specialized Studies Since World War II by Sociologists, Psychologists, and Anthropologists in the United States. New York: Foreign Area Materials Center, U of the State of New York, State Education Dept (vi,82).

1703. Fischer, Milla. "Contrastive Cultural Features in FL Teaching," SEEJ 11:302-307.

1704. Hainsworth, Jerome C. "Teaching About Communism in the American Secondary Schools," Brigham Young [PhD diss] 1967. DA 28:1983A.

1705. Jacobs, Dan N. "Area Studies and Communist Systems," SlavR 26:18-21.

1706. Parry, Albert. America Learns Russian: A History of the Teaching of the Russian Language in the United States. Syracuse: Syracuse U P (xi,205). Rev. 1706a. De Graff, Frances. SEEJ 15(1971):517-518. 1706b. Geen, Renee. MLJ 53(1969):267-268. 1706c. Legters, Lyman H. SlavR 27(1968):358-360.

1707. Sawlowski, Richard and Terlecka, Hanna. "Western Research on Russia Until 1939: I, Development up to 1914," CPS 9:145-169.

1708. Sistrunk, Walter E. "The Teaching of Americanism Versus Communism in Florida Secondary Schools," Florida [PhD diss] 1966. DA 27:3640A.

1709. Slavutych, Yar. "Ukrainian Philology in Canada," Slavs in Canada 2:247-258. [Toronto: Inter-U. Com. on Canadian Slavs.]

1710. Stolz, Benjamin A. "On Teaching a Second Slavic Language: The Problem of Serbo-Croatian," LgL 17:155-161.

1711. Terras, Victor. "A Survey of the Teaching of Russian in the US, Fall 1966, Part I: Colleges and Universities; Part II: Secondary Schools," SEEJ 11: 308-321;450-463.

1712. Turkevich, Ludmilla B., ed. Methods of Teaching Russian. Princeton, Toronto, and London: Van Nostrand (viii,216). Rev. 1712a. Baker, Robert L. SEEJ 12(1968):497-499.

1713. Wirsing, Marie E. "What an American Secondary School Student Should Know About Communism," Denver [PhD diss] 1967. DA 27:2760A.

See also 1805, 1811, 1818.

X. Science

EAST EUROPE

1714. May, Jacques M. The Ecology of Malnutrition in Central and South-Western Europe: Austria, Hungary, Rumania, Bulgaria, Czechoslovakia. New York: Hafner (xv,290).

1715. Tibensky, Jan. "The History of Science and Technology in Slovakia," T&C 8:480-484.

THE SOVIET UNION

1716. Bclousow, C.G. "Vysyxanie kaspijskogo morja," Zapiski [Fl]:181-190. [Synopsis in English: "Loss of Water in the Caspian Sea."]

1717. Cook, Earl F., ed. Tufflavas and Ignimbrites, A Survey of Soviet Studies. [Tr. by Miriam Carty.] New York: American Elsevier (xii,212). Rev. 1717a. Scott, Robert B. AJSc 265,vii:636-637

1718. Davies, Merton E., Eckman, Philip K., and Murray, Bruce C. "Planetary Contamination II: Soviet and U.S. Practices and Policies," Science 155:1511.

1719. Gill, Richard R. "Problems of Decision Making in Soviet Science Policy," M 5,ii:198-208.

1720. Graham, Loren R. "Science Policy and Planning in the USSR," Survey 64:61-79.

1721. Ivanov, A. "Nauka v Sovetskom Sojuze," NŽ 86:221-237.

1722. Langer, Elinor. "Soviet Genetics: First Russian Visit Since 1930's Offers a Glimpse," Science 157:1153.

1723. Van Allen, James A. "Are We to Abandon the Planets to the Soviet Union?" Science 158:1405.

        See also 61, 194, 212, 1445, 1448, 1693, 1694, 1697, 1698, 1845.

ENGINEERING

1724. Adabashev, Igor. "Changing Our Planet," NWR 35,i:23-26.

MEDICINE

1725. Aronson, Jason and Field, Mark G. "The Institutional Framework of Soviet Psychiatry," S. Kirson Weimberg, ed. The Sociology of Mental Disorders: Analyses and Readings in Psychiatric Sociology, Chicago: Aldine, 351-356.

1726. Field, Mark G. "Soviet and American Approaches to Mental Illness: A Comparative Perspective," James Farndale and Hugh Freeman, eds. New Aspects of the Mental Health Services, 2nd ed., London: Pergamon, 294-333.

1727. Field, Mark G. "Soviet Psychiatry and Social Structure, Culture and Ideology: A Preliminary Assessment," American Journal of Psychotherapy 21:230-243.

1728. Field, Mark G. Soviet Socialized Medicine:
An Introduction. New York: Free Press; London: Collier-Macmillan (xix,231). Rev. 1728a. Boiter, Albert.
PoC 16,iv:68-69. 1728b. Brodman, Estelle. LJ 92:
1026. 1728c. Hollander, Paul. American Scientist 55
(Mar):193A. 1728d. Rubinstein, Alvin Z. CH 53:240.
1728e. Zarechnak, Galina. SlavR 26:691.

1729. Kovacs, Helen. "Medical Libraries from
Ankara to London," BMLA 55:418-427.

See also 61.

XI. Language and Linguistics

GENERAL

1730. Birnbaum, Henryk. "On the Reconstruction and Predictability of Linguistic Models: Balto-Slavic Revisited," ScSl 13:105-114.

1731. Georgacas, Demetrius J. "Place and Other Names of Various Balkan Origins, Part IV," ZB 5:167-185.

1732. Hamp, Eric P. "On the Notions of 'stone' and 'mountain' in Indo-European," JLing 3:83-90.

1733. Kazazis, Kostas. "On a Generative Grammar of the Balkan Languages," FLg 3:117-123.

1734. Klimas, Antanas. "Balto-Slavic or Baltic and Slavic?: The Relationship of Baltic and Slavic Languages," Lituanus 13,ii:5-46. [With bibliography by G. A. Hood, pp. 38-46.]

1735. Kloss, Heinz. "Bilingualism and Nationalism," JSI 23,ii:39-47.

1736. Kučera, Henry. "Distinctive Features, Simplicity, and Descriptive Adequacy," THRJ [F7]:1114-1126.

1737. Poultney, James W. "Some Indo-European Morphological Alternations," Lg 43:871-882.

1738. Vanek, Anthony L. "The Hierarchy of Dominance Configuration in Trilingualism," Lětopis [Institut fur sorbische Volksforschung bei der Akademie der Wissenschaften zu Berlin] 14/1, Series A.

See also 1743.

INDO-EUROPEAN

ALBANIAN

1739. Pogoni, Bardhyl. "Albanian Writing Systems," Indiana [PhD diss] 1967. DA 28:2230A.

ARMENIAN

See 1920.

BALTIC

General

1740. Schmalstieg, William R. "The Vocalic Distinctive Features of Primitive East Baltic," Lituanus 13,i:61-64.

Latvian

1741. Ekmanis, Rolfs. "Aksakāl, kas jums tur atunkurā?" JGai 62:55-57.

1742. Hauzenberga-Šturma, E. "Liet. valandà un latv. valuoda," Ceļi 13:24-28.

1743. Zeps, Valdis. "Par slavismiem latviešu valodā," Ceļi 13:29-31.

See also 1734, 1737, 1913.

Lithuanian

1744. Ford, Gordon B.,Jr. "esti und yra in Vilentas' Euchiridion," ZSP 33:353-357.

1745. Francis, John M. "The Accentuation of Denominative Verbs in Lithuanian," Harvard [PhD diss] 1967.

1746. Klimas, Antonas, and Schmalstieg, William R. Lithuanian Reader for Self-Instruction. Brooklyn: Franciscan Fathers Press (iv,60). Rev. 1746a. Zeps, Valdis J. SEEJ 12(1968):104.

1747. Salys, Antanas. "The Russianization of the Lithuanian Vocabulary Under the Soviets," Lituanus 13, ii:47-62.

1748. Sánchez, José. "Films for Exotic Foreign Language Instruction," MLJ 51:195-203.

See also 1734, 1737, 1913.

Old Prussian

1749. Shopay, Olga C. "Old Prussian Adverbs in -n," SEEJ 11:296-301.

See also 1734, 1737.

MODERN GREEK

1750. Matthews, P.H. "The Main Features of Modern Greek Verb Inflection," FLg 3:261-283.

1751. Newton, B.E. "The Phonology of Cypriot Greek," Lingua 18:384-411.

See also 1748.

SLAVIC

General

1752. Andersen, Henning. "Tenues and Mediae in

the Slavic Languages: A Historical Investigation,"
Harvard [PhD diss] 1967.

1753. Benveniste, E. "Les relations lexicales
slavo-iraniennes," THRJ [F7]:197-202.

1754. Bidwell, Charles E. Alphabets of the Modern
Slavic Languages. Pittsburgh: U of Pittsburgh Inter-
national Studies Program (24). Rev. 1754a. Harrington,
Ronald V. GL 8(1968):125. 1754b. Marquess, Harlan E.
SEEJ 12(1968):379.

1755. Bidwell, Charles E. The Slavic Languages:
Their External History. Pittsburgh: U of Pittsburgh
International Studies Program (55). Rev. 1755a. Derbyshire, William W. GL 8(1968):62-64. 1755b. Marquess, Harlan E. SEEJ 12(1968):379.

1756. Ebeling, C.L. "Historical Laws of Slavic
Accentuation," THRJ [F7]:577-593.

1757. Ferrell, James. "On the Prehistory of the
Locative Singular of the Common Slavic Consonant
Stems," THRJ [F7]:654-661.

1758. Georgiev, Vladimir I. "Indoevropejskij
termin deywos v slavjanskix jazykax," THRJ (F7]:734-
737.

1759. Goɫąb, Zbigniew. "The Traces of vr̥ddhi in
Slavic," THRJ [F7]:770-784.

1760. Jakobson, Roman. "Die urslavischen Silben
ūr-, ūl-," ZPSK 20:239-241.

1761. Kuryɫowicz, Jerzy. "Slavic dambı A Problem
in Methodology," THRJ [F7]:1127-1131.

1762. Lockwood, David G. "A Typological Comparison of Microsegment and Syllable Constructions in

Czech, Serbo-Croatian, and Russian," Michigan [PhD diss] 1966. <u>DA</u> 28:655A.

1763. Matejka, L. "Generative and Recognitory Aspects in Phonology," <u>PDG</u> [F4]:242-253.

1764. Mayer, Gerald L. "A Comparative Study of the Syntax of the Cardinal Numeral in the Slavic Languages," Pennsylvania [PhD diss] 1967. <u>DA</u> 28:1420A.

1765. Milewski, Tadeusz. "The Evolution of the Common Slavic System," <u>THRJ</u> [F7]:1362-1372.

1766. Revzin, I.I. and Revzin, O.G. "K postroeniju sistemy differencial'nyx priznakov dlja slovoobrazovanija suščestvitel'nyx slavjanskix jazykov," <u>THRJ</u> [F7]:1657-1666.

1767. Shevelov, G.Y. "On Predicaments, Predictability and Futurism in Phonology," <u>PDG</u> [F4]:367-373.

See also 1730, 1734, 1909.

Old Church Slavonic

1768. Gove, Antonina F. "The Slavic Akathistos Hymm: A Comparative Study of a Byzantine Kontakion and Its Old Church Slavonic Translation," Harvard [PhD diss] 1967.

1769. Hamm, Josip. "Ainete," <u>THRJ</u> [F7]:833-839.

1770. Lightner, Theodore M. "On the Phonology of the Old Church Slavonic Conjugation," <u>IJSLP</u> 10:1-28.

1771. Mathiesen, Robert. "An Emendation to the <u>Vita Methodii</u> XV.1," <u>ZFL</u> 10:51-53.

1772. Picchio, Riccardo. "Slave ecclésiastique, slavons et rédactions," <u>THRJ</u> [F7]:1527-1544.

1773. Ševčenko, Ihor. "The Greek Source of the Inscription on Solomon's Chalice in the Vita Constantini," THRJ [F7]:1806-1817.

1774. Sotiroff, George. "Y a-t-il eu une écriture autochtone en terre slave avant le temps de Cyrille et Méthode?" CSlSt 1:79-94.

See also 1934.

EAST SLAVIC

General

1775. Bidwell, Charles E. "Phonemic Vowel Length in East Slavic?" ZFL 10:25-27.

Russian

1776. Adrianova-Peretc, V. "Zametki o leksike Slovo o polku Igoreve," THRJ [F7]:15-17.

1777. Auty, Robert. "The Gospel and Psalter of Cherson: Syriac or Russian," THRJ [F7]:114-117.

1778. Avanesov, R.I. "K istorii morfonologičeskix čeredovanij i fonemnogo costava kornevyx morfem pri obrazovanii umen'sitel'nyx suščestvitel'nyx v russkom jazyke," THRJ [F7]:118-132.

1779. Axmanova, O.S. "Nekotorye osobennosti glagol'noj giperleksemy v russkom jazyke," THRJ [F7] 141-149.

1780. Benson, Morton. Dictionary of Russian Personal Names, With A Guide to Stress and Morphology. Philadelphia: U of Pennsylvania P [2nd rev. ed.] (viii,175). Rev. 1780a. Kantor, Marvin. MLJ 52(1968): 463-464. 1780b. Zinam, Oleg. CSlSt 2(1968):280.

1781. Bielfeldt, H.H. "Russisch kustár', kustar-ja: kust wie Deutsch Stümper: Strumpf," THRJ [F7]:232-238.

1782. Birkenmayer, Sigmund S. An Accepted Dictionary of Place Names in the Soviet Union. University Park: Dept. of Slavic Languages, Pennsylvania State U (xxvii,97). Rev. 1782a. Benson, Morton. SEEJ 12(1968):372-373. 1782b. Kantor, Marvin. MLJ 52 (1968):234-235.

1783. Birnbaum, Henrik. "On the Grammatical Status of Short Form Adjectives and Some Related Problems in Modern Russian," CalSlSt 4:162-199.

1784. Birnbaum, Henrik. "Predication and the Russian Infinitive," THRJ [F7]:271-294.

1785. Bratus, B.V. The Formation and Expressive Use of Diminutives. New York: Cambridge U P (viii, 70).

1786. Clark, Ben T. Russian for Americans. New York: Harper and Row (804). Rev. 1786a. Marquess, Harlan E. SEEJ 12(1968):100-102.

1787. Conrad, Joseph L. "Aspect and American Textbooks of Russian," MLJ 51:289-294.

1788. Davison, R.M. The Use of the Genitive in Negative Constructions. New York: Cambridge U P (29). Rev. 1788a. Derbyshire, William W. SlavR 27(1968): 503-504. 1788b. Drage, C.L. MLR 63(1968):779-780. 1788c. Křižková, Helena. IJSLP 12(1969):187-191.

1789. Derbyshire, William W. "Verbal Homonymy in the Russian Language," CSlP 9:131-139.

1790. Ferguson, C.A. "St. Stefan of Perm and Applied Linguistics," THRJ [F7]:643-653.

1791. Fesenko, Andrej, and Fesenko, Tat'jana.
"Xarakternye osobennosti russkogo jazyka poslednego
desjatiletija," N̄Ž 89:244-262.

1792. Foote, I.P. Verbs of Motion. New York:
Cambridge U P (33). Rev. 1792a. Drage, C.L. MLR 63:
779-780. 1792b. Křižkova, Helena. IJSLP 12(1969):
187-191.

1793. Gallis, Arne. "Zu Syntax und Stil der geg-
enwärtigen russischen Zeitungssprache," THRJ (F7]:697-
706.

1794. Garvin, Paul L. "Heuristic Syntax in Russian-English Machine Translation," THRJ [F7]:718-725.

1795. Gribble, Charles E. "Linguistic Problems
of the Vygolesinskj Sbornik," Harvard [PhD diss] 1967.

1796. Harrison, W. The Expression of the Passive
Voice. New York: Cambridge U P (46). Rev. 1796a.
Derbyshire, William W. SlavR 27:503-504. 1796b.
Klein, Kurt A. SEEJ 12:371-372. 1796c. Křižkova,
Helena. IJSLP 12:187-191.

1797. Harshenin, A.P. "English Loanwords in the
Doukhobor Dialect: II," CSlP 9:216-230.

1798. Hays, David G., and Worth, Dean S. Toward
Exploitation of a File of Russian Text with Syntactic
Annotations. [Memorandum RM-5252-RADC.] Santa Monica:
Rand (ix,36).

1799. Henley, Norman F. "Selected Categories of
Russian Loan Words in English," Harvard [PhD diss]
1967.

1800. Holliday, Gilbert F. "Constituent Order of
the Simple Verbal Predication in Contemporary Written
Russian," Cornell [PhD diss] 1966. DA 27(1966):4237A.

1801. Iordan, Iorgu. "Notes sur les rapports lin-
guistiques russo-roumains," THRJ [F7]:958-965.

1802. Isačenko, A.V. "Frazovoe udarenie i porja-
dok slov," THRJ [F7]:967-976.

1803. Jaszczun, Wasyl and Krynski, Szymon. A Dictionary of Russian Idioms and Colloquialisms: 2,200
Expressions with Examples. Pittsburgh: U of Pittsburgh P (xiii,102). Rev. 1803a. Birkenmayer, Sigmund
S. CSlSt 1:667-669. 1803b. Sorokin, Olga. SEEJ 12
(1968):494-496.

1804. Jones, Lawrence G. "Grammatical Patterns
in English and Russian Verse," THRJ [F7]:1015-1045.

1805. Kempers, John. "The Teaching of Russian: A
Response to Nathan Rosen," SEEJ 11:71-74.

1806. Koolemans-Beijnen, Gijsbertus J.H. "A Comparative Analysis of Word Order in Contemporary Standard Russian and Polish," Stanford [PhD diss] 1967.
DA 27:4238A.

1807. Korn, David. "Genitive or Accusative After
Negation in Russian," SEEJ 11:442-449.

1808. Koubourlis, Demetrius J. "A Statistical
Analysis of the Russian Verbal Aspect," Washington,
Seattle [PhD diss] 1967. DA 29(1968):248A.

1809. Lightner, Theodore M. "On Phonetic Nasal~
a Alternations in Modern Russian Verb Forms," THRJ
[F7]:1183-1187.

1810. Lightner, Theodore M. "On the Phonology of
Russian Conjugation," Ling 35:35-55.

1811. Lippert, Henry T. "Computer-Aided Learning
and Transfer Effects of Russian Pronunciation," Illinois [PhD diss] 1967. DA 28:3028A.

1812. Long, John G. Russkoe čtenie dlja srednego urovnja. Philadelphia: Chilton (82). Rev. 1812a. Jaszczun, Wasyl. SEEJ 12(1968):236.

1813. Lotz, John. "Jakobson's Case Theory and the Russian Prepositions," THRJ [F7]:1207-1212.

1814. Lyons, John. "A Note on Possessive, Existential, and Locative Sentences," FLg 3,iv:390-396.

1815. Michailoff, Helen. New Russian Self Taught. New York: Funk and Wagnalls (372).

1816. Mihalchenko, Igor S., ed. Russian Intermediate Reader. New York, Toronto, and London: Pitman (ix,274).

1817. Miller, Herbert C. "The Fundamentals of Russian Intonation," Indiana [PhD diss] 1967. DA 28: 2229A.

1818. Morris, Seán. "Improving the Structure Drill in Russian," SEEJ 11:66-70.

1819. Mullen, J. Agreement of the Verb-Predicate with a Collective Subject. New York: Cambridge U P (13). Rev. 1819a. Derbyshire, William W. SlavR 27 (1968):503-504. 1819b. Klein, Kurt A. SEEJ 12(1968): 371-372. 1819c. Křižkova, Helena. IJSLP 12:187-191.

1820. Nicholson, John G. "Russian Verbal Aspect and 'Aktionsart'," ESEE 12:50-54.

1821. Norbury, J.K.W. Word Formation in the Noun and Adjective. New York: Cambridge U P (vi,129). Rev. 1821a. Drage, C.L. MLR 63(1968):779-780. 1821b. Korn, David. SEEJ 14(1970):105-107. 1821c. Křižkova, Helena. IJSLP 12(1969):187-191.

1822. Pilch, Herbert. "Russische Konsonantengruppen in Silbenan- und -auslaut," THRJ [F7]:1555-1584.

1823. Popov, Elisabeth A. "Semantic Structure of the Russian Diminutive," Stanford [PhD diss] 1967. DA 28:2668A.

1824. Pronin, Alexander. Russian Vocabulary Builder (By Subjects): 10 Words a Day, Book I. Los Angeles: Lawrence (iv,225). Rev. 1824a. Marcell, Noah. SEEJ 12(1968):370-371.

1825. Rakusanova, Jaromira. Complementation Characteristics of the Russian Verbs of Motion. Detroit: Research in Machine Translation Project, Wayne State U.

1826. Reformatskij, A.A. "< ž >," THRJ [F7]:1650-1656.

1827. Schmalstieg, William R. "The Analogical Spread of Russian /o/ and /e/," ISlSt 4:125-127.

1828. Sergievsky, Nicholas N. Idiomatic Russian. New York: International U P (450). Rev. 1828a. Kolb-Seletski, Natalia. SEEJ 13(1969):104-106.

1829. Shapiro, Michael. "Concatenators and Russian Derivational Morphology," GL 7:50-66.

1830. Shapiro, Michael. "K voprosu o meste udarenija v sočetanijax tipa na ruku," RLJ 21,lxxix:53-67.

1831. Shapiro, Michael. "Laws, Latitudes, and Limitations of Stress: Russian Derived Substantives," Acta Linguistica Hafniensia 11:187-200.

1832. Shapiro, Michael. "Remarks on Phonological Boundaries in Russian," SEEJ 11:433-441.

1833. Shapiro, Michael. "The Stress of Russian Substantival Composita," ScSl 13:197-210.

1834. Shaw, J. Thomas. The Transliteration of Modern Russian for English-Language Publications. Madison, Milwaukee and London: U of Wisconsin P (vii,15).

1835. Solov'ev, A.V. "Slovesnaja tkan' Zadonščiny i Slova o polku Igoreve," THRJ [F7]:1866-1875.

1836. Titelbaum, Olga A. "Morphosyntactic Patterns of Contemporary Russian Voice and Aspect," Chicago [PhD diss] 1967.

1837. Townsend, Charles E. "Voice and Verbs in -sja," SEEJ 11:196-203.

1838. Tsurikov, Alexey. "Case Selection in Clauses with Negative Transitive Verbs in Contemporary Russian," Rochester [PhD diss] 1967. DA 28:1810A.

1839. Vakar, Nicholas P. "Statistical Methods in the Analysis of Russian," SEEJ 11:59-65.

1840. Van Campen, Joseph A. "Feature Specification in Russian Morphophonemics," THRJ [F7]:2116-2125.

1841. Veenker, Wolfgang. Die Frage des finno-ugrischen Substrats in der russischen Sprache. Bloomington: Indiana U P (xvi,329). Rev. 1841a. Kiparsky, Valentin. SEEJ 12(1968):490-492.

1842. Vinogradov, V.V. "Ob omonimii služebnyx slov v sovremennom russkom jazyke," THRJ [F7]:2152-2158.

1843. Vitek, Alexander J. "Functions of Russian Adverbs: A Preliminary Transform Analysis," Michigan [PhD diss] 1967. DA 28:2235A.

1844. Waring, A.G. Russian Science Grammar:

Oxford: Pergamon (viii,174). Rev. 1844a. Guild, D.G.
MLR 63(1968):1021-1022.

1845. Whitman, Robert H. "A Textological Note on
the 1073 Izbornik," WS1 12:67-73.

1846. Whitman, Robert H. "The 1073 Izbornik: The
Manuscript and its Sources," IS1St 4:252-267.

1847. Worth, Dean S. "The Notion of 'stem' in
Russian Flexion and Derivation," THRJ [F7]:2269-2288.

1848. Worth, Dean S. "On Cyclical Rules in Derivational Morphophonemics," PDG [F4]:173-186.

1849. Worth, Gerta H. "On Word-Formation and
Semantic Change in 19th Century Russian: Their West
European Origins," THRJ [F7]:2289-2300.

1850. Yakobson, Helen B., ed. Russian Readings
Past and Present: An Intermediate Reader. New York:
Appleton-Century-Crofts (vi,153). Rev. 1850a. Dalton,
Margaret. SEEJ 12(1968):99-100. 1850b. Strong, Rob-
ert L.,Jr. MLJ 52(1968):120.

1851. Zaliznjak, A.A. "O pokazateljax množestven-
nogo čisla v russkom sklonenii," THRJ [F7]:2328-2332.

1852. Zarechnak, Michael. "A.A. Kholodovich's
Theory of Subclasses to Russian Temporal Nouns," Harvard [PhD diss] 1967.

        See also 44, 62, 1700, 1711, 1712, 1747,
1762, 1864, 1897, 2115, 2184, 2222, 2231, 2347.

Belorussian

1853. Bidwell, Charles E. Outline of Bielorussian
Morphology. Pittsburgh: U of Pittsburgh International

Dimensions Program (iv,48). Rev. 1853a. Leed, Richard
L. GL 8(1968):125-129. 1853b. Naylor, Kenneth E.
SEEJ 13(1969):271-272.

1854. Wexler, Paul N. "Purism in the Development
of a Standard Language (with Special Reference to Modern Standard Belorussian and Ukrainian)," Columbia
[PhD] diss] 1967. DA 28:2235A.

Ukrainian

1855. Bidwell, Charles E. Outline of Ukrainian
Morphology. Pittsburgh: U of Pittsburgh International
Dimensions Program (55).

1856. Foster, James M. "Some Phonological Rules
of Modern Standard Ukrainian," Illinois [PhD diss]
1966. DA 27:3858A.

1857. Gerus-Tarnawecky, Iraida. "The Watermarks
in the Pom'janyk of Horodyśce: A Comparative Historical Retrospective," WSl 12:193-198.

1858. Pritsak, Omeljan. "Non-'wild' Polovtsians,"
THRJ [F7]:1615-1623.

1859. Rudnyc'kyj, J.B. An Etymological Dictionary
of the Ukrainian Language, part 6. Winnipeg: Ukrainian Free Academy of Science (95). Rev. 1859a. Magner,
Thomas F. GL 7:162-163. 1859b. Shevelov, George Y.
Lg 44:856-875.

1860. Stieber, Zdzislaw. "L'allongement compen-
satoire dans l'ukrainien et le haut sorabe," THRJ [F7]:
1935-1940.

See also 32, 1748, 1854.

WEST SLAVIC

Polish

1861. Birkenmayer, Sigmund S. and Folejewski,
Zbigniew. Introduction to the Polish Language. New
York: Kosciuszko Foundation (190).

1862. Brooks, Maria Zagórska. "The Accusative-
Genitive Contrast in Some Polish Constructions," THRJ
[F7]:395-401.

1863. Ferrell, James. "The Nominative Singular
Masculine of the Present Participle Active in the
Kazania Swiętokrzyskie," RoczSlaw 28:69-78.

1864. Gasiński, Tadeusz Z. "A Comparison of the
Polish and Russian Case Systems," Stanford [PhD diss]
1966. DA 27(1966):4236A.

1865. Kantor, Marvin. "Phonological Rewrite Rules
for the Derivation of Contemporary Standard Polish,"
ScSl 13:211-220.

1866. Kiparsky, V. "Altpoln. abentajer 'falscher
Edelstein'," THRJ [F7]:1060-1063.

1867. Schenker, Alexander M. Beginning Polish.
New Haven: Yale U P (1x,494;336). Rev. 1867a. Glad-
ney, Frank Y. SEEJ 12(1968):222-227.

1868. Westfal, Stanislaw. Why Learn Polish?
[Plus a bibliography of the author's works] London:
Anglo-Polish Society (53).

1869. Wierzbicka, Anna. "On the Semantics of the
Verbal Aspect in Polish," THRJ [F7]:2231-2249.

See also 43, 1748, 1806.

Czech and Slovak

1870. Newman, Lawrence W.,Jr. "A Generative Approach to the Czech Verb," Harvard [PhD diss] 1967.

1871. Pauliný, Eugen. "Zum Verhältnis der Laute /i/ und /j/ im Slowakischen," THRJ [F7]:1497-1502.

1872. Pribić, Elisabeth. "Some Problems in Czech Prosody," FSUSP 1:48-53.

See also 41, 1748, 1762.

Lusatian

1873. Raede, John W. "De-Germanization of the Upper Lusatian Language," SEEJ 11:185-190.

1874. Raede, John W. "The Linguistic Importance of Lusatian," CSlP 9:231-244.

See also 1860.

Polabian

1875. Polański, Kazimierz and Sehnert, J.A. Polabian-English Dictionary. London, Paris and The Hague: Mouton (239). Rev. 1875a. Thomas, Lawrence L. SEEJ 12(1968):373-375.

SOUTH SLAVIC

See 45, 1470.

Bulgarian

1876. Aronson, Howard I. "The Grammatical Cate-

gories of the Indicative in the Contemporary Bulgarian
Literary Language," THRJ [F7]:82-99.

1877. Beševliev, V. "Protobulgarica," THRJ [F7]:
222-231.

1878. Bidwell, Charles E. "Bulgarian Syntax,"
Ling 29:5-33.

1879. Stojkov, Stojko. "The Vowel [y] in Bulgarian," THRJ [F7]:1941-1946.

1880. Topolińska, Zuzanna. "The Role of the Post-
positive Definite Article in the Bulgarian Nominal
Accentuation System," THRJ [F7]:2024-2031.

See also 40.

Macedonian

1881. Koneski, Blaže. "O jazyke makedonskoj
narodnoj poèzii," THRJ [F7]:1064-1067.

1882. LeGuillou, Jean-Yves. "La naissance d'une
langue slave littéraire moderne: Le Macédonien," ESEE
12:122-127.

1883. Miličić, Vladimir, ed. Obraten rečnik na
makedonskiot jazik. Skopje: Institut za Makedonski
Jazik "Krste Misirkov" (ii,389).

Serbocroatian

1884. Albin, Alexander. "Prilog proučavanju
jezika Stefana Rajića," PPJ 3:1-22.

1885. Beard, Robert E. "The Suffixation of Adjectives in Contemporary Literary Serbo-Croatian," Michigan [PhD diss] 1967. DA 28:211A.

1886. Benson, Morton. "English Loanwords in Serbo-Croatian," ASp 42,iii:178-189.

1887. Bidwell, Charles E. "Colonial Venetian and Serbo-Croatian in the Eastern Adriatic: A Case Study of Languages in Contact," GL 7:13-30.

1888. Brozović, Dalibor. "Some Remarks on Distinctive Features Especially in Standard Serbocroatian," THRJ [F7]:412-426.

1889. Dunatov, Rasio. "A Grammar of the Noun Declensions in Serbocroatian," Washington, Seattle [PhD diss] 1967. DA 28:1806A.

1890. Ivić, Milka. "Types of Direct Object in Serbocroatian," THRJ [F7]:989-994.

1891. Ivić, Pavle and Lehiste, Ilse. "Prilozi ispitivanju fonetske i fonološke prirode akcenata u savremenom srpskohrvatskom jeziku:III," ZFL 10:55-91.

1892. Ivić, Pavle. "The Serbocroatian Case System in Diachrony and Diatopy," THRJ [F7]:995-1008.

1893. Kocher, Margaret. "Second Person Pronouns in Serbo-Croatian," Lg 43:725-741.

1894. Moguš, Milan. "Formation of Serbo-Croat Consonants," ScSl 13:239-250.

1895. Muljačić, Žarko. "Les phonèmes italiens /ĉ/ et /ĝ/ dans les emprunts italiens du serbocroate: Problèmes de transcription et de distance phonématique," THRJ [F7]:1408-1413.

1896. Lehiste, Ilse and Ivić, Pavle. "Some Problems Concerning the Syllable in Serbo-Croatian," Glossa 1:126-136.

1897. Naylor, Kenneth E. "The Nominal Declension

in the Čakavian Serbocroatian Dialects and Literary
Serbocroatian, Compared with that of Russian," Chicago
[PhD diss] 1966.

1898. Nikolić, Berislav M. "Metanastasičeskie
sloi v govore Valevskoj Kolubary," THRJ [F7]:1430-1435.

1899. Pavlović, Mil[ivoj]. "Les interférences des
conjonctions et l'unité de la situation prédicative,"
THRJ [F7]:1503-1515.

1900. Spalatin, Christopher. "Serbo-Croatian or
Serbian and Croatian? Considerations on the Croatian
Declaration and Serbian Proposal of March 1967," JCS
7-8:3-13.

1901. Surdučki, Milan S. "English Loan Words in
Serbo-Croatian Immigrant Press," CJL 12:123-135.

1902. Van Schooneveld, C.H. "On the Meaning of
the Serbocroatian Aorist," THRJ [F7]:2126-2129.

1903. Whyte, Robert E. "Komiški, A Čakavian Dialect: Its Verbal Morphology with Texts and Concorded
Glossary," Wisconsin [PhD diss] 1967. DA 28(1968):
3171A.

See also 1470, 1710, 1762, 2305.

Slovenian

1904. Řehák, Vladimir. "Classes of Morphological
Change in Slovenian," SEEJ 11:191-195.

YIDDISH

1905. Weinreich, Max. "The Reality of Jewishness
versus the Ghetto Myth: The Sociolinguistic Roots of
Yiddish," THRJ [F7]:2199-2211.

RUMANIAN

1906. Avram, Andrei. "De la langue qu'on parle
aux enfants roumains," THRJ [F7]:133-140.

1907. Buehler, Gretchen H. "An Examination of
the Debate on Rumanian Phonemics," Pennsylvania [PhD
diss] 1966. DA 27:3028A.

1908. Petrovici, Émile. "Le neutre en istrorou-
main," THRJ [F7]:1523-1526.

1909. Rosetti, A. "Sur la chronologie des
éléments slaves méridionaux du roumain," THRJ [F7]:
1667-1668.

1910. Tamás, Lajos. Etymologisch-historisches
Wörterbuch der ungarischen Elemente im Rumänischen
(unter Berücksichtigung der Mundartwörter). Bloomington: Indiana U, The Hague: Mouton (936).

1911. Vasiliu, E. "Evolutive and Typologic Phonology: Some Remarks on the Phonology of Daco-Romanian
Dialects," THRJ [F7]:2130-2132.

See also 1801.

NON-INDO EUROPEAN

FINNO-UGRIC

See 1841.

Finnish

1912. Austerlitz, Robert. "The Distributional
Identification of Finnish Morphophonemes," Lg 43:20-
33.

1913. Lehtinen, Meri. "On the Origin of the
Balto-Finnic Long Vowels," UAJ 39:147-152.

1914. Thomsen, Vilhelm. On the Influence of Germanic Languages on Finnic and Lapp: A Historical Linguistic Inquiry. [Intr. by Thomas A. Sebeok] Bloomington: Indiana U (x,188).

Estonian

1915. Magi, Kaljo S. "A Low German-Estonian Book
of 1535," New York [PhD diss] 1965. DA 28:656A.

Hungarian

1916. Arany, A. Lazló. The Phonological System
of a Hungarian Dialect: An Introduction to Structural
Dialectology. Bloomington: Indiana U (185).

1917. Rice, Lester A. "Hungarian Morphological
Irregularities with Contributions to Feature Theory,"
Indiana [PhD diss] 1967. DA 28(1968):5039.

1918. Szépe, György. "Remarks on the Hungarian
Nominal Sentence," THRJ [F7]:1960-1972.

See also 42, 1910.

URALIC AND ALTAIC

1919. Austin, P.M. "The Etymology of 'king' in
Soviet Turkic Languages," CJL 13:34-36.

1920. Bennigsen, Alexandre. "The Problems of
Bilingualism and Assimilation in the North Caucasus,"
CAR 15:205-211.

1921. Birnbaum, Eleazar. "The Transliteration of Ottoman Turkish for Library and General Purposes," JAOS 87:122-156.

1922. Dulling, G.K. "Turkic Languages of the USSR," CAR 15:160-167.

1923. Kerns, J.C. The Eurasiatic Pronouns and the Indo-Uralic Questions. Fairborn, Ohio: J.C. Kerns (82).

1924. Krueger, John R. Mongolian Epigraphical Dictionary in Reverse Listing. Bloomington: Indiana U, The Hague: Mouton (69).

1925. Sebeok, Thomas A. "Grammatischer Parallelismus in einem tscheremissischen Segen," UAJ 39: 41-48.

1926. Anon. The First Votyak Grammar [Text in Russian, Intr. by Gyula Décsy] Bloomington: Indiana U (x,113).

GEORGIAN

1927. Gamkrelidze, Thomas V. "Kartvelian and Indo-European: A Typological Comparison of Reconstructed Linguistic Systems," THRJ [F7]:707-717.

See also 1920.

XII. Literature

GENERAL

1928. Abashidze, Irakly. "A Georgian Poet Reports," NWR 35,vii:19-21.

1929. Bida, Constantine. "Shakespeare and National Traits in Slavic Literatures (The Problem of Interpretation)," François Jost, ed. Proceedings of the IVth Congress of the International Comparative Literature Association, 273-280. The Hague: Mouton.

1930. Brody, Erwin C. "Events of the Russian Time of Troubles in Two Baroque Dramas: Lope de Vega's El Gran Duque de Moscovia and John Fletcher's The Loyal Subject," Columbia [PhD diss] 1967. DA 28:1388A.

1931. Clements, Robert J. "European Literary Scene," SatR 50,xliv:31.

1932. Filipoff, Boris and Vlach, Robert. "The Slavic Awards and Some Candidates," BA 41,i:26-27.

1933. LeRoy, Gaylord C. Marxism and Modern Literature. New York: American Institute for Marxist Studies (39).

1934. Matejka, Laidslav. "The Creative Usage of Church Slavonic," THRJ [F7]:1295-1310.

1935. Popkin, Henry. "Theatre in Eastern Europe," TDR 11,iii:23-51.

1936. Tikos, Laszlo M. "The Death of the Positive Hero," EE 16,vii:17-20.

1937. Turkevich, Ludmilla B. Spanish Literature
in Russia and in the Soviet Union, 1735-1964. Metu-
chen, N.J.: Scarecrow P (xi,273). Rev. 1937a. Weiner,
Jack. CSlSt 2(1968):138-139.

1938. Zantuan, Konstanty. "Between Author and
Reviewer," SlavR 26:308-314.

See also 30, 1774.

BALTIC

LATVIAN

1939. Akmentiņš, Osvalds. "Aspazijas lugas uz
veclatviešu skatuvēm Amerikā," Raiņa un Aspazijas
gadagrāmata, 93-99. Västeras, Sweden: RAF.

1940. Bičole, Baiba. Atrita. Shippenville, Pa.:
River Hill P (114).

1941. Birznieks, Paulis. "Saules dzija un ik-
dienas nedzeja," JGai 62:49-50.

1942. Birznieks, Paulis. "Un sieviete noliecās
noplūkt ābolu," JGai 63:49-50.

1943. Drillis, Elza. "Rūdolfa Blaumaņa literāro
darbu valoda informācijas teorijas gaismā," Ceļi 13:
16-24.

1944. Ekmanis, Rolfs. "Latviešu rakstnieki
Iekškrievijā, 1941-1945," JGai 66:21-34.

1945. Irbe, Gunars. "No sākuma līdz punktam,"
JGai 65:51-52.

1946. Ivaska, Astrīde. "Divi pārsteigumi," JGai
63:51-52.

1947. Ivaska, Astrīde. "Pokarinės latvių poezijos keliai," Metmenys 14:95-114.

1948. Jēgers, B. "Ziņas par Jāņa Reitera tautību," Ceļi 13:3-15.

1949. Kikauka, Talivaldis. Leonards. Minneapolis, Minn.: Tilts (271). Rev. 1949a. Rothrock, Ilze Š. BA 42:477.

1950. Krātiņš, Ojārs. "Istenības atspīdumi un vīzijas?" JGai 62:50-53.

1951. Krātiņš, Ojārs. "Latvieti, ak latvieti, tavu dažādību," JGai 66:49-51.

1952. Krātiņš, Ojārs. "Notikumi iztēles robež-joslā," JGai 61:52-53.

1953. Luce, Ņina. "Latviešu drāma trimdā bez Zīverta," Archīvs 8:187-204.

1954. Medne, Ausma. "Filozofiskās vadlīnijas Gunša Zariņa darbos," JGai 64:6-10.

1955. Pļavkalns, Gundars. "Apdāvināta daiļ-prozas autora vārsmas," JGai 64:54-56.

1956. Pļavkalns, Gundars. "Atspulgu pasaule," JGai 62:54-55.

1957. Pļavkalns, Gundars. "Istums un vienkāršība mūsu jaunākajā dzeja," JGai 63:25-27.

1958. Pļavkalns, Gundars. "Par kādu ķēniņu," JGai 65:50-51.

1959. Pļavkalns, Gundars. "Sensibilitāte un intellekts," JGai 64:52-54.

1960. Rungis, Aivars. Patescsi kungo, pats.
Brooklyn, N.Y.: Gramatu drangs (176). Rev. 1960a.
Kratino, Ojars. BA 42(1968):315.

1961. Salins, Gunars. Melmā saule. Brooklyn,
N.Y.: Gramatu draugs (96). Rev. 1961a. Ivask, Ivar.
BA 42(1968):316-317.

1962. Zirnītis, Edmunds. "Pravietiskais lat-
vietis," AkDz 10:5-16.

See 2078.

LITHUANIAN

1963. Angoff, Charles. "Three Lithuanian Novels,"
BR 33:42-48.

1964. Bradūnas, Kazys. Sonatos ir Fūgos. Chicago:
Mykolas Morkūnas. Rev. 1964a. Šilbajoris, Rimvydas.
Aidai 4:191-192.

1965. Donelaitis, Kristijonas. The Seasons. [Tr.
by Nadas Rastenis, ed. by Elena Tumas] Los Angeles:
Lithuanian Days Publishers (127).

1966. Jankus, Jurgis. Peilio ašmenimis. New
York: Darbinikas (261). Rev. 1966a. Šilbajoris,
Rimvydas. BA 43,i(1969):147.

1967. Mekas, Jonas. Pavieniai zodziai. Chicago:
Algimantas Mackus Book Publishing Fund (95). Rev.
1967a. Šilbajoris, Rimvydas. BA 42(1968):317-318.

1968. Mockūnas, Liutas. "Didžiausias pralaimė-
jimas-žmoniskumo praradimas," Metmenys 13:138-143.

1969. Šilbajoris, Rimvydas. "Ausserhalb der Heimat
entstandene litauische Literatur," AB 6:221-235.

1970. Šilbajoris, Rimvydas. "Kazio Bradūno
Poezija," Metmenys 14:11-31.

1971. Šilbajoris, Rimvydas. "Daži vārdi par Piecu
Stabu autoru," TV 2:50-53.

1972. Škema, Antanas. Raštai. [Ed. by A. Lands-
bergis, A. Nyka-Niliunas, K. Ostrouskas] Chicago:
Santara Šviesa Federation (500). Rev. 1972a. Šilbajoris, Rimvydas. BA 42(1968):164.

1973. Šlaitas, Vladas. 34 eileraščiai. Boston:
Kapočius. Rev. 1973a. Šilbajoris, Rimvydas. BA 43
(1969):459-460.

1974. Willmann, Asta. "The Perceptional World of
Aleksis Rannit's Poetry," Lituanus 13,i:42-60.

ESTONIAN

1975. Angelus, Oskar. "Das estnische Buch in der
freien Welt und in Sowjetestland," AB 6:75-90.

1976. Asi, Harri. Pärast plahvatust. Toronto:
Kirjastus "Libra" (189). Rev. 1976a. Valgemäe, Mardi.
BA 42(1968):309-310.

1977. Ivask, Ivar. "Recent Trends in Estonian
Poetry," BA 42(1968):517-520.

1978. Jürma, Malle. "Literātūra Igaunijā," JGai
65:42-46.

1979. Krants, Eduard. Tung alterad. Toronto:
Kirjastus "Libra" (78). Rev. 1979a. Valgemäe, Mardi.
BA 42(1968):473-474.

1980. Kuusik, Mall. "Estnische Schriftsteller im
Exil," AB 6:91-104.

1981. Oras, Anto. <u>Estonian Literature in Exile</u>.
Lund: Eesti Kirjanike Kooperatiiv (88).

See also 1974, 2262.

BULGARIAN

1982. Dinekov, Petar. "À travers les échanges
littéraires bulgaro-polonais: Penčo Slavejkov et Adam
Mickiewicz," <u>THRJ</u> [F7]:513-522.

1983. Georgiev, Emil. "Vozniknovenie starobol-
garskoj (staroslavjanskoj) stixotvornoj tradicii,"
<u>THRJ</u> [F7]:726-733.

1984. Moser, Charles A. "The Visionary Realism
of Jordan Jovkov," <u>SEEJ</u> 11:44-58.

1985. Rusev, R. "The Autobiography of Sofronij
Vračanski," <u>THRJ</u> [F7]:1683-1692.

1986. Yankov, Nikolay. "Bulgarian Writers Today,"
<u>NWR</u> 35,vi:44-45.

CZECH AND SLOVAK

1987. Haman, Aleš and Trensky, Paul I. "Man
Against the Absolute: The Art of Karel Čapek," <u>SEEJ</u>
11:168-184.

1988. Havel, Václav. <u>The Memorandum</u>. [Tr. by Vera
Blackwell] New Orleans: Tulane Drama Review. Rev.
1988a. S.H., <u>EE</u> 17,viii(1968):60.

1989. Hrabák, Josef. "Otakar Theer and the Beginnings of Czech Accentual Verse," <u>THRJ</u> [F7]:945-957.

1990. Mareš, V.F. "Stix česko-cerkovnoslavjanskoj

pesni 'Gospodine, pomiluj ny'," THRJ [F7]:1261-1263.

1991. Mňačko, Ladislav. The Taste of Power. [Tr. by Paul Stevenson, foreword by Max Hayward] New York and Washington: Praeger (235). Rev. 1991a. Harkins, William E. SlavR 27(1968):501-502. 1991b. Howe, Irving. NYR 9(12 Oct):28-30. 1991c. Stilwell, Robert L. SatR 50,xxxiii:33. 1991d. Tikos, Laszlo M. EE 16,viii:54-55. 1991e. Trensky, Paul I. SEEJ 12(1968): 487-488.

1992. Němcová, Jeanne W., ed. Czech and Slovak Short Stories. [Sel., tr. and intr. by Jeanne Němcová.] London, New York, and Toronto: Oxford U P (xv, 296). Rev. 1992a. Harkins, William E. SlavR 27(1968): 353-354. 1992b. Newman, Vivian D. LJ 92:2576.

1993. Paučo, Josef, ed. 1967 Literárny almanach Slováka v Amerike. Middletown, Pennsylvania: Časopis Slovák v Amerike (254).

1994. Pletnev, Rostislav. "The Concept of Time and Space in R.U.R. by Karel Čapek," ESEE 12:17-24.

1995. Skvorecky, Josef. "Letter from Prague," Nation (U.S.) 205:470-472.

1996. Stepanchev, Stephen. "Talk with a Czech Poet," NL 50,xix:13-15.

1997. Stern, J.P. "Kafka, Franz (1883-1924)." Encyclopedia of Philosophy 4:303-304.

1998. Szanto, George H. "Steps Toward the Phenomenological Novel: Narrative Consciousness in the Works of Franz Kafka, Samuel Beckett, and Alain Robbe-Grillet," Harvard [PhD diss] 1967.

1999. Wellek, René. "New Czech Books on Literary History and Theory," SlavR 26:295-301.

2000. Wojatsek, Charles. "Zrinyi: poète, ècri-
vain, homme d'état et soldat," ESEE 11,iii-iv:91-108.

2001.   Anon. "A Program for Czechoslovak Writers,"
[Excerpts from Literani Noviny 8 July 1967] EE 11:
26-30.

See also 1872.

GREEK

2002. Anapliotis, John. The Real Zorba and Nikos
Kazantzakis. [Tr. by Lewis A. Richards] Chicago:
Argonaut.

2003. Niketas, George. "The Axion Esti of
Odysseus Elytis-Translated, Annotated, with an Introduction," Georgia [PhD diss] 1967. DA 28:2216A.

2004. Poulakidas, Andreas K. "The Novels of
Kazantzakis and Their Existential Sources," Indiana
[PhD diss] 1967. DA 28:2260A.

2005. Yiannopoulos, Alkiviades. "The Burden of
the Whole World," [Tr. by Liza Constantinides] Char-
ioteer 9:71-78.

See also 2122.

HUNGARIAN

2006. Adams, B.S. "The Lager Verse of Miklós
Radnóti," SEER 45,civ:65-75.

2007. Alvarez, A., ed. Hungarian Short Stories.
[Intr. by A. Alvarez] London, New York and Toronto:
Oxford U P (xvi,432). Rev. 2007a. Kovacs,Imre. EE 16,
x:56.

See also 2322.

POLISH

2008. Andrzeyevski, George. The Gates of Paradise. [Tr. by James Kirkup] London: Panther (125).

2009. Bronowski, Jacob. The Face of Violence: An
Essay with a Play. [Rev. and enl. ed.] New York: World
(66).

2010. Coleman, Marion M., ed. Letters to Emilia:
Record of a Friendship. Seven Letters of Helena Mo-
djeska to a Friend Back Home. [Tr. by Michael Kwapis-
zewski, ed. and annotated by Marion Moore Coleman]
Cheshire, Conn.: Cherry Hill Books (39).

2011. Corliss, Frank J.,Jr. "Time and the Cruci-
fixion in Norwid's Vade-mecum," SEEJ 11:284-295.

2012. Domaradzki, Théodore. "Cyprien Norwid dans
les traductions et la critique de la langue fran-
çaise," ESEE 12:153-187.

2013. Dudek, Louis. "Poetry and Nationality: A
Personal View," PolR 12,i:50-58.

2014. Folejewski, Zbigniew. Maria Dąbrowska. New
York: Twayne (123). Rev. 2014a. Krzyzanowski, Jerzy
R. SlavR 29(1970):147-149. 2014b. Nowosielska,
Maryna. SEEJ 12(1968):357-358. 2014c. Thomson, Ewa
M. CL 21(1969):286-287. 2014d. Welsh, David. CSlSt
2(1968):139-140.

2015. Foleevskij, Zbignev. "Marija Dombrovskaja
i russkaja literatura," NŽ 87:96-101.

2016. Gasiorowska, Xenia. "Bolesław The Brave by
A. Gołubiew: A Modern Polish Epic," CalSlSt 4:119-144.

2017. Gömöri, George. "The Poet and the Hero Genesis and Analysis of Norwid's Bema Pamięci Żałobny-Rapsod," CalSlSt 4:145-161.

2018. Górski, Konrad. "Quelques traits caractér-istiques de la stylisation satirique dans l'oeuvre poétique de Mickiewicz en 1832-1834," THRJ [F7]:785-791.

2019. Grabowski, Zbigniew A. "S.I. Witkiewicz: A Polish Prophet of Doom," PolR 12,i:39-49.

2020. Heimer, Jackson W. "The Betrayer as Intel-lectual: Conrad's 'Under Western Eyes'," PolR 12,iv:57-68.

2021. Herling, Gustaw. The Island: Three Tales. [Tr. by Ronald Strom] New York and Cleveland: World (151).

2022. Jur'eva, Z. "Julian Tuvim po-russki," NŽ 87:323-328.

2023. Leach, Catherine. "Remarks on the Poetry of Tadeusz Różewicz," PolR 12,ii:105-126.

2024. Lourie, Richard. "A Context for Tadeusz Różewicz," PolR 12,ii:97-104.

2025. Mrozek, Slawomir. Six Plays by Slawmir Mrozek. [Tr. by Nicholas Bethell] Toronto and Vancou-ver: Clarke, Irwin and Co.; New York: Evergreen (190).

2026. Robak, Tadeusz. "Books Nobody Reads," [Excerpts from Życie Literackie 18 June 1967] EE 16, ix:21.

2027. Scherer, Olga. "Le Romantisme de Mickie-wicz," ESEE 12:3-16.

2028. Segel, H.B. "The Polish Napoleonic Cult
from Mickiewicz to Żeromski: A Rapid Survey," ISlSt 4:
128-151.

2029. Taborski, Bolesław. "Polish Plays in English Translations: A Bibliography," PolR 12,i:59-82.

2030. Thompson, John. "Stories About Terrible
Things," Com 44,vi:77.

2031. Walton, James. "Conrad and The Secret
Agent: The Genealogy of Mr. Vladimir," PolR 12,iii:28-
42.

2032. Weintraub, Wiktor. "Fraszka in a Tragic
Key: Remarks on Kochanowski's Lament XI and Fraszki I,
3," THRJ [F7]:2219-2230.

2033. Weintraub, Wiktor. "Hellenizm Kochanow-
skiego i jego poetyka," Pamiętnik Literacki 58:1-25.

2034. Weintraub, Wiktor. "In Lieu of a Discussion," SlavR 26:663-664.

2035. Weintraub, Wiktor. "Jan Kochanowski, Reader
of Latin Boccaccio and Petrarch," Mélanges de littérature comparée et de philologie offerts à Mieczysław
Brahmer, 581-589. Warsaw.

2036. Weintraub, Wiktor. "Mickiewiczowskie
'proroctwo' o Ameryce i jego angielskie paralele,"
Księga pamiątkowa du czci Konrada Górskiego, 217-223.
Toruń.

2037. Weintraub, Wiktor. "Polish Literature,"
Chamber's Encyclopaedia, Vol. XI:33-37.

2038. Weintraub, Wiktor. "The Paradoxes of Rej's
Biography," ISlSt 4:215-237.

2039. Weintraub, Wiktor. "Vilna e la mistica.
Prolegomeni Vilnensi alla poetica del profetismo di
Mickiewicz," Ricerche Slavistiche 13:173-214.

2040. Welsh, David. "Sienkiewicz versus Kra-
szewski: Observations on Novel-Writing," IS1St 4:238-
251.

2041. Wieniewska, Celina, ed. Polish Writing
Today. Baltimore: Penguin (206). Rev. 2041a. Gier-
gielewicz, Mieczyslaw. SEEJ 13(1969):263-264.

2042. Anon. "How to Promote Pegasus," [Excerpts
from Polityka 16 Sept 1967] EE 16,xii:31-33.

See also 58, 1982.

RUMANIAN

2043. Lovinescu, Monica. "The New Wave of Rumanian Writers," EE 16,xii:9-15.

2044. Stancu, Zaharia. "Notes on Contemporary
Romanian Writing," LitR 10,iv:437-526.

RUSSIAN AND SOVIET

GENERAL

2045. Abernathy, Robert. "Rhymes, Non-Rhymes, and
Antirhyme," THRJ [F7]:1-15.

2046. Edgerton, William B. "The Poetics of
Periodical Names (from Aurora to Zarja)," THRJ [F7]:
594-614.

2047. Hingley, Ronald. Russian Writers and Society. New York: McGraw-Hill (256).

2048. Žirmunskij, V.M. "On Rhythmic Prose," <u>THRJ</u> [F7]:2376-2388.

See also 1804, 2337.

OLD RUSSIAN

2049. Arant, Patricia. "Formulaic Style and the Russian Bylina," <u>ISlSt</u> 4:7-51.

2050. Costello, D.P. and Foote, I.P., eds. <u>Russian Folk Literature: Skazki. Liriceskie pesni. Byliny. Istoriceskie pesni. Duxovnye stixi</u>. New York: Oxford U P (xvii,256).

2051. Dewey, Horace W. "<u>The Life of Lady Morozova</u> as Literature," <u>ISlSt</u> 4:74-87.

2052. Gibian, George. "The New and the Old: From an Observer's Notebook," <u>PoC</u> 16,ii:57-64.

2053. Hackel, Sergei. "The Creative Scribe: A Neglected Editor of the 'Tale, Passion and Eulogy of the Holy Martyrs Boris and Gleb'," <u>MLR</u> 62:498-502.

2054. Isenberg, M. and Riha, T. "The Song of Igor's Campaign: A Poetic Interpretation." <u>CSlSt</u> 1: 105-112.

2055. LeGuillou, Jean-Yves. "Document: Le jugement Šemjaka," <u>ESEE</u> 12:44-49.

2056. Zguta, Russell. "Byliny: A Study of Their Value as Historical Sources." Penn State [PhD diss] 1967. <u>DA</u> 29(1968):197A.

See also 20, 404, 1776, 1835.

18TH CENTURY

2057. Segel, Harold B., ed. and tr. The Literature of Eighteenth-Century Russia. [2 vols.] New York:
Dutton (474,448).

See also 2329.

19TH CENTURY

2058. Craven, Kenneth. "Laurence Sterne and Russia: Four Case Studies," Columbia [PhD diss] 1967.
DA 31(1970):2872A.

2059. Delaney, Joan. "Edgar Allan Poe's Tales in
Russia: Legend and Literary Influence, 1847-1917,"
Harvard [PhD diss] 1967.

2060. Demetz, Peter. Marx, Engels, and the Poets:
Origins of Marxist Literary Criticism. [Rev. and en-
larged by the author and tr. by Jeffrey L. Sammons]
Chicago: U of Chicago P (x,278). Rev. 2060a. Bernt,
H.H. LJ 92:1625. 2060b. Pachmuss, Temira. SEEJ 13
(1969):96-97.

2061. Ekmanis, Rolfs. "Kapote un Inostrannaja
literatura," JGai 61:49.

2062. Glickman, Rose B. "The Literary Razno-
chintsy in Mid-Nineteenth Century Russia," Chicago
[PhD diss] 1967.

2063. Hagglund, Roger M. "A Study of the Literary
Criticism of G.V. Adamovič," Washington, Seattle [PhD
diss] 1967. DA 28:3669A.

2064. Hedrick, Henry R. "The Poetry of Deržavin,"
Princeton [PhD diss] 1966. DA 27(1966):2132A.

2065. Heier, Edmund. "The Second Hero of Our Time," SEEJ 11:35-43.

2066. Hughes, Olga R., Hughes, Robert P. and Struve, Gleb, eds. A Century of Russian Prose and Verse: From Pushkin to Nabokov. New York: Harcourt, Brace and World (v,217). Rev. 2066a. Roberts, Spencer E. SEEJ 12(1968):369-370.

2067. Ingram, Frank L. "Koz'ma Prutkov: His Emergence and Development as a Classic of Russian Literature," Indiana [PhD diss] 1967. DA 28:2249A.

2068. Lavrin, Janko, ed. Russian Poetry, Reader I: XVIIIth-XIXth Century Lyrics; Vocabulary to Russian Poetry Reader I. Oxford: Blackwell (153). Rev. 2068a. Dalton, Margaret. SEEJ 12(1968):99-100.

2069. Mersereau, John, Jr. Baron Delvig's Northern Flowers 1825-1832: Literary Almanac of the Pushkin Pleiad. Carbondale and Edwardsville: Southern Illinois U P (viii,267). Rev. 2069a. Gustafson, Richard F. SlavR 27(1968):347-348. 2069b. Leighton, Lauren G. SEEJ 12(1968):464-466.

2070. Setschkareff, Vsevolod. "Muratovs 'Ėgerija und die Tradition des stilisierten Romans," Festschrift für Margarete Woltner zum 70. Geburtstag, 254-261. Heidelberg: Winter.

2071. Simmons, Ernest J. Introduction to Russian Realism: Pushkin, Gogol, Dostoevsky, Tolstoy, Chekhov, Sholokhov. Bloomington: Indiana U P (ix,275). Rev. 2071a. Terras, Victor. SlavR 29(1970):555-560.

2072. Thomson, R.D. "The Non-Literary Sources of 'Roza i Krest'," SEER 45,cv:292-306.

2073. Weston, Bruce L. "The Russian Polemic of

1846-1866 on the Function of Literature," Michigan
[PhD diss] 1967. <u>DA</u> 28:2270A.

     See also 28, 432, 1193, 1194, 1213, 1225,
1227, 1229, 1256, 1259, 1262, 1265, 1269, 1270, 1271,
1804, 2015, 2176.

20TH CENTURY

2074. Annenkov, George. "The Poets of the Revolu-
tion--Blok, Mayakovsky, Esenin," <u>RusR</u> 26:129-143.

2075. Berberova, N. "Sovetskaja kritika segodnja," <u>NŽ</u> 86:105-128.

2076. Chalsma, H. William. "Russian Acmeism: Its
History, Doctrine and Poetry," Washington, Seattle
[PhD diss] 1967. <u>DA</u> 28:3633A.

2077. Cowell, Raymond, ed. <u>Twelve Modern Drama-
tists</u>. Oxford: Pergamon P (x,143).

2078. Ekmanis, Rolfs. "The Relation Between
Soviet Russian and Soviet Latvian Literatures, 1940-
1960," Indiana [PhD diss] 1966. <u>DA</u> 27(1966):2150A.

2079. Filtzpatrick, S. "A.V. Lunacharsky: Recent
Soviet Interpretations and Republications," <u>SovS</u> 18:
267-289.

2080. Friedberg, Maurice. "Soviet Writers and the
Red Pencil," <u>Midway</u> 8,iii:39-58.

2081. Gibian, George. "The Politics of Culture in
the U.S.S.R. Today," <u>SWIF</u> [F6]:111-140.

2082. Gul', Roman. "Dvadcat'pjat'let," <u>NŽ</u> 87:6-28.

2083. Karlinsky, Simon. "Surrealism in Twentieth-

Century Russian Poetry: Churilin, Zabolotskii, Pop-
lavskii," SlavR 26:605-617.

2084. Kuznetsov, Anatoly. Babi Yar: A Documentary
Novel [Tr. by Jacob Guralsky] New York: Dial P (xv,
399). [Excerpts NWR 35,i:12-19] Rev. 2084a. Horwitz,
Martin. SlavR 27(1968):686-687. 2084b. Kalb, Marvin.
SatR 50,x:37,112. 2084c. Muchnic, Helen. NYR 8(15
Jun):4-6. 2084d. Szasz, Thomas S. NRep 156,xxiii:21-
23.

2085. Lakshin, Vladimir. "The Search for Truth:
Continuity and Change in Soviet Literature," NWR 35,
ix:115-121.

2086. Maguire, Robert A. Red Virgin Soil: Soviet
Literature in the 1920's. Princeton: Princeton U P
(455). Rev. 2086a. Hendry, J.F. CSlSt 2(1968):614.
2086b. Shane, Alex M. SEEJ 13(1969):389-391.

2087. Markov, Vladimir, ed. Manifesty i programmy
russkix futuristov: Die Manifeste und Programmschrif-
ten der russischen Futuristen. München: Fink (182).
Rev. 2087a. Karlinsky, Simon. SEEJ 12(1968):471-473.
2087b. Lampl, Horst. WSlJ 14:163-164.

2088. Markov, Vladimir and Sparks, Merrill, eds.
Modern Russian Poetry: An Anthology with Verse Translations. Indianapolis, Kansas City, and New York:
Bobbs-Merrill (lxxx,842). Rev. 2088a. Bram, Joseph.
LJ 92,xi:2164. 2088b. Terras, Victor. SEEJ 12
(1968):364-365. 2088c. Wytrzens, Gunther. WSlJ 14:
159-160.

2089. Mickiewicz, Denis. "Phoebus Apollo
Musagetes: The Position of Apollon in Russian Modern-
ism," Yale [PhD diss] 1967. DA 28(1968):4181.

2090. Mihailovich, Vasa. "Hermann Hesse and Russia," Berkeley [PhD diss] 1966. DA 27(1966):2536A.

2091.   Monas, Sidney.   "In Defense of Socialist Realism," PoC 16,ii:44-56.

2092.   Morton, Miriam, ed.   A Harvest of Russian Children's Literature. [Foreword by Ruth Hill Viguers] Berkeley and Los Angeles: U of California P (xiv,474).   Rev. 2092a. Sosin, Gene.   SEEJ 13(1969): 262-263.

2093.   Muchnic, Helen.   "Three Inner Emigrés: Anna Akhmatova, Osip Mandelshtam, Nikolai Zabalotsky" RusR 26:13-25.

2094.   Panin, Gennadij.   "Ob akrostixe," NŽ 87:103-116;88:75-103. [Continuation in NŽ 88 entitled: " O russkom akrostixe."]

2095.   Pomorska, Krystyna.   "A Vision of America in Early Soviet Literature," SEEJ 11:389-397.

2096.   Sheldon, Richard R.   "Viktor Borisovič Shklovsky: Literary Theory and Practice, 1914-1930," Michigan [PhD diss] 1966.   DA 27(1966):2161A.

2097.   Slonim, Marc.   Soviet Russian Literature: Writers and Problems 1917-1967 [Rev. ed]   New York: Oxford U P (viii,373).   Rev. 2097a. Pachmuss, Temira. CSlSt 2(1968):144.   2097b. Struve, Gleb.   SlavR 27 (1968):352-353.

        See also 23, 64, 679, 1170, 1223, 1227, 1276, 1804.

RUSSIAN AUTHORS

Axmatova, A.

2098.   Driver, Sam N.   "The Poetry of Anna Axmatova,

1912-1922," Columbia [PhD diss] 1967. DA 31(1970):
1269.

Andreev, L.

2099. Woodward, James B. "Theme and Structural
Significance of Leonid Andreev's 'The Black Masks',"
MD 10,i:95-103.

Babel', I.

2100. Carden, Patricia J. "History, Justice and
Art in the Work of Isaac Babel," Columbia [PhD diss]
1966. DA 30(1970):4445.

2101. Falen, James. "A Note on the Fate of Isaak
Babel'," SEEJ 11:398-404.

Baratynskij, E.

2102. Dees, Joseph B. "Content and Expression in
the Poetry of Baratynskij," Princeton [PhD diss] 1967.
DA 28:5013A.

Belyj, A.

2103. Rou, V. [Rowe, W.] "O simvolike A. Belogo,"
NŽ 88:107-112.

See also 2104.

Berdjaev, N.

See 694, 695.

Blok, A.

2104. Ivanov-Razumnik V. Aleksandr Blok /
Andrej Belyj. Chicago: Russian Language Specialties
(179). [2nd ed. reprint of 1919 ed.]

Brjusov, V.

2105. Struve, G.P. "Istoriko-literaturnye
zametki: 1. Ob odnom stixotvorenii Valerija Brjusova.
2. K istorii polučenija I.A. Buninym Nobelevskoj
premii," Zapiski [Fl]:140-147. [Synopsis in English:
"Literary-Historical Notes."]

Bulgakov, M.

2106. Glenny, M.V. "Mikhail Bulgakov," Survey
65:3-14.

Bunin, I.

2107. de Yackovlev, Antonia L. "Bunin's Prose
Writings in Exile," Illinois [PhD diss] 1967. DA 28:
3178A.

See also 2105, 2264, 2265.

Čexov, A.P.

2108. Jackson, Robert L., ed. Chekhov: A Collection of Critical Essays. Englewood Cliffs: Prentice-
Hall (ix,213). Rev. 2108a. Bristow, Eugene. QJS 53:
90. 2108b. Bucsela, John. CSlSt 2:276-277.

2109. Lau, Joseph Shui-Ming. "Ts'ao Yu, the
Reluctant Disciple of Chekhov and O'Neill: A Study in
Literary Influence," Indiana [PhD diss] 1966. DA 27
(1966):4256A.

2110. McConkey, James. "In Praise of Chekhov,"
HudR 20,iii:417-428.

2111. Ofrosimov, Ju. "Tri sestry - Segodnja,"
NŽ 89:269-276.

2112. Rexroth, Kenneth. "Chekhov's Plays," SatR
50,xxvii:18.

See also 2247.

Cvetaeva, M.

2113. Karlinsky, Simon. "Pis'ma M. Cvetaevoj k V. Xodaseviču," NŽ 89:102-114.

2114. Šaxovskaja, Zinaida. "Marina Cvetaeva," NŽ 87:130-141.

Dal', V.I.

2115. Baer, Joachim T. "The Artistic Work of Vladimir Ivanovič Dal'," SEEJ 11:278-283.

Dostoevskij, F.M.

2116. Atkins, Anselm. "Caprice: The Myth of the Fall in Anselm and Dostoevsky," JR 47:295-312.

2117. Belknap, Robert L. "Recent Soviet Scholarship and Criticism on Dostoevskij: A Review Article," SEEJ 11:75-86.

2118. Belknap, Robert L. The Structure of the Brothers Karamazov. The Hague: Mouton (122).

2119. Daugherty, Howard A. "A Study of the Buffoon in the Novels of Dostoevskii," Washington, Seattle [PhD diss] 1967. DA 29(1968):255A.

2120. Harper, Ralph. The Seventh Solitude: Metaphysical Homelessness in Kierkegaard, Dostoevsky and Nietzsche. Baltimore: John Hopkins P (x,153).

2121. Hausamann, Rita M. "Alfred Döblin and Dostoevsky-Patterns of Literary Reaction," Harvard [PhD diss] 1967.

2122. Hoffman, Frederick J. "The Friends of God:

Dostoevsky and Kazantzakis." The Imagination's New Beginning: Theology and Modern Literature, 43-72. Notre Dame: U of Notre Dame P.

2123. Keller, Howard H. "Dostoevsky's Buffoon: A Study in Alienation," Georgetown [PhD diss] 1967. DA 28:2250A.

2124. Linner, Sven. Dostoevskij on Realism. Stockholm: Almquist and Wiksell (211).

2125. Lord, R. "A Reconsideration of Dostoyevsky's Novel The Idiot," SEER 45,civ:30-45.

2126. Mindess, Harvey. "Reappraisals: Freud on Dostoevsky," ASch 36:446-452.

2127. Močulskij, Konstantin. Dostoevsky: His Life and Work. [Tr. by Michael A. Minihan] Princeton: Princeton U P (xxii,687). Rev. 2127a. Mohrenschildt, Dimitri von. RusR 27(1968):372-373. 2127b. Terras, Victor. SEEJ 12(1968):356-357. 2127c. Wasiolek, Edward. ModA 12:321-323.

2128. Neumann, Harry. "Milton's Adam and Dostoyevsky's Grand Inquistor on the Problem of Freedom Before God," Personalist 48:317-327.

2129. Pletnev, Rostislav. "Quelques mots au sujet des néologismes de Dostoevskij," ESEE xii:55-57.

2130. Pletnev, R. "Vremja i prostranstvo u Dostoevskogo," NŽ 87:118-127.

2131. Purdy, S.B. "Poe and Dostoyevsky," SSF 4, ii:169-171.

2132. Simons, John D. "The Nature of Suffering in Schiller and Dostoevsky," CL 19,ii:160-173.

2133   Simons, John D.   "Schiller's Influence on Dostoevsky," Rice [PhD diss] 1966. <u>DA</u> 27(1966):1346A.

2134.   Stenbock-Fermor, Elisabeth.   "Stavrogin's Quest in <u>The Devils</u> of Dostoevskij," <u>THRJ</u> [F7]:1926-1934.

2135.   Terras, Victor. "Dostoevskij the Humorist: 1846-1849," <u>ISlSt</u> 4:152-180.

2136. Wasiolek, Edward, ed. <u>Dostoevsky, The Note-books for</u> The Idiot. [Tr. by Katharine Strelsky] Chicago and London: U of Chicago P (vi,254). Rev. 2136a. Neuhauser, R. <u>CSlSt</u> 3(1969):581-584. 2136b. Rosen, Nathan. <u>SlavR</u> 27(1968):625-634.

2137. Wasiolek, Edward, ed. and tr. <u>Dostoevsky, the Notebooks for</u> Crime and Punishment. Chicago: U of Chicago P (vi,246). Rev. 2137a. Frank, Joseph. <u>Com</u> 45,ii(1968):88-91. 2137b. Muchnic, Helen. <u>NYR</u> 8 (23 Mar):12-14. 2137c. Neuhauser, R. <u>CSlSt</u> 3(1969): 581-584. 2137d. Nin, Anaïs. <u>SatR</u> 50,xxiii:35,110. 2137e. Proffer, Carl R. <u>SEEJ</u> 12(1968):244-247. 2137f. Rosen, Nathan. <u>SlavR</u> 26:511-513. 2137g. Seeley, F.F. <u>SEER</u> 46,cvii(1968):502-503. 2137h. Strong, Robert L., Jr. <u>RusR</u> 26:418.

2138. Wasiolek, Edward. <u>The Brothers Karamazov and the Critics</u>. Belmont: Wadsworth (xvi,165).

2139. Webb, Donald A. "The Life and Works of Dostoevsky: A Theological and Depth-Psychological Study," Drew [PhD diss] 1966. <u>DA</u> 27(1966):2510A.

2140. Weinstock, Herbert. "Janáček on Dostoevsky," <u>SatR</u> 50,xxi:63.

See also 1287.

Družinin, A.

2141. Schulak, Helen S. "Alexandr Družinin and
His Place in Russian Criticism," California, Berkeley
[PhD diss] 1967. <u>DA</u> 28(1968):3647A.

Erenburg, I.

2142. Austin, Paul M. "Further Surgery of Eren-
burg's <u>Xulio Xurenito</u>: A Review Article," <u>SEEJ</u> 11:204-
208.

2143. Oulanoff, Hongor. "Motives of Pessimism in
Erenburg's Early Works," <u>SEEJ</u> 11:266-277.

See also 81, 2390.

Evtušenko, E.

2144. Sinyavsky, Andrei. "On Evtushenko," <u>Encoun-
ter</u> 28,iv:33-43.

Fedin, K.

2145. Struc, Roman S. "<u>Sanatorium Arktur</u>: Fedin's
Polemic Against Thomas Mann's <u>Magic Mountain</u>," <u>Re-
search Studies</u> 35:301-307.

Fet, A.A.

2146. Šilbajoris, Rimvydas. "Dynamic Elements in
the Lyrics of Fet," <u>SlavR</u> 26:217-226.

Gippius, Z.

2147. Pachmuss, Temira. "A Literary Quarrel:
Zinaida Hippius versus Tatjana Manuxina," <u>YELS</u> 4
(1964-1967):63-83.

2148. Pachmuss, Temira. "Perepiska Z.N.

Gippius s B.V. Savinkovym," <u>Vozdušnye puti</u> 5:161-167.

2149. Pachmuss, Temira. "Sergey Sergeev-Tsensky
in Zinaida Hippius's Criticism," <u>Grani</u> 63:140-153.

Gogol', N.V.

2150. Erlich, Victor. "A Note on the Grotesque.
Gogol: A Test Case," <u>THRJ</u> [F7]:630-633.

2151. Oulianoff, Nicholas I. "Arabesque or
Apocalypse? On the Fundamental Idea of Gogol's Story
'The Nose'," <u>CSlSt</u> 1:158-171.

2152. Pomorska, Krystyna. "Ob izučenii Gogolja:
Metodologičeskie zametki," <u>THRJ</u> [F7]:1590-1601.

2153. Proffer, Carl R. <u>Letters of Nikolai Gogol</u>.
Ann Arbor: U of Michigan P (vii,247). Rev. 2153a.
Holquist, James M. <u>SEEJ</u> 13(1969):383-384.

2154. Proffer, Carl R. <u>The Simile and Gogol's
Dead Souls</u>. The Hague: Mouton (206). Rev. 2154a.
Rossbacher, Peter. <u>SEEJ</u> 13(1969):247-248.

2155. Timmer, Charles B. "Dead Souls Speaking,"
<u>SEER</u> 45,cv:273-291.

2156. Vogel, Lucy. "Gogol''s Rome," <u>SEEJ</u> 11:145-
158.

2157. Woodward, James B. "The Threadbare Fabric
of Gogol's <u>Overcoat</u>," <u>CSlSt</u> 1:95-104.

Gončarov, I.

2158. Setchkarev, V. "Andrej Štolc in Gončarov's
<u>Oblomov</u>: An Attempted Reinterpretation," <u>THRJ</u> [F7]:
1799-1805.

Gor'kij, M.

2159. Borras, F.M. Maxim Gorky the Writer: An
Interpretation. Oxford: Clarendon P (xviii,195). Rev.
2159a. Folejewski, Z. SEEJ 13(1969):243-244. 2159b.
Freeborn, Richard. SEER 46,cvii(1968):506-507. 2159c.
Ignatieff, Leonid. CSlSt 2(1968):605-606. 2159d.
Shotton, M.H. MLR 63(1968):780-782.

2160. Kesich, Lydia W. "Gorky and the Znanie
Volumes, 1904-1913," Columbia [PhD diss] 1967. DA 28:
1820A.

2161. Wolfe, Bertram D. The Bridge and the Abyss:
The Troubled Friendship of Maxim Gorky and V.I. Lenin.
New York: Praeger (xiv,180). Rev. 2161a. Ermolaev,
Herman. NŽ 91(1968):295-298. 2161b. Monas, Sidney.
JMH 41(1969):288-289. 2161c. Weil, Irwin. RusR 27
(1968):361-363. 2161d. Zawacki, Edmund. SEEJ 12
(1968):355-356.

See also 2372.

Griboedov, A.

See 432.

Grigor'ev, A.

2162. Krupič, V. "Apollon Grigor'ev," NŽ 89:89-
99.

Ivanov, V.V.

2163. Stammler, Heinrich A. "Vjačeslav Ivanov's
Image of Man," WSlJ 14:128-142.

See also 2183.

Karamzin, N.

2163A. Anderson, Roger B. "Evolving Narrative
Methods in the Prose of N.M. Karamzin," Michigan [PhD
diss] 1967. DA 28:5042A.

2164. Cross, Anthony. "Karamzin Studies," SEER
45,civ:1-11.

2165. Garrard, J.G. "Karamzin in Recent Soviet
Criticism: A Review Article," SEEJ 11:464-472.

2166. Nebel, Henry M.,Jr. N.M. Karamzin: A Russian Sentimentalist. The Hague: Mouton (190). Rev.
2166a. Cross, A.G. SEER 46,cvi(1968):226-228. 2166b.
Von Wiren-Garczynski, Vera. SEEJ 12(1968):463-464.

Kuprin, A.

2167. Williams, Gareth. "Romashov and Nazanskij:
Enemies of the People," CSlP 9:194-200.

Leont'ev, K.

2168. Lukashevich, Stephen. Konstantin Leontev
(1831-1891): A Study in Russian "Heroic Vitalism".
New York: Pageant (xix,235). Rev. 2168a. MacMaster,
Robert E. SlavR 28(1969):134-135. 2168b. Simmons,
Robert W.,Jr. SEEJ 13(1969):246-247.

See also 1220.

Lermontov, M.

2169. Paganuzzi, P.N. Lermontov: Avtobiografiče-
skie čerty v tvorčestve poèta. Montreal: Monastery
(256). Rev. 2169a. Turner, C.J.G. CSlSt 2(1968):420-
422.

2170. Peace, R.A. "The Role of Taman' in

Lermontov's 'Geroy nashego vremeni'," <u>SEER</u> 45,civ:12-30.

2171. Pervushin, Nicholas V. "Lermontov's Poetic Apprenticeship," <u>ESEE</u> 12:25-43.

Leskov, N.

2172. Edgerton, William B. "Leskov's Trip Abroad in 1875," <u>ISlSt</u> 4:88-99. [Four Unpublished Letters to I.S. Gagarin.]

2173. Edgerton, William B. "Istorija odnoj bukvy," <u>NŽ</u> 89:82-86.

2174. McLean, Hugh. "Leskov and the Russian Superman," <u>Midway</u> 8,iv:105-123.

2175. McLean, Hugh. "Russia, the Love-Hate Pendulum, and 'The Sealed Angel'," <u>THRJ</u> [F7]:1328-1339.

Levitov, A.I.

2176. Matejic, Mateja. "Aleksandr Ivanovič Levitov,1835-1877: Life and Works," Michigan [PhD diss] 1967. <u>DA</u> 28(1968):5081A.

Lomonosov, M.

2177. Bucsela, John. "Lomonosov's Literary Debut," <u>SEEJ</u> 11:405-422.

Majakovskij, V.

2178. Chukovsky, Kornei. "Mayakovsky Remembered," <u>NWR</u> 35,viii:19-23.

2179. Xardžiev, Nikolaj, "Majakovskij i Xlebnikov," <u>THRJ</u> [F7]:2301-2327.

Mandel'štam, O.

2180. Brown, Clarence. "Into the Heart of Darkness: Mandelstam's Ode to Stalin," SlavR 26:584-604.

2181. Činnov, Igor'. "Pozdnij Mandel'štam," NŽ 88:125-137.

2182. Nilsson, Nils A. "Ship Metaphors in Mandel'štam's Poetry," THRJ [F7]:1436-1444.

2183. Taranovskij, K.F. "Pčely i osy v poèzii Mandel'štama: K voprosu o vlijanii Vjačeslava Ivanova na Mandel'štama," THRJ [F7]:1973-1995

See also 261, 2274.

Maršak, S.

2184. Berman, Dina. "Samuil Maršak's Verses for Children: A Computer-Aided Analysis," Pennsylvania [PhD diss] 1966. DA 28(1966):222A.

Merežkovskij, D.

2185. Stammler, Heinrich. "D.S. Merežkovskij--1865-1965: A Reappraisal," WS1 12:142-152.

Nabokov, V.

2186. Appel, Alfred, Jr. "An Interview with Vladimir Nabokov," WSCL 8,ii:127-152.

2187. Appel, Alfred, Jr. "Lolita: The Springboard of Parody," WSCL 8,ii:204-241.

2188. Bergin, Thomas J., Jr. and Bryer, Jackson R. "A Checklist of Nabokov Criticism in English," WSCL 8,ii:316-364.

2189. Brown, Clarence. "Nabokov's Pushkin and Nabokov's Nabokov," WSCL 8,ii:280-293.

2190. Bryer, Jackson R. "Vladimir Nabokov's Critical Reputation in English: A Note and a Checklist," WSCL 8,ii:312-315.

2191. Dembo, L.S., ed. Nabokov: The Man and His Work. Madison, Milwaukee and London: U of Wisconsin P (x,282). Rev. 2191a. Proffer, Carl R. SlavR 27 (1968):684-686.

2192. Dembo, L.S. "Vladimir Nabokov, an Introduction," WSCL 8,ii:111-126.

2193. Field, Andrew. "The Artist as Failure in Nabokov's Early Prose," WSCL 8,ii:165-173.

2194. Field, Andrew. Nabokov: His Life in Art, A Critical Narrative. Boston and Toronto: Little, Brown (397). Rev. 2194a. Donoghue, Denis. NYR 9 (3 Aug):4-6. 2194b. Griffin, L.W. LJ 92:2411. 2194c. Kersh, Gerald. SatR 50,xxxiv:30. 2194d. Proffer, Carl R. SlavR 27(1968):684-686. 2194e. Reeve, F.D. SEEJ 12(1968):351-353.

2195. Fromberg, Susan. "Folding the Patterned Carpet: Form and Theme in the Novels of Vladimir Nabokov," Chicago [PhD diss] 1966.

2196. Fromberg, Susan. "The Unwritten Chapters in the Real Life of Sebastian Knight," MFS 13:427-442.

2197. Gold, Herbert. "The Art of Fiction XL: Vladimir Nabokov [An Interview]." Paris Review 41:92-111.

2198. Janeway, Elizabeth. "Nabokov the Magician," AM 220,i:66-71.

2199. Karlinsky, Simon. "Illusion, Reality and
Parody in Nabokov's Plays," WSCL 8,ii:268-279.

2200. Krueger, John R. "Nabokov's Zemblan: A
Constructed Language of Fiction," Ling 31:44-49.

2201. Lee, L.L. "Bend Sinister: Nabokov's Political Dream," WSCL 8,ii:193-203.

2202. Lyons, John O. "Pale Fire and the Fine Art
of Annotation," WSCL 8,ii:242-249.

2203. Merivale, Patricia. "The Flaunting of
Artifice in Vladimir Nabokov and Jorge Luis Borges,"
WSCL 8,ii:294-309.

2204. Rosenfield, Claire. "Despair and the Lust
for Immortality," WSCL 8,ii:174-192.

2205. Stegner, Stuart P. "Escape into Aesthetics:
The Art of Vladimir Nabokov," Stanford [PhD diss] 1967.
DA 28:694A.

2206. Struve, Gleb. "Notes on Nabokov as a Russian Writer," WSCL 8,ii:153-164.

2207. Uphaus, Robert W. "Nabokov's Kunstlerroman:
Portrait of the Artist as a Dying Man," Twentieth
Century Literature 13,ii:104-110.

2208. Williams, Carol T. "Nabokov's Dialectal
Structure," WSCL 8,ii:250-267.

2209. Williams, Carol T. "The Necessary Ripple:
The Art of Vladimir Nabokov," Wisconsin [PhD diss]
1967. DA 28(1968):3203A.

See also 2224.

Nekrasov, N.

2210. Birkenmayer, Sigmund S. "N.A. Nekrasov:
A Glimpse of the Man and the Poet," ESEE 12:188-200.

2211. Birkenmayer, Sigmund S. "The Peasant Poems
of Nikolaj Nekrasov," SEEJ 11:159-167.

2212. Peppard, M.B. Nikolai Nekrasov. New York:
Twayne (192). 2212a. Birkenmayer, Sigmund S. SEEJ
13(1969):397-399. 2212b. Gregg, Richard. SlavR 28
(1969):172-174.

Ofrosimov, Ju.

2213. Gul', Roman. "Ju. V. Ofrosimov," NŽ 89:266-
268.

Oleša, Ju.

2214. Beaujour, Elizabeth K. "The Invisible Land:
A Study of the Artistic Imagination of Iurii Olesha,"
Columbia [PhD diss] 1967. DA 31(1970):1259A.

Pasternak, B.

2215. Kalb, Marvin. "Pasternak's Russia," SatR
50,x:70-72,84-87.

2216. Levin, Elena. "Nine Letters of Boris Pasternak," HLB 15:317-330.

2217. Magidoff, Robert. "The Life, Times and Art
of Boris Pasternak," Thought 42:327-357.

2218. Rowland, Mary F. and Rowland, Paul. Pasternak's Doctor Zhivago. [Preface by Harry T. Moore]
Carbondale and Edwardsville: Southern Illinois U P
(xiv,216). 2218a. Coates, Carrol F. SEEJ 12(1968):
353-354. 2218b. Hughes, Robert P. RusR 27(1968):496-

497. 2218c. Šilbajoris, Rimvydas. <u>BA</u> 43(1968):279.

2219. Šilbajoris, Rimvydas. "Pasternak and
Tolstoj: Some Comparisons," <u>SEEJ</u> 11:23-34.

2220. Terras, Victor. "Boris Pasternak and Roman-
tic Aesthetics," <u>PLL</u> 3:42-56.

2221. Zaslove, Jerald. "<u>Dr. Zhivago</u> and the
Obliterated Man: The Novel and Literary Criticism,"
<u>JAAC</u> 26,i:64-80.

See also 67.

Pil'njak, B.

2222. Kuzmich, Ludmila R. "Language and Stylistic Characteristics of Boris Pilnjak's Novel <u>The Naked
Year</u>," New York [PhD diss] 1967. <u>DA</u> 29(1969):231A.

Puškin, A.S.

2223. Call, Paul. "Puškin's <u>Bronze Horseman</u>: A
Poem of Motion," <u>SEEJ</u> 11:137-144.

2224. Clark, A.F.B. "Nabokov's Pushkin," <u>UTQ</u> 36:
302-308.

2225. Clébert, Jean-Paul. <u>The Gypsies</u>. [Tr. by
Charles Duff] Baltimore: Penguin (282).

2226. Meyerson, E.F. and Weiner, Jack. "Cervan-
tes' 'Gypsy Maid' and Puškin's 'The Gypsies'," <u>ISlSt</u>
4:209-214.

2227. Nesaule, Valda. "Tatiana's Dream in Puškin's <u>Evgenij Onegin</u>," <u>ISlSt</u> 4:119-124.

2228. Shaw, J. Thomas, ed. <u>The Letters of Alexander Pushkin</u>. Madison: U of Wisconsin P (880).

2229. Vickery, Walter N.   "Byron's Don Juan and
Puškin's Evgenij Onegin: The Question of Parallelism,"
ISlSt 4:181-191.

See also 2481.

Remizov, A.M.

2230. Burke, Sarah A.   "Salient Features in the
Writings of A.M. Remizov," Texas [PhD diss] 1966. DA
27(1966):3037A.

Šoloxov, M.

2231. Schaarschmidt, Gunter.   "Interior Monologue
in Šoloxov's Podnjataja celina," SEEJ 11:257-265.

2232. Stewart, D.H. Mikhail Sholokhov: A Critical
Introduction. Ann Arbor: U of Michigan P (viii,250).
Rev. 2232a. Folejewski, Z. SEEJ 13(1969):91-94.

Solugub, F.

2233. Selegen, Galina V.   "The Russian Symbolist
Novel (Fedor Sologub's Melkij bes)," Indiana [PhD
diss] 1967. DA 28(1968):3684A.

Solženicyn, A.

2234. Koehler, Ludmila.   "Alexander Solzhenitsyn
and the Russian Literary Tradition," RusR 26:176-184.

2235. Rossbacher, Peter.   "Solzhenitsyn's
'Matrena's Home'," ESEE 12:114-121.

2236. Solženicyn, Aleksandr.   "An Open Letter to
the 4th Congress of Soviet Writers from Alexander
Solzhenitsyn," Survey 64:177-181.

Tolstoj, A.K.

2237. Berry, Thomas E. "Satire in the Works of
A.K. Tolstoj," Texas [PhD diss] 1967. DA 27:4215A.

Tolstoy, L.N.

2238. Archambault, Reginald. "Tolstoy on Education," Midway 8,i:57-67.

2239. Bayley, John. Tolstoy and the Novel. New
York: Viking (316). Rev. 2239a. Frohock, W.M. YR 57,
i:131-135. 2239b. Matlaw, Ralph E. SlavR 26:510-511.
2239c. Muchnic, Helen. NYR 9 (14 Sep):3-4. 2239d.
Pachmuss, Temira. SEEJ 12(1968):253-254. 2239e.
Rosenthal, Raymond. NL 50,v:20-21. 2239f. Šilbajoris,
Rimvydas. BA 143(1968):438. 2239g. Strong, Robert L.
RusR 26:308.

2240. Christian, R.F. "The Passage of Time in
Anna Karenina," SEER 45,civ:206-210.

2241. Feuer, Kathryn. "Alexis De Tocqueville and
the Genesis of War and Peace," CalSlSt 4:92-118.

2242. Friedberg, Maurice. "The Comic Element in
War and Peace," ISlSt 4:100-118.

2243. Lednicki, Waclaw. "Tolstoy Between War and
Peace," CalSlSt 4:73-91.

2244. Matlaw, Ralph, ed. Tolstoy: A Collection
of Critical Essays. Englewood Cliffs: Prentice-Hall
(178). Rev. 2244a. Minerof, Arthur. LJ 92:2412.

2245. Noyes, George R. Tolstoy. New York: Dover
(395).

2246. Phillipson, Morris. The Count Who Wished
He Were a Peasant: A Life of Leo Tolstoy. New York
and Toronto: Pantheon (v,170).

2247. Simmons, Ernest J. "Tolstoy and Chekhov,"
Midway 8,iv:91-104.

2248. Simmons, Ernest J. "Tolstoy's Dramatic
Writings," Midway 8,ii:57-72.

2249. Spence, Gordon W. Tolstoy the Ascetic:
Biography and Criticism. New York: Barnes and Noble
(xiv,154). Rev. 2249a. Lee, C. Nicholas. SEEJ 13,
(1969):244-245.

2250. Troyat, Henri. Tolstoy [Tr. by Nancy
Amphoux] Garden City: Doubleday (x,762). Rev. 2250a.
Buyniak, Victor O. CSlP 10(1968):399-400. 2250b.
Littlejohn, David. Reporter 38,iii(1968):41-43.

2251. Wiener, Leo, tr. Tolstoy on Education.
[Intr. by Reginald D. Archambault] U of Chicago P
(xx,360). Rev. 2251a. Rudy, Peter. SEEJ 14(1970):92.
2251b. Šilbajoris, Rimvydas. BA 43(1969):136-137.

    See also 1213.

Turgenev, A.

2252. Hollingsworth, Barry. "Alexandr Turgenev
and the Composition of 'Khronika russkogo': A Note and
a Query," SEER 45,cv:531-536.

Turgenev, N.I.

2253. Silverman, Lawrence F. "N.I. Turgenev: His
Life and Works from 1789-1824," Harvard [PhD diss]
1967.

Tvardovskij, A.

2254. Pervushin, Nicholas. "Les deux Vassili
Terkine de la littérature russe," CSlSt 1:113-116.

Vjazemskij, P.

2255. Markov, Vladimir. "Russkie čitatnye poèty: Zametki o poèzii P.A. Vjazemskogo i Georgija Ivanova," THRJ [F7]:1273-1287.

Xlebnikov, V.

See 2179.

Zamjatin, E.

2256. Brown, Edward J. "Eugene Zamjatin as a Critic," THRJ [F7]:402-411.

2257. Fischer, Peter A. "A Tentative New Critique of E.I. Zamjatin," Harvard [PhD diss] 1967.

Zoščenko, M.

2258. Von Wiren-Garczyński, Vera. "Zoščenko's Psychological Interests," SEEJ 11:3-22.

AUTHORS TRANSLATION

2259. Adamovič, Georgij. Edinstvo: Stixi raznyx let. New York: Russkaja Kniga (54). Rev. 2259a. Ivask, George. BA 42:300-301. 2259b. Gul', R. NŽ 89:277-279.

2260. Antonov, Sergei. The Pen'kovo Affair: Delo bylo v Pen'kove [Intr. and notes by A. Dressler] Oxford: Pergamon (xx,172).

2261. Axmatova, Anna. "Poema bez geroya," SEER 45,cv:474-496.

2262. Axmatova, Anna. Requiem. Anna Axmatova - Marie Under. [Intr. by A. Rannit, epilogue by F.

Moriak] New York: Meždunarodnoe Liter. Sodružestvo.
Rev. 2262a. Petrovskaja, T. NŽ 90(1968):291.

2263. Bulgakov, Mixail. The Master and Margarita.
[Tr. Mirra Ginsburg] New York: Grove P (x,402); [Tr.
Michael Glenny] New York: Harper & Row (vi,394). Rev.
2263a. Babenko, Victoria A. SEEJ 12(1968):478-480.
2263b. Rosenthal, Raymond. NL 50,xxiii:18-19. 2263c.
Simmons, Ernest J. SatR 50,xlv:35-36;56. 2263d.
Solotaroff, Theodore. NRep 157,xxiii:26-29.

2264. Bunin, I.A. "Neizvestnye stixi I.A. Bunina,"
NŽ 89:19-23.

2265. Bunin, I. "Rassypannyj nabor (pis'ma I.
Bunina)," NŽ 86:135-138.

2266. Chekhov, Anton. The Island: A Journey to
Sakhalin. [Intr. by Robert Payne, tr. by Luba and
Michael Terpak] New York: Washington Square P (xxxvii,
374). Rev. 2266a. Brown, Clarence. NRep 157,xvii:
26-32. 2266b. Friedberg, Maurice. SatR 50,xl:35-36.

2267. Chukovskaja, Lydia. The Deserted House.
[Tr. by Aline B. Werth] New York: Dutton (144). Rev.
2267a. Bradley, Thompson. SlavR 27(1968):688. 2267b.
Ermolaev, Herman. SEEJ 13(1969):99-101. 2267c.
Schmidt, Albert C. Reporter 38,i(1968):44-47.

2268. Cooper, Joshua. Russian Companion. 2 vols.
Oxford: Pergamon P (xxiv,315);(vi,284).

2269. Gončarov, Ivan. Oblomov. [Tr. with an
intr. by David Magarshack] Baltimore: Penguin (485).

2270. Harley, Nadezhda. Russian Tales. New York:
Cambridge U P (65).

2271. Kataev, Valentin. The Holy Well. [Tr. by
Max Hayward and Harold Shukman] New York: Walker and
Co. (160).

2272. Krotkov, Jurij. I Am From Moscow: A View
of the Russian Miracle. [Tr. by author and Mark B.
King] New York: Dutton (213). Rev. 2272a. Hill,
Steven P. SEEJ 13(1969):261-262. 2272b. Ivsky, Oleg.
LJ 92:3033-3034.

2273. Krotkov, Jurij. "Pis'mo Misteru Smitu," NŽ
86:244-285.

2274. Mandel'štam, Osip. Sobranie sočinenij. [Ed.
by G.P. Struve and B.A. Filippov] 2nd ed. vol. 1:
Stixotvorenija [Intr. essays by Clarence Brown, G.P.
Struve and E.M. Rais] Washington: Inter-Language Lit-
erary Associates (cv,553). Rev. 2274a. Ivask, George.
SlavR 29(1970):155-156.

2275. Nekrasov, Viktor. Kira Georgievna. [Intr.
by Militsa Greene, notes by Hector Blair and Militsa
Green] Cambridge: Cambridge U P (152). Rev. 2275a.
Isotov, Nicholas D. SEEJ 12(1968):239-240.

2276. Ofrosimov, Ju. "Rifmovannye dogadki: O
poèzii D. Klenovskogo," NŽ 88:114-122.

2277. Oleša, Jurij. Love and Other Stories. [Tr.
with an intr. by Robert Payne] New York: Washington
Square P (xxv,230). Rev. 2277a. Czerwinski, Edward
J. SEEJ 12(1968):482-485.

2278. Pasternak, Boris. My Sister My Life. [Tr.
by Phillip C. Flayderman] New York: Washington Square
P (xxxi,170). Rev. 2278a. Czerwinski, Edward J. SEEJ
12(1968):481-485. 2278b. Šilbajoris, Rimvydas. BA 42
(1968):333-334.

2279. Paustovskij, Konstantin. Selected Stories
[Intr. and notes by Peter Henry] Oxford: Pergamon P
(xxxvii,143). [In Russian.] 2279a. Dalton, Margaret.
SEEJ 12(1968):99-100.

2280. Pil'njak, Boris. The Tale of the Unextinguished Moon and Other Stories. [Tr. by Beatrice Scott, intr. by Robert Payne] New York: Washington Square P (xx,267). Rev. 2280a. Czerwinski, Edward J. SEEJ 12 (1968):482-485.

2281. Puškin, Aleksandr. "Count Nulin," [Tr. by Anthony D. Briggs] SlavR 26:286-294.

2282. Šoloxov, Mixail. One Man's Destiny and Other Stories, Articles, and Sketches 1923-1963 [Tr. by H.C. Stevens] New York: Knopf (271). Rev. 2282a. Muchnic, Helen. NYR 8(15 Jun): 4-6. 2282b. Shane, Alex M. SEEJ 13(1969):101-102. 2282c. Weil, Irwin. SatR 50,xxiv:33.

2283. Šoloxov, Mixail. Selected Tales from the Don. [Intr. and notes by C.G. Bearne] Oxford: Pergamon P (xviii,102)[In Russian]. Rev. 2283a. Dalton, Margaret. SEEJ 12(1968):99-100.

2284. Soluxin, Vladimir. A Walk in Rural Russia. [Tr. by Stella Miskin] New York: Dutton (254).

2285. Tendrjakov, Vladimir. Three Novellas. [Intr. and notes by J.G. Garrard] Oxford: Pergamon P (xxviii,199).

2286. Terc, Abram. Fantastičeskie povesti: V cirke, Ty i ja, Kvartiranty, Grafomany, Gololedica, Pxenc ; Sud idët ; Ljubimov ; Čto takoe socialisticeskij realizm. New York: Inter-Language Literary Associates (454). Rev. 2286a. Friedberg, Maurice. SEEJ 12(1968):478.

2287. Ul'janov, N. "O suti," NŽ 89:67-78.

2288. Voznesenskij, Andrej. Antiworlds and The Fifth Ace [Ed. by Patricia Blake and Max Hayward, foreword by W.H. Auden] New York: Basic Books (xxiv, 296; Garden City: Doubleday (xxiii,296).

2289. Voznesenskij, Andrej. "Poem With a Footnote," [Tr. by Louis Simpson with Vera Duncan] NYR 8,
9(18 May):21.

2290. Yevtushenko, Yevgeny. Bratsk Station and
Other New Poems. [Tr. by Tina Tupikina-Glaessner,
Geoffrey Dutton, and Igor Mezhakoff-Koriakin, intr.
by Rosh Ireland] Garden City: Doubleday (xxvi,214).
Rev. 2290a. Holquist, James M. SEEJ 12(1968):480-482.
2290b. Neiswender, Rosemary. LJ 92:245.

2291. Yevtushenko, Yevgeny. Poems Chosen by the
Author. [Tr. by Peter Levi and Robert Milner-Gulland]
New York: Hill and Wang (96). Rev. 2291a. Bram,
Joseph. LJ 92:2045-2046. 2291b. Hirschberg, W.R.
BA 42(1968):335.

2292. Yevtushenko, Yevgeny. "Rome," [Tr. by
George Reavey] SatR 50,xxix:24-27.

2293. Zamjatin, Evgenij. The Dragon: Fifteen
Stories. [Tr. and ed. by Mirra Ginsburg] New York:
Random House (xx,291). Rev. 2293a. Deneau, Daniel P.
SSF 5,iii(1968):313-315. 2293b. Ehre, Milton. NL 50,
vi:22-23. 2293c. Holquist, James M. SlavR 28(1969):
175-177. 2293d. Kern, G. NŽ 87:328-330. 2293e.
Muchnic, Helen. NYR 8(15 Jun):4-6.

2294. Zamjatin, Evgenij. My [Intr. by Evgenij
Žiglevič, afterword by Vladimir Bondarenko] New
York and Washington: Inter-Language Literary Associ-
ates (223).

2295. Zoščenko, Mixail. Ljudi. [Intr. by Hector
Blair, notes by Hector Blair and Militsa Greene]
Cambridge: Cambridge U P (66). Rev. 2295a. Isotov,
Nicholas D. SEEJ 12(1968):239-240.

2296. Zoščenko, Mixail. Pered Vosxodom Solnca,
Povest'. [Intr. by Vera von Viren-Garczinski and

Boris Fillipov] New York: Inter-Language Literary Associates (208). Rev. 2296a. Glade, Henry. BA 43
(1969):133-134. 2296b. McLean, Hugh. SEEJ 12:475-
477.

See also 72, 81, 91, 105, 112, 2084.

YUGOSLAV

GENERAL

2297. Mihailovich, Vasa D. "Yugoslav Literature
since World War II," LitR II,ii:149-161.

2298. Stankiewicz, Edward. "The Legend of Opulent
India, Marin Držić, and South Slavic Folk Poetry," ZB
5:120-128.

2299. Vujica, Nada K. "Literary Portrait of Sida
Košutić" JCS 7-8:14-30.

MACEDONIAN

See 1883.

SERBOCROATIAN

2300. Držić, Marin. Uncle Maroje. [Tr. by Sonia
Bićanić] and Grižula [Tr. by Ljerka Djanješić] Zagreb:
Summer Festival Dubrovnik (52,96). Rev. 2300a.
Czerwinski, Edward. BA 43,i(1969):137.

2301. Jasenovic-Nusinov, Ludmilla. "Laza K.
Lazarević comme homme et écrivain," Montreal [PhD
diss] 1966.

2302. Kadić, Ante. "Krleža's Tormented Vision-
aries," SEER 45,civ:46-64.

2303. Pavlovitch, K. St. "Yovane Doutchitch,
prince de poètes serbes," ESEE 12:99-113.

2304. Stolz, Benjamin A. "Historicity in the
Serbo-Croatian Heroic Epic: Salih Ugljanin's 'Grčki
rat'," SEEJ 11:423-432.

2305. Vuković, Jovan. "The Structure of Njegoš's
Decasyllabic Verse Compared with the Decasyllabic
Verse in Epic Folk Poetry," ISlSt 4:192-208.

See also 1252, 1275, 1282, 2298.

SLOVENIAN

2306. Kreft, Bratko. "Prešeren et Puškin: Frag-
ment d'une étude," THRJ [F7]:1094-1113.

UKRAINIAN

2307. Andrusyshen, C.H. "Publications in Other
Languages," [General Discussion of Ukrainian Literature and Life] UTQ 36:545-556.

2308. Olynyk, Roman. "Panteleimon Kulish and his
Yevgenij Onegin nashego vremeni," CSlP 9:201-215.

2309. Rudnytsky, Ivan L. "A Publication of the
German Writings of Ivan Franko," SlavR 26:141-147.

2310. Slavutych, Yar. "Istoriosofija Jevhena
Malanjuka," Northern Lights 3:123-130.

2311. Slavutych, Yar. "Osnovni temy u tvorčosti
M. Oresta," Zapysky Naukovoho Tovarystva imeny Ševčenka 177:191-196.

2312. Slavutych, Yar. "Sobornyc'ki ideji Ivana

Franka," <u>Zapysky Naukovoho Tovarystva imeny Ševčenka</u>:
<u>Ivan Franko</u> 32:171-178.

　　　　See also 48, 1228.

YIDDISH

　2313.　Buchen, Irving H.　"Isaac Bashevis Singer
and the Revival of Satan," <u>TSLL</u> 9:129-142.

　2314.　Singer, Isaac B.　<u>The Manor</u>, New York:
Farrar, Straus and Giroux (442).　Rev. 2314a. Wain,
John.　<u>NYR</u> 9(26 Oct):32-36.

　　　　See also 186.

XIII. Folklore

GENERAL

2315. Oinas, Felix. "Varoitussarjat iamerensuo-
malaisissa ja slaavilaisissa kansanrunoissa,"
Kalevalaseuran Vuosikirja 47:89-102. [Warning sets in
Finnic and Slavic folk songs.]

EAST EUROPEAN

2316. Brastiņš, Arvīds. Māte Māra: Māras
dziesmu sakārtojums un apcerējums. Cleveland: Māra
Pubs. (311). [Table of contents and intr. also in English (297-310).]

2317. Dömötör, Tekla. "Animistic Concepts and
Supernatural Power in Hungarian Folk Narratives and
Folk Customs," JFI 4:127-137.

2318. Durham, Mae. Tit for Tat and other Latvian
Folk Tales Retold. [Tr. of Skaidrite Rubene-Koo, notes
by Alan Dundes, illus. by Harriet Pincus] New York:
Harcourt, Brace and World (126).

2319. Feldon, Victoria. "On American and Lithuanian Folk Art," Litua 14,ii:63-72.

2320. Johansons, Andrejs, ed. Vecrīgas ziņgu
grāmata. New York: Grāmatu Draugs (214).

2321. Kurman, George. "Pseudomythology in Estonian Folklore," CSlSt 1:474-481.

2322. Leader, Ninon A.M. Hungarian Classical

Ballads and Their Folklore. New York: Cambridge U P
(xii,367). Rev. 2322a. Cushing, G.F. SEER 46,cvi
(1968):223-224. 2322b. Oinas, Felix J. EEQ 2(1968):
333-335.

2323. Oinas, Felix. "Nõuandeist 'Kalevipojas',"
Tulimuld 18:96-97. [On the instructions to the warrior
in the epic Kalevipoeg.]

2324. Pop, Mihai. "Le mythe du 'Grand Voyage'
dans les chants des cérémonies funèbres roumaines,"
THRJ [F7]:1602-1609.

2325. Ruches, P.J., coll. and tr. Albanian His-
torical Folksongs 1716-1943: A Survey of Oral Epic
Poetry from Southern Albania with Original Texts.
Chicago: Argonaut (ix,126).

2326. Šmits, P., comp. and ed. Latviešu tautas
teikas un pasakas, Vol. 8-9. Otru izdevumu ar ievadu,
vesturiski bibliografisku parskatu un motivu raditaju
sagatavojis H. Biezais. Waverly, Iowa: Latvju Gramata.
(493,29;545,28).

2327. Szirmai, Palma. "A Csángó-Hungarian Lament."
Em 11:310-325.

2328. Ward, Donald. "Solar Mythology and Baltic
Folksongs," D.K. Wilgus, ed., with assistance of Carol
Sommer, Folklore International: Essays in Traditional
Literature, Belief, and Custom in Honor of Wayland
Debs Hand, 233-242. Hatboro, Pa.: Folklore Associates.

See also 1925, 2298, 2333.

SLAVIC

2329. Bogatyrëv, P.G. "Improvizacija i normy
xudožestvennyx priemov na materiale povestej XVIII v.,

nadpisej na lubočnyx kartinkax, skazok, i pesen o
Ereme i Fome," THRJ [F7]:318-334.

2330. Djoudjeff, Stoyan. "Esquisse d'une méthode
musicologique pour l'étude des vers populaires," THRJ
[F7]:523-540.

2331. Levin, Isidor. "Vladimir Propp: An Evaluation on his Seventieth Birthday," JFI 4:32-49.

2332. Lord, Albert B. "The Influence of a Fixed
Text," THRJ [F7]:1199-1206.

2333. Obrębska-Jabłońska, Antonina. "The Rough
Copies of Byelorussian Songs in the Federowski Collection," THRJ [F7]:1445-1457.

2334. Oinas, Felix J. "The Relationship Between
the Slavic and Finnic Heroic Epic," The American
Philosophical Society Year Book 1966:681-683.

2335. Pozdneev, A. "Vremja složenija russkix
skazok," THRJ [F7]:1610-1614.

2336. Unbegaun, Boris O. "Der Schrecken der
Heuschrecken im moskovitischen Russland," Festschrift
für Margarete Woltner zum 70. Geburtstag:254-261.
Heidelberg: Carl Winter Universitätsverlag.

2337. Yeoman, John, tr. and ed. The Apple of
Youth and Other Russian Folk Stories. [Illus. by Barbara Swiderska.] New York: Oxford U P (63).

        See also 1298, 1732, 1883, 2049, 2050, 2056,
2298, 2304, 2305.

                        OTHER

2338. Arnold, Hermann. "Some Observations on
Turkish and Persian Gypsies," JGLS 46,iii-iv:105-122.

2339.   Austerlitz, Robert.   "Two Gilyak Song-
Texts," THRJ [F7]:99-113.

2340.   Başgöz, Ilhan.   "Dream Motif in Turkish Folk
Stories and Shamanistic Initiation," Asian Folklore
Studies 26,i:1-18.

2341.   Başgöz, Ilhan.   "Rain-making Ceremonies in
Turkey and Seasonal Festivals," JAOS 87:304-306.

2342.   Fraser, Angus M.   "The 'Turkish Spy' on
Gypsies," JGLS 46,iii-iv:132-141.

2343.   Maranda, Elli K.   "The Cattle of the Forest
and the Harvest of Water: The Cosmology of Finnish
Magic," June Helm, ed., Essays on the Verbal and Vis-
ual Arts: Proceedings of the 1966 Annual Spring Meet-
ing of the American Ethnological Society, 84-95.
Seattle: U of Washington P (215).

2344.   Radloff, V.V.   South-Siberian Oral Literature: Turkic Texts. [Vol. 1. Intr. by Denis Sinor]
Bloomington: Indiana U (xvi,xxiv,419).

2345.   Valtonen, Pertti. "Finnish Gypsy Texts,"
JGLS 46,iii-iv:82-97.

See also 702.

XIV. The Arts

GENERAL

2346. Daniel, Oliver. "On Discovering Szymanow-ski," SatR 50,xxv:54-55.

2347. Kaldor, Ivan L. "Slavic Paleography and Early Russian Printing: The Genesis of the Russian Book," Chicago [PhD diss] 1967.

2348. Kundziņš, Pauls. "Latviešu tautas celt-niecība starptautiskā jomā," Archīvs 8:83-94.

2349. Stafford, Cronelius. "The Nights of Pula," EE 16,i:51-53.

2350. Tarassuk, Leonid. Russian Pistols in the Seventeenth Century. York, Pa.: George Shumway (35).

2351. Anon. "A 'Happening' in Prague," EE 16,x: 13-15.

See also 618, 717, 1170, 2319.

MUSIC

2352. Apkalns, Longīns. "Padomju mūzikas ētosa dilemma," JGai 63:28-38.

2353. Bartók, Bela. Rumanian Folk Music [Ed. by Benjamin Suchoff]. The Hague: Nijhoff. VI(704);VII (756);VIII(660). Rev. 2353a. Lang, Paul H. MQ 54, iv:543-549.

2354.   Bernheimer, Martin. "The Bolshoi at Montreal," Opera 18:891-892;909.

2355.   Bratuz, Damiana. "1 The Folk Element in the
Piano Music of B. Bartók. 2 Schumann: Great Sonata in
F Minor, an Analytical and Historical Study," Indiana
[PhD diss] 1967.

2356.   Brown, Malcolm H. "The Symphonies of Sergei
Prokofiev," Florida State [PhD diss] 1967. DA 28
(1968):2706A.

2357.   Crohn, Harris N. "A Study of the Opera
Katja Kabanova by Leos Janáček," Rochester [PhD diss]
1967.

2358.   Cutter, Paul F. "A Program of Renaissance
and Baroque Music by the Slovenian Composers Jacobus
Gallus and Joannes Baptista Dolar," FSUSP 1:100-105.

2359.   Daniel, Oliver. "From the Banks of the
Vlatava," SatR 50,viii:76-77.

2360.   Freeman, John W. "Opera in Brno," EE 16,ii:
17-20.

2361.   Garden, Edward. Balakirev--A Critical Study
of his Life and Music. New York: St. Martin's (352).

2362.   Gelatt, Roland. "A Polish Musician for Our
Time," Reporter 37,vii:53-54.

2363.   Gelatt, Roland. "The Russians are Coming,"
Reporter 36,xi:44-46.

2364.   Green, Stanley. "The New Russian Hit Pa-
rade," SatR 50,xxxiv:66.

2365.   Harris, Charles D. "Keyboard Music in Vienna During the Reign of Leopold I, 1658-1705," Michigan
[PhD diss] 1967. DA 28(1968):5091A.

2366.   Henrotte, Gayle A.   "The Ensemble Divorti-
mento in Pre-Classic Vienna," North Carolina [PhD
diss] 1967.   DA 28(1968):5091A.

2367.   Kolodin, Irving.   "Passion by Penderecki,"
SatR 50,xlvii:87.

2368.   Kopczyńska, Zdzisława.   "La dispute sur
l'octave en Pologne au début du 19ième siècle," THRJ
[F7]:1068-1083.

2369.   Mason, Madeline.   "Paderewski: 'Music is
Oratory'," MJ 25,iv:38-39;73-74.

2370.   Pone, Gundaris.   "Jaunās mūzikas forma un
doma, 1950-1960," JGai 62:6-19.

2371.   Sahlmann, Fred G.   "The Piano Concertos of
Serge Prokofiev: A Stylistic Study," Rochester [PhD
diss] 1967.

2372.   Šaljapin, Fedor I. [Chaliapin] Chaliapin,
an Autobiography as Told to Maxim Gorky [Tr. by Nina
Froud and James Hanley] New York: Stein and Day
(320).

2373.   Seaman, Gerald.   History of Russian Music
Vol. I: From Its Origins to Dargomyzhsky.   New York:
Praeger (xv,351).   Rev. 2373a. Dukelsky, Vladimir.
RusR 27(1968):481-482.   2373b. Velimirovic, Milos. MQ
55(1969):408-417.

2374.   Stravinsky, Igor.   "Stravinsky at Eighty-
Five: An Interview," NYR 8,x:12-16.

2375.   Vlad, Roman.   Stravinsky. [Tr. from Italian
by Frederick and Ann Fuller] London, New York and
Toronto: Oxford U P (vii,264). [2d ed.]

2376.   Walker, Alan, ed.   Frédéric Chopin: Profile

of the Man and the Musician. New York: Taplinger
(334).

2377. Weinstock, Herbert. "An Authentic 'Prince
Igor'," SatR 50,xlvii:84.

See also 96, 1668, 1687, 2140, 2327, 2330.

DRAMA AND THEATER

2378. Burian, Jarka M. "Theatre in Czechoslovakia: Reflections of a Participating Visitor," DS 6,
i:92-104.

2379. Clurman, Harold. "Theatre in Europe II,"
Nation (U.S.) 205:29-30.

2380. Clurman, Harold. "Theatre in Europe III,"
Nation (U.S.) 205:60-62.

2381. Coleman, Marion M. "To Play, or Not to
Play?--Modjeska and the St. Petersburg Engagement,"
PolR 12,iv:44-56.

2382. Den, Peter. "Notes on Czechoslovakia's
Young Theater of the Absurd," BA 41:157-163.

2383. Grynberg, Henryk. "Why I Left the State
Jewish Theatre in Poland," Ms 14,iii:39-43.

2384. Rozov, Victor. "The Soviet Theater Today,"
NWR 35,vii:41-46.

2385. Vaškelis, Bronius. "Contemporary Lithuanian Drama," Lituanus 13,iii:5-27.

2386. Witkiewicz, Stanislaw I. "On a New Type of
Play," [Tr. by C.S. Durer and Daniel C. Gerould] DS 6,
ii:173-180. [Polish plays.]

See also 1935.

VISUAL ARTS

2387. Alpatov, M.W., ed. Art Treasures of Russia.
[Comm. by O. Dacenko, tr. by Norbert Guterman] New
York: Abrams (178). Rev. 2387a. Il'inskaja, N. NŽ 90
(1968):292-296.

2388. Alpert, Hollis. "Hollywood in Budapest,"
SatR 50,li:20-21;38-39.

2389. Congrat-Burlar, Stefan, comp. Posters of
the Russian Revolution, 1917-1929, from The Lenin
Library, Moscow. [Photographic research by Caio Gar-
ruba; historical notes, captions, and chronology comp.
by Stefan Congrat-Butlar.] New York: Grove P. Rev.
2389a. de Saint-Rat, André. CSlSt 2:271-273.

2390. Èrenberg, Il'ja. "Tribute to Picasso," NWR
35,ii:34-37.

2391. Forman, Miloš. "Chill Wind on the New
Wave," SatR 50,li:10-11,41.

2392. Gheorghiu, Miknea. "Young Faces, Young
Hearts," SatR 50,li:16-17.

2393. Glynn, Thomas. "Adversity's Geniuses: Polish Artists Today," EE 16,iii:9-14.

2394. Gross, Priva B. "Some Aspects of Medieval
Church Architecture in Poland," PolR 12,ii:41-67.

2395. Ipsiroglu, M.S. Painting and Culture of the
Mongols. [Tr. by E.D. Philips.] New York: Abrams (112).
Rev. 2395a. Sisson, Jacqueline. LJ 92:2147.

2396. Kandinskij, Vasilij. O duxovnom v iskusstve.

CForeword by Nina Kandinskaja.] New York: Inter-Language Literary Associates (159).

2397. Karsavina, Tamara. "Diaghilev and Other Partners," Dance 57,676:196-197,202.

2398. Knight, Arthur. "The Bright Spring, the Bleak Winter," SatR 50,1i:12-13.

2399. Kozinstev, Gregori. "The New Film-Makers," SatR 50,1i:15,43-44.

2400. Kundziņš, Pauls. "Tagadnes architektūras meklējumi," JGai 64:17-23.

2401. Lawson, Joan. "Red Army Ensemble," Dance 57,680:409-410.

2402. Mead, Igor and Sjeklocha, Paul. Unofficial Art in the Soviet Union. Berkeley and Los Angeles, U of California P (xv,213). Rev. 2402a. Kovarsky, Vera. RusR 27(1968):364-366. 2402b. Sprague, Arthur. SlavR 27(1968):677-678. 2402c. Wright, A.C. CSlP 11 (1969):394-395.

2403. Nonn, Thomas I. "Modern Hungarian Painting," New York CPhD diss] 1966. DA 28(1966):561A.

2404. Rácz, István. Art Treasures of Medieval Finland. CPhotographs by István Rácz, intr. and notes by Riitta Pylkkänen, and tr. by Diana Tullberg and Judy Beesley.] New York, Washington, and London: Praeger (15,12 notes,245 plates). Rev. 2404a. Lunde, Karl. SlavR 28(1969):170-171.

2405. Rácz, István. Early Finnish Art: From Prehistory to the Middle Ages. CPhotographs by István Rácz, intr. by C.F. Meinander, notes on the illustrations by Pirkko-Liisa Lehtosolo, tr. by Diana Tullberg] New York, Washington, and London: Praeger. (19

12 notes,159 plates.) Rev. 2405a. Lunde, Karl. SlavR
28(1969):170-171.

2406. Reklaitis, Povilas. "Die bildende Kunst der
litauischen Emigration 1945-1966," AB 6:237-259.

2407. Richards, J.M. A Guide to Finnish Architecture. New York and Washington: Praeger (112,177
plates). Rev. 2407a. Fitch, James M. SlavR 27:356-
357.

2408. Roslavleva, Natalia. "To Have and to Lose--
Asel' at the Bolshoi," Dance 57,683:581-584.

2409. Roud, Richard. "Through an Ideology
Darkly," SatR 50,1i:13-14,42.

2410. Sihare, Laxmi P. "Oriental Influences on
Wassily Kandinsky and Piet Mondrian, 1909-1917," New
York [PhD diss] 1967. DA 30(1970):4892A.

2411. Simon, John. "The Czechs are Coming," NL
50,xiv:22-24.

2412. Smith, Desmond. "Filming the New Revolution," Nation (U.S.) 204,ix:268-272.

2413. Souritz, Elizabeth. "News from U.S.S.R.,"
DM 41,v:96-98.

2414. Swift, Sister Mary Grace. "The Art of the
Dance in the Union of Soviet Socialist Republics: A
Study of Politics, Ideology, and Culture," Notre Dame
[PhD diss] 1967. DA 28:4069A.

2415. Valenti, Jack. "Film-making Behind the Iron
Curtain," SatR 50,1i:8-9,39-40.

2416. Vorkalis, Antons. "Neilis ir latviešu Klē,"
JGai 61:30-31,47.

2417. Voyce, Arthur. The Art and Architecture of
Medieval Russia. Norman: U of Oklahoma P (xii,432).
Rev. 2417a. Gebhard, David. LJ 92:2755. 2417b. Ham-
ilton, George H. RusR 27(1968):376-377. 2417c. Koll-
mann, Jack E. CSlSt 3(1969):728-735. 2417d. Schmidt,
Albert J. Historian 30(1968):479-480. 2417e. Teholiz
Leo. SlavR 28(1969):347-349. 2417f. Terras, Victor.
SEEJ 12(1968):259-260. 2417g. Vejdle, V. NŽ 89:286-
287.

See also 104, 136.

Index

Numerals refer to item numbers in this bibliography.